THE END OF THE

TWENTIETH

CENTURY

The Great Powers and Eastern Europe

Tocqueville: The European Revolution and
Correspondence with Gobineau *(editor)*

A History of the Cold War

Decline and Rise of Europe

A New History of the Cold War

Historical Consciousness

The Passing of the Modern Age

The Last European War, 1939–1941

1945: Year Zero

Philadelphia: Patricians and Philistines, 1900–1950

Outgrowing Democracy: A History of the United
States in the Twentieth Century

Budapest 1900: A Historical Portrait
of a City and Its Culture

Confessions of an Original Sinner

The Duel: 10 May–31 July; The Eighty-Day
Struggle Between Churchill and Hitler

JOHN
LUKACS

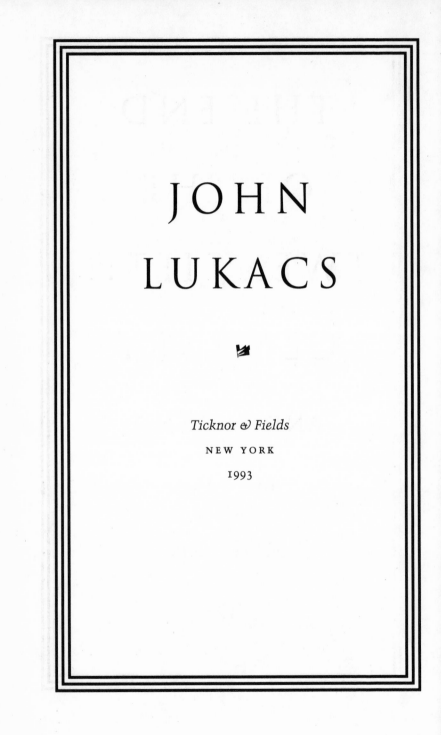

Ticknor & Fields

NEW YORK

1993

THE END

OF THE

TWENTIETH

CENTURY

AND THE END

OF THE

MODERN

AGE

For information about permission to reproduce selections
from this book, write to Permissions, Ticknor & Fields,
215 Park Avenue South, New York, New York 10003.

Library of Congress Cataloging-in-Publication Data

Lukacs, John, date.
The end of the twentieth century and the
end of the modern age / John Lukacs.
p.   cm.
ISBN 0-395-58472-8
1. History, Modern — 20th century.   2. Nationalism — History —
20th century.   3. World War, 1914–1918 — Influence.   4. World War,
1939–1945 — Influence.   I. Title.
D421.L85   1993
909.82 — dc20   92-34081
CIP

Printed in the United States of America

AGM   10   9   8   7   6   5   4   3   2   1

Book design by Anne Chalmers

Portions of Chapters V and VI appeared, in different forms,
in *Harper's Magazine, The Wilson Quarterly* and *Philadelphia.*

THIS BOOK IS DEDICATED
TO MICHAEL VON MOSCHZISKER

CONTENTS

I. THE END OF THE TWENTIETH CENTURY I

II. THE REVOLUTIONARY IO

III. THE END OF THE COLD WAR:
GOOD-BYE TO ALL THAT? 21

IV. RUSSIA. THE FRONTIER. 44

V. GERMANY. THE CENTER. 79

VI. BETWEEN TWO WORLDS III

VII. EUROPE . . . EUROPE? 170

VIII. NATIONALISM, NATIONALITY, NATIVISM,
NATIONAL FEELING, NATIONAL CHURCHES,
NATIONAL RELIGION 203

IX. THE STATE AT THE END OF
THE MODERN AGE 242

X. THE END OF THE MODERN AGE 272

Manches Herrliche der Welt
Ist im Krieg und Streit zerronnen
Wer bewähret und erhält
Hat das schönste Los gewonnen.

(Great creations in this world
Were destroyed by war and strife.
Who protected and preserved
Have won the most beautiful prize.)

— Goethe

❧ I ❧

THE END OF THE
TWENTIETH CENTURY

THE TWENTIETH CENTURY is now over. It was a short century. It lasted seventy-five years — from 1914 to 1989. Its two main events were the two world wars. They were the enormous mountain ranges that dominated its entire landscape. The Russian Revolution, the atomic bomb, the end of the colonial empires, the establishment of Communist states, the dominion of the two world superpowers the United States and the Soviet Union, the division of Europe and of Germany: all of these were the consequences of the two world wars, in the shadow of which we have been living. Until now.

The nineteenth century lasted ninety-nine years, from 1815 to 1914, from the end of Napoleon's wars to the start of the First World War. The eighteenth century lasted one hundred and twenty-six years, from the beginning of the world wars between England and France (of which the American War of Independence was a part) until their end at Waterloo. The seventeenth century lasted one hundred and one years, from the destruction of the Spanish Armada in 1588 (of which the establishment of a united France was one important consequence) to 1689, the year after the so-called Glorious Revolution in England, when the main threat to England became France and no longer Spain.

At that time, three hundred years ago, the very word "century" was hardly known. The *Oxford English Dictionary* notes its first usage, in English, in 1626. Before the middle of the seventeenth century, "century" meant a Roman military unit of one hundred men. Then it acquired another meaning, that of one hundred years.

That was one of the symptoms of the beginning of our modern historical consciousness. Another of its symptoms was the creation of the terms "ancient" and "modern." The three historical ages Ancient, Medieval and Modern became accepted notions three hundred years ago. (One example: they appear in the texts of two second-rate German chroniclers, Hornius and Cellarius, in the 1680s.) So in 1689 some people thought that the Middle Ages were over, though no one thought then that the world order of the seventeenth century had ended. In 1815, too, no one knew that the end of the Atlantic world wars between England and France had come. Everyone, both enemies and sympathizers of the French Revolution, were concerned with the prospect of great revolutions erupting again. There were revolutions after 1815; but the entire history of the nineteenth century was marked by the absence of world wars for ninety-nine years. Its exceptional prosperity and progress were due to that.

We know that the twentieth century is over. We know this, at least in part, because of the evolution of our historical consciousness — which is something different from a widespread knowledge of history. That evolution, and that evolution alone, may be the most essential ingredient of the history of our minds.

The twentieth century will end officially on the last day of the year 2000. But the true turning points (and turning points are different from milestones) in the lives of civilizations, of nations, of a single person, do not coincide with the decimal calendar. Also, history is not of one piece; the turning points are not absolute. So many violent symptoms of the cracking up of the Edwardian or Victorian order were present before 1914. So many of the habits, physical and mental, of the Middle Ages lived on after the seventeenth century. The end of the twentieth century is not absolute. The shadows of the two world wars have not yet disappeared. But they are retreating: they no longer dominate the historical landscape. *That* is why, by and large, the twentieth century *is* over.

June 1989. *"We must be aware of the dangerous temptation of seeing history mainly from the viewpoint of the present, while we must be equally conscious of the condition that what we know at present is an inescapable ingredient of our view of the past." Today I wrote this sentence for a chapter in a book on which I am now working. It is not a particularly profound observation; but it has a bearing on my situation now.*

I am a participant historian, unable to avoid thinking about what is happening now. (Knowledge is neither objective nor subjective — that Cartesian separation is both illusory and outdated. Our knowledge is inevitably personal, and participant.) Or, as Goethe once wrote: "The beginning and the end of all literary activity is the reproduction of the world that surrounds me by means of the world that is in me." "Literary activity": the writing of history is surely a literary activity; but Goethe's statement applies to the study and to the consciousness of history as well. That consciousness has made me a historian and not a novelist.

Right now I am thinking of something other than my present work. I am not only conscious — I know that the twentieth century is over. The evidences of this accumulate in my mind. They assume something like a serried order. During dinner I tell S. some of this. Attentive as she is, she is not particularly interested in my details. Women know something that men rarely do: that terms (as distinct from words) do not really matter, that descriptions are more telling than definitions, that whatever there is that is general is there within what is particular. She finds it more interesting when I say that I think the Berlin Wall will be gone soon.

(A few months later The Wall came down. So many people, including entire governments, were surprised. They shouldn't have been.)

I am a person of the twentieth century. There is a fearful chronological symmetry to my life. I was born ten years after 1914, when the twentieth century truly began. I am sixty-five in 1989, and I know that it is over. That gives me a certain perspective, but not much more than that. I was fifteen when the Second World War broke out, and then came the decisive years, including the formative years of my own mind. I hope that God allows me another fifteen years. By that time my perspectives will hardly matter.

Some people think that the twentieth century is over because the cold war is over. This idea appeals to those who see the entire history of the century ruled by the struggle between Democracy and Communism, incarnated, respectively, by the United States and the Soviet Union, beginning in 1917. That perspective is wrong. The twentieth century began with a bang, in 1914 — the Big Bang, of which the Russian Revolution in 1917 was but one of the consequences. The main political force in the twentieth century has been nationalism, not Communism.

I have a weakness for coincidences. I was born in 1924, seven days after Lenin had died and two days before Woodrow Wilson would die. The ideas, indeed the personalities, of these ephemeral protagonists of the early twentieth century belonged to the nineteenth. In 1914, by the time the twentieth century opened, their views of the world were already outdated. That their ideals seemed to triumph for a very short time, when they seemed to be the two different and opposite architects of a new world, was not inconsequential; but they did not matter much in the long run. To think that the world could be made safe for democracy (or, more precisely, that democracy would make the world safe) was a shortsighted and self-serving idea. So was that of International Communism. That is obvious in 1989, at the end of the twentieth century; but it was already evident in 1914, at its very beginning.

In 1914 Marxism suffered a huge blow from which it never really recovered. Marx, his followers and successors, including Lenin, believed that classes were more important realities than were nations (Marx had paid no attention to nations at all, he confused them with states); that the economic motive determined what people thought and believed. The very opposite was true. In 1914 a German workingman had more in common with a German factory owner than with a French workingman. The same was true of French or British or American workingmen and their managers. In 1914 international socialism melted away at once in the heat of nationalist enthusiasms, especially in Germany. But already two years before that, the young Mussolini discovered that he was an Italian first and a socialist only second. (He *was* a man of the twentieth century, born in the same year that Marx had died.) There was a Communist revolution in Russia in 1917; but what Lenin achieved was not an international revolution. To the contrary, it was Russia's withdrawal from Europe. To survive the civil war in Russia, Lenin had to let International Communism go by the board. His government survived, but the Soviet Union remained the only Communist government in the world. Whenever Communists attempted a successful revolution elsewhere, they failed. Except for the Soviet Union (well, add their satellite border "state" of Outer Mongolia) there were no Communist states in the world until after the Second World War. Then Communist states were erected in Eastern Europe, but not because of revolutions or because of the popular appeal of Communism. They were put there because of the national triumph of Russia over Germany, with the result of the Russian occupation of most of Eastern Europe.

In 1914 Wilson, too, thought that the outbreak of the war in Europe was a reactionary event, a consequence of the outdated political and social order of the Old World. He was wrong: the carnage of that war became terrible because of nationalism and democracy. It was no longer a war between traditional armies of traditional states. Entire nations were rushing at each other, fighting to the end, making any kind of a compromise peace impossible. After the war Wilson was repudiated by the majority of his countrymen; years before his death he was, like Lenin, a broken man, and not only physically; and his idea of the War to End Wars, as well as the League of Nations, proved to be the sorriest of failures.

Yet — such is the irony of history — the ideas of this pale Presbyterian professor-President were more revolutionary than those of the Bolshevik radical from the middle Volga region. Wilson's propagation of the idea of national self-determination helped to bring about the destruction of entire empires in 1918. Seventy-odd years later that idea of national self-determination is destroying some of the very states that Wilson helped to create: Yugoslavia and Czechoslovakia, for example. It has also destroyed the structure of the Soviet Union, that inheritor of the old Russian empire. Communism is dead, but national self-determination is very much alive.

This means — again, contrary to those who see the history of the twentieth century governed by the cold war — that we are witnessing not only the end of the division of Europe that had been tacitly accepted at Yalta in 1945. We are beginning to witness changes in the political geography of Europe that was established in the first years of the historical century, in 1919 at Versailles.

The twentieth century is gone; and 1917 is now very far away. In Russia it is no longer only Stalin and Stalinism, it is Leninism and Lenin that are being repudiated. To a lesser — though as yet not clearly visible — extent this is happening with Wilsonianism in the United States too.

It was a tragedy for Russia that her great conservative statesman Stolypin was assassinated in 1911; and it was a tragedy for the United States that in 1912 its most popular leader, Theodore Roosevelt, was cheated out of his presidential nomination by the Republican party. So in 1914 America was governed not by him but by Woodrow Wilson, with the result that it was Wilson and not Roosevelt who established the ideology of American internationalism in the twentieth century; for not only Franklin Roosevelt but Herbert Hoover, as well as John Foster Dulles, Richard Nixon and Ronald Reagan were avowed Wilsonians. There is a difference now, in 1992, when many Americans are no longer attracted to the idea of national self-determination; they realize that the breakup of states is latent with immeasurable and perhaps endless dangers. This uneasy sidling away from Wilsonian internationalism is new. Whether it will have enduring consequences I cannot tell.

It took a long time, almost an entire century, for this dying of the Communist appeal and this fading of Wilsonianism; but this was not because of their innate strength. It had taken so long because, despite superficial impressions, the movement of ideas in this democratic century has been very slow. Consider only how, in the face of contrary evidence, intellectuals all over the world could or would not revise or abandon their sympathies for Marxism long after its failures had become ever more obvious. That unwillingness of so many people to change their minds has been typical of this century, and not only in its politics. Seventy years ago not only Marx but Darwin, Freud, Picasso, Stravinsky, Einstein were seen as the intellectual giants of our times. So they were fifty or sixty years later; most of them even now. Compare this stagnant list with that of the so-called stodgy nineteenth century. What a difference between Goethe and Nietzsche, Scott and Wilde, Chateaubriand and Ibsen, Rossini and Debussy — not to speak of Wagner . . .

Wagner lives on. So does nationalism, mass nationalism, the main political and social phenomenon of the twentieth century. Its most radical incarnation was Hitler, whose unwillingness to compromise, whose ideas and whose determination to carry them out were more unyielding and radical than those of any other famous revolutionary leader, like Lenin or Stalin or Mao.

Consider but this single, disturbing evidence: at the end of this century there are almost *no* believing Communists anywhere, not many even in the lands of the Soviet Union, where the remnant party men are merely nationalist bureaucrats. Yet there are Nazis still, admirers of Hitler, not only the remnants of an old generation but new adherents, young men and women, some open, others tight-lipped, in many countries of the world, not only in Germany and Austria.

We must not exaggerate their numbers or their influence — for many reasons, including the condition that Hitler, too, belonged to the twentieth century and not to something more enduring or greater. A greater Germany may arise again; new versions of National Socialism may rise again; but not in their Hitlerite forms.

Still: if the mountain ranges dominating the landscape of the twentieth century were the two world wars, 1940–41 was the highest point of those mountain ranges. It was then that Hitler came very near to winning the Second World War — nearer than Germany in 1914 or in 1918. If he had done so, with what consequences! In a way, much of the twentieth century before 1940–41 led up to Hitler. And so much of the rest of the century, from 1941 on, was the consequence of the Second World War that he alone had begun and that was dominated by his presence until its end.

✄ II ✄

THE REVOLUTIONARY

IN MARCH 1989 I went to Hitler's birthplace.

The town of Braunau, where Adolf Hitler was born one hundred years ago, is off the tourist-beaten track — that is, distant from the Munich-Salzburg-Linz-Vienna superhighway. It is in the Innviertel, a region of the province of Upper Austria, which, even before the Autobahn, had few tourist attractions comparable to the pretty shining lakes farther to the south, on the shores of which innkeeping had become a source of income for Austrians during the nineteenth century. About forty miles north of Salzburg and seventy miles east of Munich, Braunau is a good two-hour drive from both, on two-lane roads. There are few local trains between Munich and Simbach, the German frontier town across the Inn River. The train no longer comes to Braunau.

Partly because of this relative remoteness Braunau has been undamaged by the tempestuous ravages of the Second World War and by the less tempestuous but more endemic ravages of modern architecture. In 1874, three years after Hitler's father had come to take up his post as a customs official there, many of the wooden buildings of Braunau were destroyed by fire. But most of the houses of Braunau, built of stone, still stand in tight rows along the main city square, which serves as an open-air market once a week. They jut out more irregularly in some of the side streets. Many of them are buildings of the seventeenth and eighteenth centuries, and some even older. There are two particularly handsome prospects in Braunau. One is the remnant of the city wall (Braunau was a fortified town for centuries), with a few ramshackle gardens and houses set atop the grey stone ramparts in the cracks of which clumps of greenery have pushed their way through. The other is the view east from the large market square whose eastern edge is unobstructed by buildings and slopes slightly downward. The prospect is of a range of green-brown mountains under an unusually wide expanse of sky. But that bright lightness opens up away from Braunau, many of whose narrow streets, including the small square around its high-spired church, are seldom washed by sunlight. What is perhaps unusual is this combination: Braunau is both handsome and somber.

The somber quality resides in the darkness of some of its old houses, with their heavy buttresses. Their appearance is but a representation of the history of this town and of the complicated story of the loyalties of its inhabitants. The Inn River is the boundary between Austria and Germany; but that was not always so. For centuries Braunau was a Bavarian frontier town facing Austria. In 1706 it was a center of a peasant rebellion against the Habsburgs. It passed back and forth from Bavarian Wittelsbach to Austrian Imperial Habsburg rule. It was in Braunau that in 1810 Napoleon's new bride, the Archduchess Marie Louise, was festively transferred from her Austrian to her French entourage. During his campaigns against Austria in 1805 and again in 1809 Napoleon spent the night in this frontier town — in the same House Schüdl (and presumably in the same second-story rooms) where seventy years later Hitler's father came to live. It is a well-proportioned building on the south side of the large market square.

The house where Adolf Hitler was born stands a hundred yards farther down on the main street. In 1889 it was the Gasthaus zum Pommer, one of the two main inns of Braunau, an old hostelry once owned by a brewery — that is, a "Brauhaus." Hitler's father moved often, at least until he could buy his own house during the last years of his life; before that he had often preferred to live in inns. The Gasthaus zum Pommer is partially occupied now; it houses a hostel for handicapped children. Earlier it was a kind of public library. After Hitler had annexed Austria, Martin Bormann bought it for the purpose of ceremonial preservation. At that time, and also during the war, it was a place of pilgrimage for many people, most of them coming from Germany to contemplate the Führer's birthplace in awe. The house has something of a dual aspect now, almost as if it were divided against itself. The ground-floor façade is heavy and Germanic; the top two storys have the pale wash of yellow Austrian stucco. The back of this L-shaped house, with its arched corridors of the upper storys, seems abandoned and in poor repair. During my visit to Braunau the building was closed. I could not ascertain the location of the room where Adolf Hitler was born.

People in Braunau do not seem to be divided against themselves. They are a fairly homogeneous people, which is somewhat unusual, since during the 1940s (near the end of the war and for several years afterward) millions of the German-speaking peoples of Central Europe had moved from north to south and from east to west, leaving their great bombed cities, fleeing before the avenging Russian armies, expelled from their once homelands among other Eastern European peoples, eventually establishing themselves in postwar West Germany and Austria. (By 1950, for example, most of the inhabitants of Munich were no longer its natives.) But this great inchoate migration of peoples touched the Innviertel only marginally. Its people are stubby, gnarled, muscular, with some of the marks of inbreeding. (Hitler's father and mother, too, were second cousins.)

I came to Braunau in early March. A friend had reserved a room for me in the main hostelry of the town, Hotel zur Post, an old inn with gloomy rooms and a good sturdy cuisine. I ate my dinner alone, behind a table occupied by locals, including the owner, a man of a long line of Braunau innkeepers. I knew that they knew why I had come to their town; I was obviously a forerunner of the many journalists who had booked the Post solid for the nineteenth and twentieth of April. Their conviviality eventually spilled over the low back of the bench separating my table from theirs. As the dining room of the inn was emptying, one of them, a wiry little man, a bit in his cups, stepped over to sit with me. I told him that I was not a professional journalist but a historian, something that impressed him not at all. What seemed to impress him — and, I fear, not altogether agreeably — was that I knew something about the history of his town. I asked him where the Gasthaus zum Pommer was. We went out in the pelting rain. We looked at it. Then he invited me to go on drinking in another tavern. "My father was a Nazi," he said. "I don't know about myself." Then he added: "I am an engineer." At breakfast next morning the owner came over to sit with me. He started the conversation by telling me that "der Hitler" had lived but the first three years of his life in Braunau. (Actually he lived there even less than that.) Then he went on to say that, yes, there were people around here who had been Nazi sympathizers in the 1930s, but this had been a depressed region then, and people were influenced by the prosperity and the high level of employment of factories in German Simbach, a few hundred yards away across the Inn.

That was typical of the few conversations I had with people in Braunau — which is why I write that people in Braunau do not seem to be divided among themselves. There is, at the same time, a division, a kind of split-mindedness, within their minds. When it comes to memories of the Hitler years, they are defensive but not remorseful. When it comes to foreigners, the attitude reflects what, to them, is a commonsense skepticism: foreigners cannot, and will not, understand those things. But this is not an attitude of the people of the Innviertel in particular; it is an attitude still widespread among the people of Austria at large. What is particular about the people of Braunau and the Innviertel is their insistence that Adolf Hitler was not a typical son of their city and their land, that he was not really one of them. And in this they are, at least to some extent, correct.

There are three things in Hitler's early years about which he misled people: about Braunau, about his father and about his years in Vienna.

He dictated — dictated rather than wrote — *Mein Kampf* in the winter and spring of 1924–25. *Mein Kampf* consists of (and originally was to be printed in) two volumes, of which the first is autobiographical. Hitler declared this in his preface: from his own history "more can be learned than from any purely doctrinary treatise" about the development of himself and of the movement. Now he had "the opportunity to describe my own development, as far as this is necessary for the understanding of the first as well as the second volume, and which may serve to destroy the evil legends created about my person by the Jewish press."

Mein Kampf begins with a paean to Braunau. "Today I consider it my good fortune that fate designated Braunau on the Inn as the place of my birth." Again: "this little town on the border appears to me the symbol of a great task." And again: "this little town on the River Inn, gilded by the light of German martyrdom." Yet it is not only that the Hitler family moved away from Braunau in the third year of Adolf Hitler's life. All of his repeated emphasis on his native roots notwithstanding, he did not return to Braunau until his forty-ninth year.

He came back to Braunau on the twelfth of March in 1938,

on a Saturday, the day of the week when he was born. That Saturday in 1889 had been grey. Now Braunau was washed by the sun. The resistance of the Austrian government had collapsed the day before. That night people poured into the streets; there was a triumphant torchlight parade. A large swastika banner was draped over the stone carving of the Habsburg Imperial double-headed eagle at the top of the arch of the old city gate. From the early morning of the twelfth German army units were coming over the bridge, passing through Braunau, cheered on by the crowd. A little before four in the afternoon there was a hush. In a big open Mercedes touring car Hitler came slowly across the bridge. He received a large bouquet of flowers. His face was unsmiling. The automobile halted before the house where he was born. He did not descend; he did not wish to enter. Braunau did not mean much to him. He never saw it again. After March 1938 party officials and other enthusiasts designed embellishments and commemorative erections in Braunau. Hitler was not interested.

That afternoon he drove on, in the direction of Linz. His triumphant progress followed, by and large, the route of his family during his childhood and early youth. The year after his birth his father was posted from Braunau to three different places in Upper Austria, eventually settling in Leonding, a suburb of Linz. On the thirteenth of March in 1938, more than one hundred thousand people crowded into Linz to cheer Hitler. Their frenetic jubilation made him change his original plans; he proclaimed the union of Germany with Austria then and there. Till the end he had a soft place for Linz in his heart. A few days before killing himself in the Führerbunker in Berlin, he looked dreamily at a plan of a future Linz that he had wished to make into a great cultural center (and to which in his personal will he had donated most of his paintings). Leonding is on the way from Braunau to Linz; yet it was Linz first and Leonding second. From Linz Hitler drove to pay a short

visit to his parents' grave, in the parish churchyard of Leonding. I saw that grey gravestone, with his father's photograph
set in it under glass. In May 1945, after American troops had
set them free from the concentration camp in nearby Maut-
hausen, a schoolmate of mine and a friend had their memorable first picnic lunch sitting on the wall of that churchyard.
They saw an enormous wreath left on the grave of Alois and
Klara Hitler, with a wide ribbon: the homage of the party of
the district. In March 1989 there were two small pots of flowers on the grave.

Across the street from the churchyard stands an ocher-stuc-
coed one-story house where the Hitler family lived for eight
years. Not far from the other side of the church stands another
ocher-colored building, the tavern where Hitler's father was
sitting when he was struck dead by a stroke. Adolf Hitler was
thirteen years old then.

Hitler wished to obscure certain things in his youth. Unquestionable is the evidence of his love for his mother, a sad-
eyed, oval-faced woman, the third wife of his father. This was
a filial love about which Dr. Bloch (Klara Hitler's Jewish phy-
sician in Linz) said that he had seen nothing like it in his
career. What remains contradictory (and these contradictions
exist within Hitler's own statements) is his relationship to
his father. Alois Schicklgruber was the first of his line to rise
in the world. He was better situated and better off than his
son would later admit. Without anything more than a lower-
school education he rose to be a customs official in Braunau.
He was a sanguine, willful, respectable civil servant: his photographs exhale the picture of an official of the Habsburg Empire, self-confident almost to the point of caricature. He was
an illegitimate son (something that was neither rare nor particularly demeaning among Austrian peasant families at the
time) and changed his name from Schicklgruber to Hitler
thirteen years before his son Adolf was born. For this alone

Adolf should have been grateful. (The reminiscences of his schoolmate Kubizek sound convincing: Hitler said that "Schicklgruber impressed him as too rough, too peasantlike; besides, too long and impractical.") He inherited other things from his father, too: the latter's restlessness (Alois's frequent moves), perhaps also some of his attractiveness to women; his handwriting and his signature resembled his father's for a long time. Yet he was vexed, perhaps painfully, about his father throughout his life. In *Mein Kampf* he wrote about his father with glowing respect, in phrases of superficial sentimentality that are otherwise absent in that book. "I honored my father and loved my mother," he wrote. But during a long nocturnal conversation, replete with memories, with the Austrian general Edmund von Glaise-Horstenau (who was also born in Braunau) in April 1939 Hitler said something different: "I feared my father, but I loved him not at all."

He wished to distance himself from his family as soon as he could. As he told Glaise-Horstenau that night, he wanted to break away, "with the definite aim to become something really great." In this, as also in many other things, Hitler was very different from Napoleon, whose ties to his family had accompanied him (often burdensomely) throughout his life. Yes, Hitler was an Austrian who wished to be a great German, just as Napoleon the Corsican wanted to become a great Frenchman, or Stalin the Georgian a great Russian, or Alexander of Macedon the greatest Greek. Yet Hitler was perhaps less influenced by Austria than Napoleon had been influenced by Corsica, or Stalin by Caucasian Georgia.

He wrote at length in *Mein Kampf* about his progress from Braunau through Linz to Vienna, insisting that it was in Vienna that his entire ideology had crystallized. Most of his biographers and commentators have, by and large, accepted his explanation, emphasizing his Austrian background and his experiences in Vienna. There is some truth in these explanations, but not enough. Yes: his five years in Vienna influenced him in many ways. The life of a great city opened his eyes, in more ways than one. He read all kinds of political and ideological publications and he was, at least to some extent, impressed with their contents. But there is evidence that even before coming to Vienna he thought of the Austrian state as corrupt and ramshackle, while he admired the power of Germany. When he was twenty-three he left Vienna forever. The painstaking researches of certain German historians have since established that the picture he drew of himself of a poverty-stricken young man in Vienna was not correct. His small inheritance provided him with more money than he would assert later. It is questionable, too, whether his encounter with Jewish people in Vienna (where 90 percent of the Jews of Austria lived at that time — he had known no Jews in Braunau or Leonding and very few in Linz) was as decisive as he declared in *Mein Kampf,* since we have virtually no evidence of his essential anti-Semitism before 1919. It seems that the sudden crystallization of his world view came relatively late, in his thirtieth year, in early 1919 in Munich. It was then and there that the critical mass of Hitler's ideology congealed, out of his feelings about the defeat of his beloved Germany but even more out of what he saw as hateful and ugly in the few agitated months of the short-lived Munich "Soviet Republic." The other matter that this formerly shy and reticent young man had discovered within himself was this: he was a gifted public speaker, a *Redner.*

He was not a typical son of the land he had been born in; not in his elective affinities, not in his temperament or even in his appearance. In that part of Upper Austria there is a sun-bleached toughness in the faces of the people: a subalpine race, taciturn, suspicious of authority, conservative in their traditionalism, combative but not revolutionary. But Hitler was very far from being a traditionalist or a conservative. He was that frighteningly modern phenomenon, the revolutionary nationalist. "I was a nationalist; but I was not a patriot," he wrote. That distinction, that difference between nationalism and patriotism, is often obscured in our modern usage. The two terms are often used interchangeably. Yet "patriotism" is an old English word, while "nationalism" is a relatively new one, appearing first in the 1840s. The difference between patriots and nationalists has marked some of the deepest rifts in the history of the twentieth century. Patriotism is traditionalist, deeply rooted, introverted and defensive; nationalism is populist, extroverted, aggressive and ideological. Adolf Hitler chose to uproot himself from his family and his homeland. He wanted to identify himself with Germany, and he did.

Consequently Hitler did not have an identity problem. But an increasing number of Austrians did. The political manifestation of Austrian nationalism was born in the same decade in which he was born — among other things, in the form of Georg von Schönerer's Pan-German party, which strove for the union of Austria with Germany and, implicitly, for the dissolution of the traditional Habsburg monarchical state. Thereafter a paradoxical linguistic usage came into being. *Ein Nationaler*, a nationalist, in Austria was someone who wished to see the abrogation of an independent Austria and of a distinct Austrian nationality, in favor of their absorption into a German *Volk* and state. When in 1918 the Habsburg monarchy ceased to exist and Austria remained a truncated state, many Austrians thought that such a small country was not viable. Not every Austrian who thought so was a Nazi; conversely there were Nazis who wanted to maintain some kind of separate Austrian identity. Especially after Hitler had risen to power in Germany, a difference emerged among the Austrian people, between patriots who struggled to maintain the independence of Austria, and nationalists who fought for its union with the Third Reich. Added to this division between themselves there was a split-mindedness within themselves. The last Austrian chancellor who tried to maintain the independence of Austria from the Third Reich felt compelled to say that he stood for a "German and Catholic" Austria. After Hitler had marched into Austria, he chose to sanctify the union of Germany and Austria with a plebiscite. On 10 April 1938 only 5 people out of nearly 3,600 voted against Hitler in Braunau.

That was the year of his greatest and most convincing political triumphs. He was the greatest revolutionary of the twentieth century, whose entire political career was a refutation of Marx. In that year Simone Weil wrote this refutation of Marx: "It is not religion, it is revolution that is the opium of the people" — words fitting Hitler all too well.

Twenty miles to the south of Braunau, in the small village of St. Radegund, only one man voted against Hitler. I shall return to him near the end of this book.

⚜ III ⚜

THE END OF THE COLD WAR:

GOOD-BYE TO ALL THAT?

THE COLD WAR was the result — one of the results — of Hitler. He foresaw that. As early as November 1941 — almost three weeks before Pearl Harbor and the halt of the German advance before Moscow (that was *the* turning point of the Second World War, two great events simultaneously, one in a semitropical setting, the other amidst snow and ice, half a globe apart) — Hitler told a few of his generals that the war might have to end with something like a compromise.* The lightning-war period was over. Now his entire world strategy changed. Like his idol Frederick the Great, he would split his enemies. Germany would be so strong and tough (only then did Hitler decide to put the German economy on a full war scale) and inflict such defeats on one or the other of its enemies that their artificial coalition would break apart sooner or later. He knew that the Anglo-American-Russian coalition was an alliance of disparate peoples, with different purposes. This belief governed his military and political strategy up to the end.

He was both right and wrong. The grand alliance of Britain and Russia and the United States fell apart — but not until he

---

* From the diary of General Franz Halder, 19 November 1941: "the recognition, by both of the opposing coalitions, that they cannot annihilate each other leads to a negotiated peace." 23 November: "we must face the possibility that neither of the principal opponents [Germany and England] succeed in annihilating, or decisively defeating, the other."

was dead and his Third Reich a smoking hulk. He had painted himself into a corner. No matter how consequential their differences, none of his three enemies was inclined to make peace with him. The German people (and probably Hitler, too) thought that they had less to fear from the Americans than from the Russians and even from the British. The reconstruction of the secret (and some not so secret) German attempts to make some kind of contact with all kinds of Americans in 1944 and 1945, always with the purpose of provoking trouble between them and the Russians, still awaits its master historian. Most of these efforts were undertaken by Himmler behind Hitler's back, but it is by no means certain that they were undertaken against Hitler's wishes. Yet till the very end, as the wording of his last testament shows, Hitler said that he could not really state (surely not publicly) whether American or Russian rule over a conquered Germany would be preferable for the German people.

It is perhaps interesting that a few days before his death, Mussolini, too, put a similar rhetorical question to one of his remaining minions. "What would you prefer," he asked, "Italy becoming a British colony or a Soviet republic?" As behooves a former socialist and radical, Mussolini answered himself: "I'd prefer the latter." He failed to see that the era of British colonization was gone. Italy became neither British nor Russian but a kind of American satellite after the war. But not because of direct American pressures, but because that was what most Italians wanted at that time.

Italy — not the Italian people but the geographical position of Italy in Europe — had something to do with the origins of the cold war, though not very much. The cold war was the result of the division of Europe, which was the consequence of the war that Hitler had begun and fought. Not only was he the greatest revolutionary of the century, but the new German army that he inspired and helped to create proved to be the most powerful armed force in the world. For the total defeat of the Third Reich both Russian and Anglo-American power together were needed. That Churchill and Stalin and Roosevelt and Hitler understood. Their differences lay in their prospects of what Germany's defeat would lead to: what forms would the division of Europe take? As early as 1943 some people at the highest level of American policy planning were worried lest the Soviet Union acquire undue influence in an Italy liberated by the Anglo-American armies; they tried to limit Russian participation in Italian affairs. They need not have worried: Stalin's interest in Italy* was minimal. At the same time Stalin was worried lest the British or the Americans acquire undue influence in some countries of Eastern Europe that were to be "liberated" by the Russian armies. He need not have worried: the British, and especially the American, willingness to treat Eastern Europe as an important area of interest to themselves hardly existed at all.

By the time Hitler died, the division of Europe was accomplished. The upheaval at the end of the war was enormous; but there was nothing very revolutionary about that division. The eastern half (actually, one third) of Europe and of Germany was occupied and controlled by the Russians; it was to be ruled by them and by people who were subservient to them. In Western and Southern Europe, and in western Germany, the Anglo-American presence (after 1947 more and more American, less and less Anglo) helped to restore, or to establish, liberal and democratic governments. During the next forty-five years of the cold war there would not be a single pro-Communist coun-

---

* Or in France. In 1944 he told de Gaulle that the latter might as well allow the French Communist leader Thorez to return from Moscow to Paris. Thorez will make no trouble, Stalin said. He was indifferent to de Gaulle's disarming of the French Communist partisans. In 1944 it was the Americans who feared that de Gaulle might be too soft on the French Communists, while it was Stalin who cared not a whit for them.

try in Western Europe and not a single anti-Communist country in Eastern Europe (except for Greece, which in 1944 was
liberated not by the Russians but by the British).

Why, then, the cold war at all? Because of a mutual — or,
more precisely, reciprocal — misunderstanding. Soon after
1945 the Americans came to believe, and fear, that Stalin,
having brutally forced Communist governments on Eastern
Europe, was ready and willing to push Communism farther
into Western Europe (and western Germany). Conversely, Stalin believed, and feared, that the Americans, having established themselves in Western and Southern Europe, were
willing and ready to challenge his rule in Eastern Europe.
Both sides were wrong. The crude unscrupulousness of the
Russians and of their Communist satellites — their obsessive
propaganda and the brutality of their behavior — was a decisive contribution to these perceptions. But, then, so was the
ideological appeal of anti-Communism, concentrating on Communism rather than on Russian national interests — and unable to recognize that precisely because of the weakness of the
Communist appeal the iron curtain, that barbed-wire incarnation of the division of Europe, could not last.

I have written often about the origins of the cold war, a
reiteration of which is not now my purpose. There is, however,
one additional and important element that I must mention
here, where my theme is not the beginning of the cold war but
its unraveling and ending. It involves some of the original
perceptions of its duration. In 1945 Roosevelt and the American government thought, and hoped, that the military situation at the end of the war would be temporary: that after the
withdrawal of the occupying armies from most of Europe Stalin would be satisfied with the presence of pro-Russian, though
not necessarily Communist, governments in Eastern Europe.
That was not what Stalin wanted. He was well aware of the
weakness of the Communist appeal outside the Soviet Union,

which is why he preferred to have the states of Eastern Europe ruled by people whose inferior character was such that they were entirely, indeed abjectly, subservient to him. Very few Americans were aware of this inherent weakness, though Churchill was: as early as New Year's Day in 1953, when Stalin was still living and the dangerous tensions of the American-Russian cold war were at their peak, he told his secretary that if he (John Colville) lived his normal span he "should assuredly see Eastern Europe free of Communism." That meant the 1980s. Churchill's prediction was astonishingly precise. But it was long before the 1980s that the cold war — its original character, and its conditions — had changed, and drastically, even though so many people were either unable or unwilling to recognize that.

There is another prescient remark that Churchill made, already during the war, in November 1944, which has not received the attention it deserves. It was recorded by de Gaulle in his war memoirs. In answer to the latter's anxious query Churchill said: Yes, the Americans were rather thoughtless in not considering seriously the dangers of Russian expansion in Europe; yes, Russia now was a hungry wolf in the midst of sheep. "But after the meal comes the digestion period." Russia would not be able to digest the peoples and their states in Eastern Europe.

Digestive problems involve one of two matters — the unaccustomed quantity or the unusual quality of what had been ingested — or, in some cases, both. That was the case with the Russian ingestion of Eastern Europe from the beginning. By quantity I mean the territory they wanted to control: the geographical extent of their sphere of interest. It was too much — not only for the safety of Europe, not only for the sake of the world balance of power, but for the Soviet Union itself. Stalin knew that. He did not want more territory than had fallen to him in 1945; that was plenty enough. Not because he was modest: his principal interest, governing his policy till the day he died, was to make sure, brutally sure, to keep all that he got. The problem for his successors, then, was how to avoid the occurrence of violent disgorgements. Their insistence on a complete conformity to Russian ideological and political practices gradually weakened. The domestic independence of Eastern European states gradually increased, until Gorbachev gave up Eastern Europe without a fight.

But we must realize that this Russian territorial retreat from the middle of Europe — I repeat, it is territory that mattered and still matters, not ideology — had begun almost immediately after the war, more than forty years before that Eastern European *annus mirabilis*, 1989. In 1948 Tito's Yugoslavia broke away from the Soviet orbit. Because Stalin could not threaten Yugoslavia directly, having no common frontier with that country, his power was restricted to objurgations and subversive threats. The worst four years of the cold war followed; the iron curtain became a horrid physical reality; Eastern Europe (like the Soviet Union) was sealed away from the rest of the world through barbaric and despicable measures.

The Germanies were different. An East German satellite state came into existence in 1949; but across Germany, and Berlin, an iron curtain providing for a complete separation did not yet exist, because Stalin thought that the future of Germany might still be negotiable. He was sufficiently worried by the prospect of an American-German alliance to propose, in 1952, that he might give up the East German Communist state in exchange for a reciprocal American withdrawal from West Germany — for a neutral and unaligned, united Germany, in sum. The West German government and the Western powers did not respond. Some of the recently available East German files confirm that the possibilities for such an alternative were entertained by Stalin's successors almost until 1961, before the erection of the Berlin Wall. We also know that immediately after Stalin's death in 1953 some members of the Politburo, unsure and worried as they were, inclined to suggest to the Americans that a renegotiation of the division of Germany, or perhaps even of Central Europe, was a possibility. The aged Churchill thought that, too; but he was overruled by Eisenhower and Dulles, who did not wish to negotiate — nor did Chancellor Adenauer of West Germany.

Meanwhile the Soviet leaders were well aware of their digestive problems. The first open revolt against Communism broke out briefly in East Berlin in 1953; even before that, the new rulers in Moscow ordered a reformation of the Communist leadership in Hungary. The main spokesman for such a renegotiation was Stalin's feared and hated secret-police boss Beria. (It is almost always the head of the secret police who is most knowledgeable about potential troubles, and consequently willing to negotiate with a powerful enemy: Fouché during the last phase of Napoleon's and Himmler of Hitler's rule.) Khrushchev and his friends had Beria shot; but they felt constrained to go on with a policy of cautious territorial retreats. In 1954 they opened the way for a renegotiation of the division of Austria, meaning a reciprocal withdrawal from the Russian and Western zones of occupation there. Having overcome the resistance of the suspicious Dulles, in 1955 the Russian and the American (and British and French) occupation troops left Austria. A "neutral" (but decidedly Western and non-Communist) Austria came into being. One of the Russians' reasons for acceding to this was their — diminishing — hope that the Austrian model might be applied to Germany, that it would arouse the interest of the West Germans. This did not happen; but the first definite phase of a Russian retreat from the center of Europe had begun. (Within the same year they gave up their naval base in Finland and made up with Yugoslavia.)

All of this had consequences soon: the riots and revolts in Poland in 1956 and the more fundamental and dynamic national rising in Hungary (which could not have happened if Russian troops had still been present in eastern Austria). In any event, 1956 was *the* turning point of the cold war. Perhaps even the end of it, if by "cold war" one means the direct prospect of an actual war between American and Russian armed forces in Europe. Surely 1956 was the end of the most critical phase of their confrontation. The Hungarian Rising threw the Russian leadership into an unprecedented crisis, their greatest since the German invasion of their country in 1941. For a few days at the end of October in 1956 it seemed that the entire Soviet sphere was on the verge of dissolution. Then the Russians reacted: they chose to reconquer Hungary with their army. There was one principal element in their decision. They saw that, save for propagandistic activity, the Americans would not intervene; that, in sum, the United States was unwilling to risk any changes in the division of Europe — that is, in the status quo. Thus Khrushchev (who had already denounced Stalin during the Party Congress earlier that year) was reassured that Stalin had been wrong. The United States did not really wish to challenge the Russian sphere of interest in Eastern Europe, surely not at the risk of war. (Or at the risk of renegotiating the division of Europe: when the Russians put down the Hungarian Rising, Eisenhower and Dulles were relieved.) Thus, despite the justified universal hue and cry about the brutal Russian suppression of the Hungarian Rising, the conditions for an improvement of American-Russian relations were in the making; and less than three years later Khrushchev himself would arrive in Washington, a visit that he had desired above everything else.

There were two other consequences of these events in 1956 that I must mention at this point. It was in 1956 that the final erosion, the last phase in the history of the appeal of Communism in Europe, began. Many intellectuals in the West were now leaving the Communist parties in droves (in my opinion, too late to be to their credit). It was also the beginning of that opportunistic and increasingly meaningless hybrid called Eurocommunism. In Eastern Europe, particularly in Hungary, some of the more intelligent Communists had become the most determined anti-Communist thinkers, writers, resisters, dissidents.

There was another, related consequence that may deserve attention. That was the rise of Andropov — and, ultimately, that of Gorbachev — in the Soviet hierarchy (since the latter eventually became the former's protégé). Andropov was the Soviet ambassador to Budapest during the Hungarian Rising. The post of a Soviet ambassador in one of the minor satellite capitals was an unimportant one. But Andropov had his eyes open; and he never forgot what he saw in those days. Twice during that rising two of the highest Kremlin personages, Mikoyan and Suslov, had flown into Budapest, without being able to stem the rapid course of events; but it was Andropov who helped to save the Russian bacon. It may be that he invented the Kádár solution, meaning that he found a Hungarian Communist leader who was willing to lead a new pro-Soviet government and party in Hungary, though not one who would turn the clock back and restore all of the instruments of the myopic Communist terror that had ruled the country before 1956. The Politburo was grateful to Andropov, whence his rise to higher and higher posts of the Soviet government, eventually to the headship of the state police apparatus and, in 1982, to his leadership of the entire Soviet Union. But — probably because of his experiences in 1956, too — Andropov also knew how corrupt and dangerously unpopular the rule of a narrow and selfish Communist party hierarchy could be. Had he not died in 1983, there is evidence that some of the reforms that Gorbachev then began to institute would have been made by Andropov himself. It was not only that Gorbachev was someone whose political and administrative talents he had recognized, that Gorbachev was his protégé; it was that Gorbachev had learned from Andropov, as indeed Andropov had learned from what he had seen in Budapest in 1956. So ran the thread from the successful architect of the Soviet suppression of Hungarian democracy in 1956 to the man who thirty-odd years later made parliamentary democracy in Hungary possible and removed the last Soviet troops from there. "God writes straight with crooked lines." I am reluctant to cite my oft-quoted favorite Portuguese proverb; but I think that in this instance it is appropriate.

How did the cold war come to an end? Since 1956 — perhaps even after 1953 — it was winding down. Yet the digestive problems of the Russians were insufficiently understood in the West, and especially misconstrued in the United States. From the Russians' bad table manners people concluded that their appetite was insatiable, whereas the opposite was rather true: their digestion was poor. And this condition no longer involved only political geography, the excessive quantity of their sphere; it involved, inevitably, the essence of Communism — that is, the quality of it. All over Europe, very much including Eastern Europe and also in the Soviet Union, the remnant belief in Communism was evaporating until, in the 1980s, the realities of that evaporation became so obvious that even a Ronald Reagan could no longer ignore it. In Western Europe the Communist parties shrank year after year; in countries such as Italy and Spain they had become small-bourgeois capitalist parties, Communist in name only. *Mutatis mutandis*, the same thing happened in Eastern Europe. There a class of party members still formed the governments, but true Communist (or even Marxist) believers among them existed no longer. They were a new class of functionaries and bureaucrats, interested in nothing other than the maintenance and security of their power — for which, in a crisis, their only guarantee seemed to be the power of the Soviet Union. Some of them, as Ceauşescu in Rumania, became extreme nationalists; that helped their popularity, at least for a while. By 1985–86 it became evident that while the United States no longer challenged their legitimacy, the Eastern European Communist leaders could not count on the unequivocal support of Moscow even when in trouble. In 1989 all of them gave up their power without risking, let alone firing, a shot. (The only exception was Rumania, where there was some — not much but a little — fighting, since the security services of the Ceauşescu tribe were very large. They consisted not of Communists but of nationalist thugs serving the national dictator.)

Much of this was true of the Soviet Union too, where, during the years of the decaying Brezhnev rule, it was increasingly obvious that the most corrupt and inefficient element in the government was the party itself. There the last believing Communists dwindled to a small minority by the time Gorbachev appeared. His most ominous opponents were not former rock-ribbed Communists but nationalists, both without and within the Russian ethnic mass: military men and ideological nationalists, bitter as they witnessed the demolition not of Communist ideology but of the external and internal bulwarks of the Soviet state.

It is with the above in mind that we ought to consider the real nature of the occasional crises that punctuated Russian-American relations since 1956 — hiccups in the digestion, delaying the winding down of the cold war. In 1960 the Russians shot down an American spy plane, the U-2; but they shot it down over their own country, after having tolerated the crisscrossing flights of American spy planes over the Soviet Union for years. In 1961 came the Berlin Wall: but that monstrous thing was built to contain, not to expand; to keep tens of thousands of East Germans from filtering through to the West. In 1962 came the Cuban missile crisis: but that came about because the Russians had to do something for Castro, since they had been unwilling to guarantee him against an American invasion that seemed to be more and more within John Kennedy's plans; and the evolution of the crisis showed that nothing was further from the Kremlin's purposes than to risk a war with the United States over Cuba. In 1968 Brezhnev sent troops into Czechoslovakia; but only after he had become sure that the Czechs would not put up a fight and that the Americans would not react; he overcame his reluctance to act when he began to worry that the disappearance of Communism in Czechoslovakia might spill over into the latter's neighbors, including the Ukraine, part of the Soviet Union. In 1980 the Russians moved troops into Afghanistan, where one of their tribal chieftains, nominally a Communist, had been murdered by another nominally Communist tribal chieftain; but also because they — wrongly — feared that Jimmy Carter was about to invade the neighboring state of Iran. By that time Brezhnev's military advisers had built a large Russian war fleet, for the first time in Soviet history; but the presence of that fleet meant little or nothing in the Mediterranean. It was the American Sixth Fleet that patrolled the Persian Gulf and the Lebanese coast, landing Marines there in 1982, six thousand miles from Norfolk and only a few hundred miles from the state frontiers of the Soviet Union. The powerful Russian fleet stood by at a very respectable distance, doing nothing at all.

I wish not to be misunderstood. A bully, when feeling threatened, will act aggressively; he does not cease being a bully. The leaders of the Soviet Union were neither modest nor pacifist. But their most startling acts of intervention were made because of purposes that were defensive; they had more troubles of their own than people suspected or were willing to admit; their appetite for more foreign expansion and conquest was something quite different from being insatiable. With all the technological and analytical information at their disposal, people in charge of the enormous bureaucratic labyrinths in Washington, Experts — and, increasingly, intellectuals in high government positions — either did not see these things at all, or surely not clearly enough. Worse: when people do not see something, this often means that they do not wish to see it — a condition that may be comfortable and profitable to them. That was true of many of our presidents during the cold war, from Eisenhower to Reagan; of popular political figures, from Joe McCarthy to Oliver North; and of experts such as Henry Kissinger, who began his grand public career by touting the existence of a — as we now know, nonexistent — Missile Gap. Consequently, the cold war lasted longer than it should have, and the United States became transformed into the very military-industrial state the prospect of which in 1960 a speechwriter put in one of Eisenhower's last public speeches — the end result being that while it is not now arguable that the Soviet Union lost the cold war, it may be arguable whether the United States has won it.

But then, the United States and Russia never fought a war — indeed, during most of the two world wars they were allies.

One of the main, perhaps *the* main reason that the cold war did not become a hot war or a Third World War was that the great mass of the American and Russian peoples have had no historic antipathy between them. Distant, they knew little about each other, they did not hate each other. That factor was probably even more important than the existence of the dreadful atomic weapons when after 1945 great wars between the superpowers became almost unthinkable. Despite the overwhelming sentiment of anti-Communism, and despite the existence of certain anti-Russian ethnic groups within the

United States who were pushing for ever more aggressive American interventions against the Soviet Union, the great majority of Americans were not only unwilling to contemplate a Third World War; they had none of the feelings and the memories that historically hostile neighboring peoples so often harbor against each other. Perhaps even more important were the sentiments of the Russian people — indeed, of most of the people making up the Soviet Union. It is wrong to believe that public opinion (or popular sentiment) does not exist under totalitarian dictatorships. All dictators, including Stalin, are aware of the larger and deeper currents of the sentiments of their peoples. For two centuries Russians have liked Americans perhaps more than they have liked any other people. (That their affection for Americans and for things American has often sprung from illusory or insubstantial knowledge is beside the point.)

We have seen that 1956 was the turning point of the cold war, but that it took more than thirty years to wane and disappear. One of the main reasons for the continuation of the cold war — indeed, for some of its bloodiest episodes — was the unexpected appearance of Communist regimes in unexpected places of the globe. Until 1960 every Communist government, except for Yugoslavia and Albania, was a neighbor of either the Soviet Union or China (or, like East Germany, occupied by the Soviet army). From 1960 on, beginning with Cuba, Communist or pro-Communist governments came into being in the oddest places: Abyssinia, Angola, Suriname, Mozambique, Nicaragua, Afghanistan, Grenada. Some of these soon devolved into blood-encrusted tribal tyrannies — some of them *were* bloody tribal tyrannies from the beginning. Their self-invented "Communist" label confirmed the American belief that the entire history of the twentieth century was marked by the titanic struggle of Democracy vs. Communism. Yet the Soviet Union had nothing to do with these "Communist" revolutions. Unlike the Russian-imposed Communist governments in Eastern Europe, these revolutions or coups were spontaneous, surprising Moscow as well as Washington. Often they were not even the results of local Communist agitation, of local Communist parties, of local Communist revolutionaries: Fidel Castro, for example, did not even know (or say) that he was a Communist until well after he had marched into Havana. He was a "Communist" because he was anti-American, not the reverse. (Had he arisen twenty years earlier, when the adversaries of the United States were Germany and Italy, Castro would have surely declared himself a "Fascist." Among other things, he was a great admirer of General Franco, at whose death in 1975 he declared a week of national mourning in Cuba.)

The leaders of the Soviet Union felt compelled to assist most of these newfangled allies — for a while. Yet the importance of their relationship with the United States had an absolute priority over their relations with their faraway supplicants. Russia did not have the slightest intention of establishing important Soviet bases in the Western hemisphere or in Africa. During the last ten years more of these "Marxist" governments gave up, except for Cuba, whose *líder maximo* had had his bitterest disappointments with the Soviet Union well before the 1980s. After all, the Russians had left him in the lurch in 1962, unwilling from the very first moment of the missile crisis to come even close to risking a war with the United States over Cuba. (That it took more than twenty years for the time-servers of the Kennedy court to recognize this, let alone to admit it, is another story.)

Nearly two centuries ago, some thirty years after the American Revolution, some people in South America were sufficiently inspired by the example of North America to declare their own independence from the distant and weak Spanish motherland. One hundred and sixty years later few people in

Washington were willing to recognize that the one common element in most of the revolutionary movements sputtering in the oddest places of the so-called Third World was a tribal hatred of foreign, in most cases white, power. That this kind of hatred was, in most instances, as unjustified as it was short-sighted is another matter. But I have to mention it here, since among other things it proves again that the ideas and the appeal of anti-colonialism (more precisely, tribal nationalisms) have been more enduring than the idea of the proletarian revolution of the international working class; and that for two hundred years at least, the main agent of anti-colonialism has been the United States rather than Russia — in the twentieth century Wilson and Franklin Roosevelt rather than Lenin and Stalin.

Soon after the Cuban missile crisis subsided, another set of crises broke into the open in another part of the world. Washington chose to see America threatened by the increasing incursions of North Vietnamese into South Vietnam — that is, by the prospect of portions of Indochina falling to "Communism"; hence it became engaged in a war in Vietnam. The Russians showed no interest in Vietnam, they intervened not at all, and sent but the meagerest supplies to the North Vietnamese brethren — in the Russians' view, no relatives of theirs, distant supplicants at best. But while the United States got bogged down in the Indochinese morass, the Russian leaders felt suddenly threatened on two fronts. Communist China had acquired its own atomic bombs; and there were Chinese pressures on Mongolia, Sinkiang and all along the four thousand miles of inadequately marked and often indefensible Asian frontier between the Soviet Union and China. In early 1968 an actual bloody battle erupted along the Russian-Chinese border. Closer to home, Communism was then unraveling in Czechoslovakia. Brezhnev chose to suppress it (we have seen that the agonizing decision to intervene in Prague was made in the Kremlin once it was sure that the Czechs would not fight). At the same time Moscow suggested to Washington a query: would the United States remain indifferent if Russia mounted a preventive attack on China (probably restricted to the nuclear plants of the latter)? Of course the national security people in Washington rejected any such Russian suggestion with horror. It was at that moment that Richard Nixon, a provincial and small-minded politician at first, decided that he would become a World Statesman (insisting on this avocation ever since that time). His global vision was assisted by the globular Kissinger, whose ideas of a world balance of power impressed Nixon. He would make an Opening to China, playing the Chinese card against the Russians. (Probably it was the obverse of what they ought to have done: they ought to have said to the Russians that the United States would be indifferent to what Russia might do to China, in exchange for which the Russians should let a more liberal Czechoslovakia be — in which case the final unraveling of the cold war might have proceeded twenty years earlier than it did.)

Kissinger and Nixon's (and Ford's and Reagan's and Bush's) playing of the China card did not amount to much — it was the Chinese who knew how to play the American card. In any event, American notions about China being a Great Power and the greatest possible foreign market for U.S. goods are old American illusions going back long before the calculations of recent presidents. The key to the cold war was Eastern Europe, not Asia. Throughout the twentieth century the realities of power and politics in the Far East have been more changeable than those in Europe, where, after all, twice the United States fought a war allied with Russia against Germany. Throughout the twentieth century the kaleidoscope of the Far East changed much more, and more often. There were times when the United States was allied with Japan against an unfriendly Russia; other times when it was allied with Russia against Japan; yet other times when it was allied with China against Japan; again other times when it was allied with Japan against China; and there was a transitory period during the 1970s and most of the 1980s when the United States cultivated good relations with Japan as well as with China, while the Russians were unable to do so. This transitory phase is now over. American relations with Japan are not what they were; nor are those of Japan and China, which is the more important of these permutations. The last two may be growing closer to each other, mostly because the Japanese wish to see that happen. If they succeed — and there is no certainty that they will — a Japanese-Chinese alliance may become the greatest power in the world, threatening, at least potentially, America and Russia alike. Then America and Russia will become allies again.

I began this subchapter by recalling the existence of popular opinion in Russia even under Stalin; and I must conclude it by recalling one of its most extraordinary eruptions during the entire history of the Soviet Union. This occurred before the American embassy on 9 May 1945, Russia's V-E Day. It was a spontaneous demonstration, involving perhaps as many as two hundred thousand Russians, unplanned and unorganized: the true outburst of a people who, joyful as they were because of the end of a terrible war, wished to express their gratitude and affection for the United States. It was much more than huzzahing an ally; it was a mighty chorus of thanks.

Forty-six years later the elements of this kind of empathy still exist, at a time when the government of the United States faces what may be its greatest problem in the long run: what would the United States do and how should Americans look at the prospect of the potential dissolution of the Russian empire itself?

☙

17 August 1991. *I was an early anti-Communist. At the age of seventeen I read Marx, and found him almost always unrealistic, at times unreadable. I wrote about this intellectual experience in my* Confessions of an Original Sinner, *and about error after error in Marxist philosophy elsewhere. I shall not sum up these things here. I left my native country and my family in 1946, at the age of twenty-three, even before Hungary became entirely Communist-ruled; I knew that this would happen because of the Russian presence, and soon. The future, including my own future, was America. I hoped against hope that the United States might do something to force the Russians out of Hungary; but I was almost certain that this would not happen. Still I hoped and argued for some American intervention in Eastern (more precisely, Central-Eastern) Europe. Somewhat later I changed my mind, or rather my desiderata. Perhaps alone among my émigré countrymen I had convinced myself that the hopeful prospect for my native country was not a further worsening but an improvement of the relations between the United States and Russia — because the American threatening of Russia about Eastern Europe would make the Russian grip there tighter, not weaker; because those threats would not be translated into direct action; because the United States would no more risk a world war with Russia over Hungary (and it shouldn't) than would the Russians risk a world war with the United States over Cuba; because the improvement of American-Russian relations might lead to a renegotiation of the division of Europe, which could involve Hungary. This*

did not happen; but after a little more than forty years the Russians gave Hungary up. Forty years before, I thought that they would remain in Hungary for at least fifty years; I was ten years off, thank God.

Forty years earlier no one, including myself, thought that we could ever return to our native country while the Russians were still there. Here I must mention an interesting psychic phenomenon (interesting to me, too, because it is yet another denial of the Freudian dogma according to which dreams are always and necessarily the products of the subconscious; to the contrary, they are reappearances of consciousness). After I had fled Hungary, I had a dream that recurred every few weeks. After a while this dream came to trouble my sleep every few months; and about thirty years ago it ceased altogether. In this dream I was back in Hungary, on a visit, but painfully aware that I had been reckless and foolish to return; I saw that on the faces of all my friends and relatives; the Communist police were closing in on me; I would be arrested soon and never allowed to leave again. I then learned that many of my fellow émigrés were plagued by the very same dream (a phenomenon that goes against the grain not only of the Freudian but also of the Jungian dogma, since it had nothing to do with the Collective Unconscious; it was the product of the consciousness of similar experiences and similar fears). These dreams disappeared because of the passage of time, but also because the iron curtain itself was corroding. For at least twenty years before the final, and actual, demolition of the iron curtain something became possible that we had not dared even to dream about: we could visit our native country, fairly safely. Most of us did this, myself included, several times. One common conscious experience remained: the relief every one of us felt at the moment when we were leaving Hungary, passing the last Hungarian frontier post and glimpsing the first Austrian border marker or customs barrier from our rented car or through the window of our train slowly gathering speed.

Now this is gone too. I had come back to Hungary for short visits until I would spend more than two months there in 1987, closeted in the new national library, reading and researching for my Budapest 1900 book. I was almost certain then that the last vestiges of Communist rule would be gone soon and that, at the most, some Russian military bases would remain. My friends in Hungary were more pessimistic, but that is perhaps a result of the traditional national temperament. Three years later I returned again, to witness the opening of a freely elected Hungarian parliament, about which more anon. In early 1991 I returned to teach a semester at the university in Budapest. In June 1991, a few days after I left my native country for home (consider but the meaning of these juxtaposed terms that sound as if they were an oxymoron, which they are not), the last Russian troops were to leave Hungary. A great national celebration was proposed for that day, a national fête, all church bells ringing. I was not pleased with this. It was not necessary to insult the Russians. Russia would remain a great country, and a neighbor of Hungary after all. I never had any particular liking for Russians, and I never had anything but contempt for Communism. But I knew, all my life, and in the United States as well as in Hungary, plenty about the dangerous stupidities of anti-Communism, its obsessive elevation into a popular ideology, as if it were synonymous with patriotism, which it is not.

"The insane fear of socialism throws the bourgeois headlong into the arms of despotism." Tocqueville wrote that in 1852, four years after he stood up against the socialist workers and the radical revolutionaries in the streets of Paris. A century later anti-Communism was due to more than insane fear, and it was not restricted to the bourgeois. Often it was most popular among the workers themselves, especially in the United States. (Marx ignored not only the nationalism of the proletariat — that antiquated word — but also their addiction to respectability.) Mussolini and Hitler and an endless host of dictators could not have come to power without the popular appeal of anti-Communism.* It is foolish to think that the mainspring of anti-Communism is the concern of people for their financial security. It has been far more popular and emotional than that.

The psychology of anti-Communism is a complex matter that has not yet received the attention it deserves. A dedication to truthfulness, a measure of honesty and, yes, bravery (more precisely, a contempt for and a revulsion of official and prevalent untruths) are the qualities present in almost every private (or, rarely, public) expression opposed to Communism in countries and in places where Communists or their satellites are in power. Where they are not, a self-identification with anti-Communism suggests a kind of self-satisfaction, the source of which is, more than often, the desire for respectability, the wish to assert that one belongs within the mainstream of public opinion, and within the authentic community of the nation. I have seen plenty of opportunistic Communist fellow travelers in my life (and not only in the twilight years of 1945–46 in Hungary); I have, alas, seen even more opportunistic

---

* Late in November 1932, Hitler to Hindenburg: "The Bolshevization of the masses proceeds rapidly." He knew that this was not true. He also knew that this was the kind of argument that would impress Hindenburg and the conservatives. Unlike nine years before, when his *Putsch* was shot down in the Munich streets, he would become the ruler of Germany legally, constitutionally, democratically, not against but with the support of the most respectable elements in Germany — at least in part because of their anti-Communism.

anti-Communists in the United States, many former leftists among them. I may have written a few things about this unsavory phenomenon elsewhere. Here I only insist that the ideology of anti-Communism contributed to the protracted nature of the cold war. The identification of anti-Communism with American patriotism did, on occasion, damage to traditional American liberties,* and it contributed powerfully to the establishment of the American military-industrial state. The obsession with Communism obscured the main condition of the cold war, which had little to do with Communism. That condition was the presence of Russian armed power where it did not belong. And now, when the cold war is over, the temptations of many of these questionable patriots persist: unappeased by the Russian withdrawals, they go on with their propaganda to promote the dissolution of the traditional Russian state proper, trying to convince themselves and others that it is the prime interest — and task! † — of the United States to propagate and impose its system of government and philosophy on most of the world, including Russia, half a globe away.

---

* A few examples from my files. The antimilitarist (but Germanophile) Mencken in 1947: we should go to war against "the Russian barbarians." When Truman fired MacArthur, 1951, a Resolution of the Michigan State Legislature: "World Communism achieved its greatest victory of the decade." (In Los Angeles the city council ordered the American flag flown half-mast.) Joe McCarthy about the same event: "the greatest victory the Communists have ever won." Senator William Jenner of Indiana: "Agents of the Soviet Union" were actually in charge of the Truman Administration.

† Midge Decter: "America should be the policeman of the world." A statement by an American intellectual, *anno* 1991.

⚔ IV ⚔

RUSSIA. THE FRONTIER.

19 August 1991. At eight in the morning the telephone rings. Jim McBride calls with the news that Gorbachev is out, a new state committee of emergency took power in Moscow, with Yanayev. My first reaction: it will not last.

20 August, afternoon. It seems to me that this coup is already fading.

21 August. The coup has failed. This is remarkable and good; but the real problems and troubles are only beginning. George Kennan says that this is even more remarkable than was 1917. This is true in one important sense: I, too, am heartened by the resistance put up by young Russian people in Moscow and Leningrad: this may be something new in the history of that vast, unfortunate country.

The final end of Communism, etc. But Russia? The Russian empire? Isn't it — in a way — like March 1917? Except that there is more to Gorbachev and Yeltsin than there was to people like Kerensky. Also: there is no strong leader among the Russian nationalists, surely not now.

But this entire coup, these three days, was only a short blip in the history of the dissolution of the Russian empire.

On a May evening in 1991 I was at Budapest's East Station, the Keleti, waiting for my stepson to arrive on the Vienna train. On one of the two main departure tracks I saw a large train, Budapest-Lwów-Moscow, full of Soviet soldiers, officers, their wives, leaving Hungary. The big green Russian coaches were crowded, soiled, people were heaving their cheap suitcases and bundle after bundle up the carriage steps and through the corridor windows. There was something pathetic in the shabby quality of their uniforms, of the women's clothes, their baggage, the train. They were settling in, elbowing their way through the packed corridors to their compartments, leaving their garrison lives in Hungary without regret.

They were not attractive, these Russians. Yet they were preferable to the underworld that now inhabits the once so monumental, romantic halls of the Keleti, one of the architectural wonders of Central Europe one hundred years ago: an underworld of petty criminals, pickpockets, many Arabs, Rumanians, Gypsies, mixed with the scouring of the now borderless ghetto of the criminal populace of Budapest; a sinister crowd. They were the bad lot of the homeless, homeless by choice, not because of a cruel fate. The Russians — they were going home.

Those Russians on the Russia train were the last frothy surf of a receding tide. The Eastern people milling in the station were the first froth of an incoming tide from the east, nomadic or near-nomadic, a tide whose extent is still unforeseeable and immeasurable — a great migration that may overwhelm Hungary and Europe. Another tide; and perhaps behind them a great Asian tide, rolling westward — in which event Russia will be the outer breastwork, the shield. The Russians: the bulwark of Western civilization, of the white race in Europe. This is a prospect no longer unthinkable, no longer implausible.

In 1943 Louis-Ferdinand Céline wrote that the German army at the Volga was the last bulwark of Europe; after that the deluge, les Chinois à Brest. He meant not Brest-Litovsk on the Polish-Russian frontier but Brest at the westernmost *tip of Brittany, of Europe. He lamented that the Germans lost the battle at Stalingrad and that their retreat westward then began. He was wrong about that. The Chinese are not in Brittany and even the Russians are out of Berlin — indeed, out of Eastern Europe. And once Uzbeks, Turkmens, Mongols, the advance guard of "les Chinois," begin surging westward, it will be the Russians whose historic task will be to hold them up. Russia, the new frontier of what remains of Western civilization. During the last Mongol invasion of Europe, in the thirteenth century, the fall of Kiev preceded the Battle of Liegnitz. That sequence may not repeat itself. But I am a historian, not a prophet.*

Russia and the United States. Tocqueville wrote one hundred and sixty years ago about these great powers beyond Europe, one standing for freedom, the other for servitude, each powerful enough "to sway the destinies of half the globe." This is over now. The United States is no longer the unique incarnation of a free democracy; and servitude in Russia, especially the kind of servitude that still existed there in Tocqueville's time, is gone too. (The servitude imposed by technology and bureaucracy and the internal and external rise of the New Barbarians threaten both; but that is another story, the problem of the twenty-first century.)

As I wrote before: Russia and the United States never fought a war. They were allied in the two world wars, against Germany. (And, in a way, against Japan.) Also: it is not only that the Russian and American peoples have never disliked each other. They also have some characteristics in common.

An interesting element: the great Arctic and subarctic relationship of Russians and Americans on the northern rim of the

Pacific. Alaska and Siberia. The Russians were willing to let Americans have Alaska for a pittance in 1867 (hoping thereby — in vain — to embroil the United States with Great Britain in the far west). The fantastic stories of Alaskan-Siberian contacts from 1919 to 1924 still await their full historical treatment. The iron curtain (twenty-five years before Churchill would use that famous term) had already clanged down on the western frontiers of the diminished Russian empire. But in the Far East it took another three to five years until Moscow's rule was consolidated. In the meantime all kinds of fascinating contacts existed between Alaska and eastern Siberia, involving fur traders, buccaneers, roustabouts, ambitious criminals of all sorts. (Not to speak of the fact that the emphatic American military and naval presence in Vladivostok till late 1920 was meant to keep the Japanese from snatching a portion of the Russian Far East for themselves.) Even now I read of the decision of the Alaskans to ship thousands of tons of Alaskan salmon as a gift to the Russian people.

When the Russo-Japanese War had broken out in 1904, the American press and public opinion were anti-Russian because of what they had heard about Tsarist persecutions, including pogroms. Cartoons abounded: "The gallant little Jap pummeling the Russian bear," etc. The Russian foreign minister Witte came to New York, trying to counteract it. But Theodore Roosevelt was statesman enough. The Japanese were winning on the Korean-Manchurian front, they had won the naval war hands down, but at Portsmouth Roosevelt succeeded in delimiting their conquests. It was not in the American interest to see Russian power in the Far East crumble, to be replaced by a gigantic Japanese empire.

In 1945 all of the American military, very much including all the later so vocal anti-Communists, including General MacArthur, praised the Red Army to the skies, wishing for

Stalin to enter the war against Japan. In 1905 Lenin had re-joiced in the Japanese victory over Tsarist Russia. In August 1945 Stalin's Order of the Day to the Russian Far Eastern Army called its officers and soldiers to expunge the shame of Russia's defeat by Japan forty years before.

Stalin was a Russian nationalist. It was not Communism, not Communist revolutions, but Stalin's wish to make the Russian conquest of Eastern Europe, including parts of Central Europe, solid and permanent that led to the division of Europe and the cold war. Much of this was (and often still is) obscured by the ravages of ideological thinking and propaganda, of pro-Communism as well as of anti-Communism. During and for some time after the war, an uncritical appreciation of Russia contributed to the American unwillingness to define the lim-its of Stalin's conquests. Franklin Roosevelt's politic idea to position himself midway between Stalin and Churchill (and to distance himself from the latter on crucial occasions) corre-sponded to the then widespread American view that American democracy, historically, politically, perhaps even socially, stood and moved somewhere between an older world incar-nated by Britain and the somewhat crude but in some ways admirable radical pioneer experiment of the Soviet Union. In 1942 *Life* magazine (whose publisher, Henry Luce, had pro-claimed the American Century) printed a full-page picture of Lenin with the text: "This Is Perhaps the Greatest Man of the Century." In 1953 the editors of *Life* theologized that Com-munism was "mortal sin," while McCarthyism was only "ve-nial sin." Many Americans seem to have forgotten that, had it not been for the Russian army, Hitler might have won his war. To many anti-Communism had become not only an ingredient of, but identical with American patriotism — an ideology propagated by honest people as well as by converted intellec-tuals, time-servers, by a widespread fauna of opportunists. It was the ideological cement that bound the American "conservative" movement and the Republican party together — a cement that may be dissolving now.

Still, the Russian-American relationship is simpler, less complicated than the Russian-European relationship. There is the element of distance: Russia borders on Europe, not on the United States, except at that faraway, marginal Alaskan-Siberian tip. There is the long haul of history: one thousand years of contacts, enmities, alliances, deeply felt differences and attractions between Russia and Europe. Such contacts between the United States and Russia during two hundred years were fewer and less important. (Culturally, too: the Russian interest in second-rate American writers such as Jack London and Hemingway. Poe's influence on Baudelaire was more profound.) The Russian-American enmity of the cold war, the two governments regarding each other as principal enemies in the world (and in the skies), was but a short chapter in their history, now closed. Even then (despite all of those missiles) they did not directly threaten each other.

In the one thousand years of Russian and European enmity and friendship, revulsion and attraction, fear and hope, invasions and retreats, isolation and participation alternate. And "Europe," of course, is not of a piece, as is the United States. At times Russia was allied with Prussia and Germany, at the expense of Poland; at times aligned with Poland against Germany; at times allied with Britain (or France); at times threatening Britain (and even at war with Britain and France, in the Crimea, 1854–56). In 1612 the Poles were in Moscow. In 1814 Cossacks were galloping up and down the Champs-Elysées and four districts of Paris had Russian military governors. In 1941 the Germans stood before Moscow, in 1942 they reached the Volga and the Caucasus. In 1945 the Russians took Berlin. None of these geographical extremes would last. But this is not the place to sum up the history or the complicated elements of Russia's relationship with Europe, including their cultural relationships, about which thoughtful books have been written. Here one thing stands out. No matter what happens, Russia not only borders on Europe; she is the frontier of Europe — and Asia. The Communist regime in Russia was an anomaly. All of the great alternating fluctuations notwithstanding, history does not move like a pendulum. There is no precise returning, no repetition of things where they once were. In the long run Russia is becoming more European (and American too).

What happened in Petrograd in November 1917 was more than a Communist coup. It was Russia's withdrawal from Europe. The makers of that revolution proclaimed that the old Russia was too "Asiatic" — that is, not European enough. They claimed that Marxism, the most radical of all the revolutionary ideologies coming from "Europe," must be adapted to Russia. The opposite happened. Russia withdrew from Europe — geographically, physically, politically, socially, ideologically. Already Lenin was compelled to do so. His successor Stalin disdained European ideas, including International Communism. Unlike Lenin, who was a revolutionary but not a statesman, Stalin was a statesman, not a revolutionary. (Revolutionaries seldom make good statesmen.)

In 1939 Stalin's Russia reentered Eastern Europe. Stalin, the lone master of the only Communist state in the world, his Russia a pariah in the eyes of many governments and peoples, suddenly found that his alliance was coveted by France, Britain, even by Hitler's Germany, in view of a coming war. He found that his Russia could profit more from a deal with Hitler — the apostle of anti-Communism — than from France and Britain. He had more respect for Hitler than for the democrats and liberals and capitalist leaders of Western Europe. So his Russia regained almost half of Poland, the Baltic states, a slice of Finland, Bessarabia and Bukovina from Rumania — almost all that Lenin had forfeited. On one occasion Stalin told Hitler's foreign minister that he, Stalin, understood Asia and Asiatics better than Europeans understood them (which may have been true). On another occasion, in 1941, he told the visiting Japanese foreign minister, with whom he signed a treaty: "We are Asiatics, too." Hitler — whom he liked, admired, respected, feared — attacked him in 1941. For a moment it seemed to Stalin that all was lost. Then came a change. The Russian soldiers, the Russian people, the Russian mud and snow and ice — and the knowledge that they were not alone, that they had the British and the Americans for their allies — stopped the Germans. By 1945 the Russians were in Berlin, Vienna, Prague, and were the masters of much of Eastern Europe. They entered Central Europe with a vengeance. Forty-five years later they retreated from it again.

But this was not the whole story. As so often in Russian history, the external and the internal, the physical and the mental relations of Russia to Europe, have not been synchronized, they have been contradictory.

Peter the Great tried to make Russia a European state. He took his primitive, loutish Russia by the scruff of the neck and pushed it forward (that is, westward). He pushed Russia into the Baltic, he conquered what today are Estonia and Latvia from Sweden, he created a new capital city, St. Petersburg, in the fens and marches. This military and geographic movement toward Europe went apace with the Tsar's creation of institutions emulating European ones. Yet Peter's methods (and even the character of some of his novel institutions) remained remote from the habits, customs and practices of most of the European states of his day. He "Europeanized" Russia, with non-European methods.

Still, the Russian state — not the country, not the nation,

not the people, not the church — became part of the European system of states in the eighteenth century when the entry of Russian armies into European wars and countries was requested, arranged and, at times, paid for by various European powers during the century from the death of Peter the Great to that of Napoleon. On occasion Russian soldiery trooped through Prussia, Bohemia, Saxony, Hungary, as far west as Switzerland, Holland, Italy, France. But they did not stay; and these short-lived military movements did not correspond with inward Russia, a country that remained almost as remote and alien from Western Europe as before.

In a more lasting way, the westward movement of the Russian empire itself went on: the Crimea, Moldavia, much of Poland, present-day Lithuania and Finland were acquired by Peter's successors. During the nineteenth century there came a change. Russian music, Russian literature, Russian art, and learning became enjoyable, intelligible and accessible to Europeans and Americans for the first time. That expansion was remarkable both in its extent and in its qualities. At the same time, during the nineteenth century the advance of the Russian frontier toward Europe largely stopped. Russia was expanding in the Causasus, in Asia, to the south and east. The double pull of Europe and Asia was there. (It is seldom known that the division of "European" and "Asiatic" Russia became an accepted notion only in the 1830s, when a German geographer defined the eastern border of "Europe" along the Ural Mountains and the Caucasus; but that main frontier along the Urals did not and does not correspond to any administrative boundary within Russia itself.)

In 1918 the Russian state withdrew from Europe geographically as well as politically. The 1917 revolution occurred in St. Petersburg but, mostly because of military exigencies, in 1918 the Bolsheviks moved the capital back to Moscow, where it had been before Peter the Great's time. It stayed there. After a brief "Petrograd" denomination, St. Petersburg became "Leningrad." In 1991 it became St. Petersburg again.

But it is unlikely that it will become the capital of Russia again. The oscillation between "European" and "Eurasian" Russia, between the Petersburg and Moscow periods of Russian history, is now over. The exact place of the Russian–Eastern European frontiers has fluctuated through the centuries, and it may still fluctuate; yet has Russia no other choice but to become more and more "European" — in the good as well as the bad sense of the word? That will depend on Europe, not on Russia; on what "Europe" — and "America" — will mean.

The sympathizers as well as the obsessed enemies of Communist Russia have not understood this. The former saw Russia for a long time as an ideological prototype of a pioneer Marxist socialist society, overlooking the fact that a nation is a *cultural* prototype — that, after all was said, the Russians remained very Russian indeed. The latter saw Russia as the incandescent focus of international revolution, long after Stalin had shown that he was hardly interested in that.

Few statesmen in the twentieth century were as contemptuous of International Communism as was Stalin. Under his regime we may detect a last example of the curiously unsynchronized nature of and the differences separating Russian foreign and internal policy. Because of the rising power and threat of the Third Reich, Stalin's Russia signed an alliance with France (and Czechoslovakia) in 1935; at the same time the Communist International adopted the so-called Popular Front policy, calling for an alliance of all "anti-Fascist" forces. But that, for Stalin, was all foreign matter. Within the Soviet Union his purges began. Their horrible evidences were lamentably and dishonestly ignored not only by pro-Communists but by all kinds of other people in the Western world.

That is now well known. What remains misunderstood is Stalin's main purpose with the purges (misunderstood even by anti-Communists, beginning with Koestler's melodramatic and nonsensical interpretation in *Darkness at Noon*). Most commentators and historians have seen the purges as the manifestations of a dictator's paranoia. There *was* something to that. But what the purges essentially accomplished was the replacement of an older Communist party (and military) bureaucracy by a newer kind of state bureaucracy with one common denominator: its complete subservience to Stalin and his state. Between 1935 and 1939 Stalin's foreign commissar Litvinov was still allowed to preach and promote "Collective Security" against Hitler and "Fascism," respect for the League of Nations, cooperation with all democratic and liberal forces and statesmen in the West. At the same time within the Soviet Union tens of thousands of internationalists and other old Bolsheviks within the Communist party were arrested, imprisoned and murdered. By 1939 this discrepancy was over; the purges ended; "Collective Security" and Litvinov were gone, too; and Stalin opted for an alliance with Hitler.

The world, in the long run, has received one benefit from the brutal and insensate cruelties that Stalin visited upon his own people. Had he not done so, he would be more revered by his people than he is now. The long-range consequences of his crimes have made his name, like Hitler's, anathema.

For seventy years Communism retarded the normal progress, the Europeanization, the gradual liberalization and material improvement of Russia, which had begun under the last Tsars. There is one exception to this. In 1917, facing a German army slowly advancing, nibbling at the western edges of their empire, the people of Russia grew tired of the war; they gave up. In 1941, facing almost the entirety of the greatest German war

machine in the history of the world, which reached the out-
skirts of Moscow and Leningrad, the Russian people fought
on. Their resistance was unpredictable and unexplainable. It
sprang and grew from many sources. A generation of impoverished, stupefied, downtrodden masses stood the test better
than their previous generation during the First World War.
Their resistance and victory over the Germans was their greatest — no, their *only* great — achievement during the seventy-
four years of Soviet Communism.

Oddly enough, they are not of one mind about this — and I
mean the Russians, not some of the nationalities that actually
welcomed the German victories.

Again this involves Stalin's place in their history. Stalin's
diplomacy before June 1941 was cowardly. He was unwilling
to believe that Hitler would invade Russia; he left most of his
military machine unprepared until the last hour (and in some
instances even a few hours beyond that). He was badly shaken
in the beginning of the war, apathetic and mute for nearly ten
days. In September he actually wrote Churchill that the Soviet
Union was "on the verge of collapse"; he asked Churchill for
the most senseless and impractical kind of help, including the
sending of twenty-five British divisions to southern Russia.
There are some indications that he would have responded to a
German proposal for an armistice, had there been any. Still,
during the great panic of October–November 1941, when the
government was fleeing Moscow, where the inhabitants may
have been ready to surrender to the Germans, Stalin kept his
head. In the end, he thought it better to stick with his alliance
with Roosevelt and Churchill — no doubt, too, because he
knew that Russia would get much out of that.

He was not enthusiastic about that alliance; and it behooves
us to remember that there were many Russians of like mind.
There is a kind of American parallel here. There were and still

are Americans who thought, and for a long time, that Roosevelt's alliance with Britain and Russia was a mistake, that it was against American interests to go to war with Germany. There were, and there still are, Russians who preferred, and prefer, Germany over the English-speaking world. Add to this their rejection of all that was Communism. In the United States we have rehabilitated the poet Ezra Pound, which is inconsequential on the larger scale of events. In Russia a rehabilitation of General Vlassov would not be inconsequential.

General Vlassov was a very Russian figure — a Dostoyevskian one. He fought with distinction during the first winter of the war. In June 1942 he suddenly chose to go over to the Germans. That conversion occurred because of his hatred of Stalin, and of Communism. There has been no comparable event in the history of the Second World War, otherwise replete with men changing camps, surrenders, betrayals. There were French, Czech, Yugoslav and Greek generals who surrendered to the Germans, who even sided with them politically; but there were none who were willing to join the Germans and assist the Germans in the war against their own country. Vlassov formed a Russian nationalist army. For a while Hitler would not accept such an army; eventually he relented. The Vlassov brigades included some of the worst criminals of the war among their ranks; some of them distinguished themselves (if that is the word) by committing the vilest cruelties against the heroic Poles during the Warsaw Rising in 1944. Vlassov himself was not an unattractive personage. He was a Russian idealist, a military intellectual with high Slavic cheekbones, a sorrowful countenance behind thick horn-rimmed glasses. In the end, the Allies turned him over to the Russians; he was tried and executed in 1946 in Moscow.

He was undoubtedly one of Stalin's major victims. It is almost certain that his reputation will rise now — together with those of some of the other Russians and Ukrainians and Cossacks who fought not only with Vlassov but in units of the SS till the end of the war. To what extent? That will be a symptom for the immediate future of Russia. Will Vlassov's reputation rise above or at least equal that of Russia's best generals during the Second World War, of Zhukov, for example, who had his troubles with Stalin but who was Stalin's marshal, after all? If that happens, it will be a worrisome thing; another, even though indirect, rehabilitation of Hitler's cause in retrospect, and the symptom of future where "the West," for Russians, will mean Germany above all.

In 1948 Yugoslavia was the first state to break away from the Soviet sphere. In 1991 Yugoslavia was the first formerly Communist country breaking apart in a brutal civil war. There is a lesson in this somewhere.

The main division in Europe (and in England) through the nineteenth century was that between conservatives and liberals. These terms have become imprecise and they are often employed not only imprecisely but illegitimately. For more than one hundred years two major forces have replaced them: nationalism and socialism.

Not in Russia. There, too, the two old terms do not quite fit; but there is a corresponding, perhaps even deeper and stronger division: that between Westernizers and Slavophiles.

This Russian duality does not correspond to the Eastern-Western oscillation of Russian history (in the seventeenth century, from Ivan the Terrible to Peter the Great, by and large an Eastern period; thereafter a Western period, from Peter the Great to Lenin). The roots and sources of the Russian duality between West and East (not so much between Europe and Asia as between Europe and non-Europe) derive from a remoter past, incarnated in the history of the Russian Church and its religion, Byzantine but not Western Christian from its very beginning. Even the schisms *within* the Russian Church (especially during its crisis in the dark seventeenth century) are full of significant details.

It was during the nineteenth century, when Russia grew, albeit often slowly and erratically, more and more European, that the two opposing groups of Westernizers and Slavophiles crystallized. They represented the two poles around which the intellects of Russia gathered then — in some ways even now. Before 1917 the Westernizers were the pro-Europeans: aristocrats, liberals, radicals and intellectuals who thought that Russia was backward, that she had to shake off the remnants of a barbaric and semi-Asiatic past to catch up with the progressive, liberal, advanced civilizations and institutions from Europe. The Slavophiles were the anti-Europeans, at times deep-thinking conservatives who thought that most nations and beliefs of Europe were rotten within, that Moscow was the third Rome and that the Russian people, leaders of all Slavs, were Chosen People of God, uncorrupted by the rest of an immoral and heretical Europe.

Toward the end of the nineteenth century the war between these ideological schools of thought abated somewhat. Among other things, a new, not really Slavophile, conservative group formed (around an excellent journal, *Vekhi*), full of promise. But the Westernizers, the liberals and the radicals, seemed to have won. By 1914 the intelligentsia and the upper-class culture of Russia seemed more Western, more European than ever before. The Communists, too, took their ideology — their Marxism, their atheism, their materialism, their idea of progress — from the West. They succeeded in gaining control over Russia; they won the Russian civil war. Then it became apparent — to those who saw deeper than the surface — that the Russia that congealed under Bolshevik rule was full of non-

European, Slavophile characteristics. The capital was moved back to Moscow. There came the struggle at the top between Trotsky and Stalin. (The young Trotsky once called the Bolsheviks "slavophilizing Marxists"; but then he elected to become a bloody Bolshevik.) It is not in the least surprising that Stalin beat him out of power, forcing him into exile; for even though Stalin was born in Georgia, he was the more typically Russian of the two, a kind of Slavophile, to boot.

Russia is different now. Not many Russians see themselves as the Chosen People of God. Also: Communism killed pan-Slavism, or at least wounded it deeply. The trust and faith that any Eastern European Slavic peoples have had in Russia for centuries is gone (except perhaps in Serbia). Also: "Westernizer" no longer connotes only pro-European; it also means pro-American. (The cultural relationship of Russia and America is a great open question for the future.) Still, beneath the categories of conservatives and liberals, religious and agnostics, the division between Westernizers and Slavophiles somehow endures. Peter and Ivan, Chaadayev and Khomyakov, Turgenev and Dostoyevsky, Witte and Pobedonostsev, Milyukov and Rasputin, Trotsky and Stalin, Litvinov and Molotov . . . and, during the second half of the twentieth century, Pasternak and Sholokhov, Sakharov and Solzhenitsyn . . . Soon, new protagonists will emerge.

In America there has been a similar division, between isolationists and internationalists, Redskins and Palefaces (it may be significant that these two labels were invented by Philip Rahv, an American critic of Russian birth): Bancroft, Whitman, Mark Twain, Vachel Lindsay, Robert Frost Redskins; Prescott, Henry James, F. Scott Fitzgerald Palefaces (the list is mine, not Rahv's). Still the categories leak, they are imprecise. Every American was a bit of a Redskin, every isolationist a bit of an internationalist, every American idealist a bit of an American imperialist — and the reverse.

Even more so in Russia — Tolstoy, for example (about whom the Marquis de Vogüé wrote that he was "a mixture of chemist and Buddhist," and Chesterton: "the mixture of an inhuman puritan and a presumptuous savage"). Isaiah Berlin's celebrated essay separating Tolstoy the hedgehog from Tolstoy the fox, the artist from the philosopher, was all wrong. It is not that Tolstoy was a hedgehog at one time and a fox at another; he was always, and simultaneously, both (if the hedgehog-vs.-fox metaphor is really apt, which it isn't). What is more important: the movements of opposites in relation to each other are indications of their relative strengths. Many more outstanding Russians became Slavophiles after having been Westernizers than the other way around. The Slavophiles were more stubborn than the Westernizers, whose ideas changed throughout the nineteenth century, depending on the principal intellectual and political currents coming from Europe, while the ideology of the Slavophiles remained in essence constant.

And — this is important — even the isolationist Slavophiles got many of their original ideas from Germany. (The ideology and even the terminology of the early Russian Marxists also came from Germany.) The emotional and sentimental exaltation of the *Volk* ("folk," *narod*), the nationalist romanticism of German thinkers of the Fichte type, formed many of the foundations of the Slavophile ideology. Dostoyevsky's Francophobia and Turgenev's Francophilia were not superficial or accidental. (The influence of German literature on Dostoyevsky has been considerable; he cribbed entire plots from E. T. A. Hoffmann and other German gothic tale-tellers.)

The great history of Russian-German relations, profound with tragedies and attractions and meaning, is not closed. A new chapter has been opening. It now depends not on literature or ideology but on the suddenly enormous question of the immediate future of the Russian state.

In my writing and teaching I have almost always preferred "Russia" and "Russians" to "the Soviet Union" and "Soviets." I know that this is imprecise — as is "America," too, for the United States, and "Americans" for United Statesians (so are "English," "British," "Irish," on occasion). But "Soviet Union" is even less precise than "Russia." It comprised fifteen (at times twelve, at times fourteen) "republics" and hundreds of nationalities. But the essential factor in the history of this century is still that of the state, and its relationship with other states. Stalin's and Khrushchev's and Brezhnev's state, no matter what its name or constitution, was a continuation of the age-old Russian state, made by Ivan and Peter and Catherine and Alexander and Nicholas, not by Marx or Engels or Lenin. By now (September 1991), besides its imprecision, the term "Soviet Union" had declined to the level of near-absurdity. The name of the Holy Roman Empire gradually meant less and less in the late seventeenth and eighteenth centuries, before the final demise of that title in 1806; but even during the last phase of its existence it was a more meaningful title than that of the Soviet Union during its final demise. And the Holy Roman Empire lasted one thousand years, the Soviet Union only seventy.

But *Russia* lasted one thousand years. It may last another thousand. And *Russian?* Well, millions of the inhabitants of that state and empire were not Russians, but their official or at least their second language and much of the culture and most of their institutions were Russian, and so they are even now. The disappearance of Communism in 1991 is an event of very small importance when compared to the dissolution, or even to the regression, of the ancient and traditional great Russian state. Communism is gone; Russia will remain. How much of that empire, how much of that state? *That* is the big question, and not for Russia alone — for Europe, for America, for the world. A *Russian* Russia is now coming into being, but what will its extent be? and its function?

The name of Leningrad reverts to St. Petersburg; but it is not *entirely* impossible that the extent of Russia may be reverting to something it was before Peter.

The first Russian state was Kievan *Rus*. Then came the Tartar invasion. Then the Grand Duke of Muscovy became the Tsar of Russia. During all of those centuries the history of Russia, its government, its monarchy and its society were fundamentally different from those of European states. Then came Peter, who wanted to make Russia into a state — primarily, though not entirely, in the European way. He also conquered lands and their peoples who were not Russian. His successors, Tsarinas and Tsars, went on to extend the Russian empire in Poland, along the Baltic and the Black seas, in the Caucasus and in Asia. That was not entirely unlike the English conquest of Wales and Scotland and Ireland, or the French conquest of Alsace and Lorraine, or the American acquisition of French Louisiana, Spanish Florida, the Southwest. The empire endured not only because the Russians were strong but because their state institutions and even their culture were stronger than those whom they had incorporated (the Poles and the Finns having been probably the only exceptions to that). In most cases the Tsars had conquered lands — often largely empty lands — inhabited by peoples who were not yet nations. The Tsar's government held it all together. There was — often not because of Russian moderation but because of a certain Russian carelessness — a considerable cultural (and sometimes even political) autonomy for some of these non-Russian peoples under the last Tsars. Their stirrings of nationalism, with their ultimate desire for an independent national state, had begun (and not even everywhere) only a century or so ago, agitated by a few intellectuals and revolutionists.

Lenin thought that the latter were working for him. There were many non-Russians among his Bolsheviks. He thought that what happened in Russia would simply repeat itself among the non-Russian peoples of the former empire. He was wrong: anti-Communists won in Finland, the Baltics, Poland, among peoples who were allergic to Muscovites, to Russian conditions and institutions and ideas that they considered and felt inferior. In the Ukraine, in Georgia and Armenia, in the Caucasian and Asiatic portions of the old empire, Lenin and his allies won. Tribal nationalism there was not strong enough to resist or defeat the superior power of the Russians.

The Communist party became the cement that held the institutions of the Soviet Union together. Stalin, who started out as a commissar of the nationalities, understood the problem. He tried to Russify some of the nationalities as much as he could, using alternately the carrot and the stick. The carrot was, among other things, the enlargement of their territories. The Ukrainian nationalists ought to be thankful to Stalin, who made a Ukraine larger than it had ever existed before, including Polish lands and the important slice of the so-called Carpatho-Ukraine, beyond the Carpathian Mountains, belonging to a Russian-speaking state for the first time in history. The Lithuanians owe him a measure of thanks too: their capital and principal city, Vilnius, had been taken by Poland in 1920, but in 1939 Stalin gave it to Lithuania — geographical conditions all but forgotten now.

But that cement of the party, and of the "Union of Soviet Socialist Republics," was not enough. Nationalism reached even the most remote and backward of Soviet "republics." That may be *the* principal problem of the next quarter century or more. It is not certain whether the majority of their peoples really want independence and sovereignty, that they wish to be entirely detached from Russia. Yet that may not matter. Plebiscites, referendums and national elections may only becloud the issue — except that in this democratic age they bequeath a kind of legitimacy to the "independence" of a new nation. People enjoy their national flags and other symbols that range from the sublime to the ridiculous, such as national airlines, national license plates and so on. The image is as important as is the reality. The reality is armed power. If the Russians cannot cajole them back into some kind of federation or confederation with Russia, will the Russians resort to force to bring some of them back, or at least keep them politically in line (not to speak of the purpose of protecting millions of Russians living in these "republics")? The image is important: are these people ready to die for their new flags? All this may lead to bloody civil wars — but on the guerrilla level, not to wars of entire national armies fighting along definite fronts. The texture of history has changed. Perhaps the emotions of nationalism will not erupt on battlefields; the flag may be fought for during bloody riots in crowded stadiums above football fields. Perhaps not.

Contrary to the accustomed beliefs, all this depends little on economics. Small states can survive very well. Switzerland or Luxembourg are better off than Britain or the United States. Georgia and Armenia may become like Syria or Rumania, the Asian republics more or less like Iran or Afghanistan. I can foresee a bubbling new Levantine world, a subcivilization ruled by brigands and traders — another reversion to something that existed before the Modern Age.

The Russian concept of the state is peculiar, both stronger and weaker than the idea of the state in the Western world.

The origin and the essence of that is Constantinism. The emperor Constantine was probably the greatest political benefactor of the Christian Church in two thousand years. He sided with the Christians and put an end to their persecution. But he was not himself a Christian and he led a crude and licentious life. Consequently, to the eternal honor of the Western Church, he was not beatified, not elevated to sainthood. In the Eastern churches, in Byzantium, whence Christianity had come to Russia, he *is* a saint. So is Saint Vladimir, the Kievan ruler who forced his people to immerse themselves in the Dniester River for their mass conversion (rare in the West, where conversion and baptism are individual, not collective). Vladimir is a saint in Russia and the Ukraine, but not in the West. (A German chronicler recorded a descriptive phrase of the person of Vladimir in his time: *fornicator immensis et crudelis.*)

That Constantinian and Byzantine element is the origin of the union of state and church among the Orthodox peoples of Eastern Europe and Russia: autocephalous and Caesaropapist. Other peoples, in the West, have not been immune to the temptations of Caesaropapism or of a nationalist church. There were plenty of bishops who were willing to pay homage to German emperors, to Henry VIII, Louis XIV, Napoleon, Mussolini and, on occasion, to Hitler. (Consider, too, the nationalism of many religious leaders in the history of the United States.) Still, Constantinism in the West is not the rule. Popes and bishops defied not only Henry VIII but a succession of monarchs and dictators. Consider but one important difference between Poland and Russia. In the former the Catholic Church was a bulwark against Communism, retaining much of its spiritual and religious independence. In Russia the Orthodox Church collapsed in 1917; save for certain admirable exceptions it could produce no focus of resistance amidst an otherwise superstitious and religious people. Stalin knew this. During the war and after he restored many of the privileges of the Orthodox Church, and he forced a return to Orthodoxy on the (superficially) Rome-related Ukrainian Uniates (i.e., "Catholics of the Eastern rite"). Stalin was once an Orthodox seminarian; on occasion he would privately express his belief in the existence of God. He was no true Christian of course; but neither was Peter the Great, who had, however, insisted on the complete unity of the Russian Church with his state, meaning the subordination of the former to the latter, a supreme law that remained in force until 1917.

"Church" as well as "state" were bad words to Lenin. He was a quintessential Russian revolutionary atheist. Yet Caesaropapism came back under Stalin, and so did the cult of the state. I wrote earlier that what the purges led to was Stalin's replacement of an old party bureaucracy with a state bureaucracy that was entirely subservient and obedient to him. That corresponded with the reappearance of the respectful usage of the word "state" in Soviet terminology, journalism and propaganda by the late 1930s. By that time "state interests," "state security," "state organs," etc., became sacrosanct terms, superseding references to party and ideology on important occasions. The Bolsheviks' secret police itself — renamed often — eventually became the state security organization. Its personnel was not composed of ideologues, radicals and revolutionaries, but by policemen and bureaucrats who had quotas to fulfill. Like all policemen and agents, they had to make work for themselves. It was not fanaticism or dedication to the ideals of Communism that explained, at least in great part, the senselessness of the arrests during the purges. What Joseph Conrad wrote about his secret agent was applicable to radical anarchists and revolutionaries circa 1900; but I once found Anthony Trollope's description of an English detective (in *He Knew He Was Right*) in those dear, lawful, sedate Victorian years which is applicable to every state security official in the twentieth century, including the personnel of the OGPU-NKVD-MVD-KGB: "He was a man loving power, and specially anxious to enforce obedience from those with whom he came in contact by the production of the law's mysterious authority. In his heart he was ever tapping people on the shoulder."

In Russian the word for a citizen is *grazhdanin*, meaning the inhabitant of a state, not of a city. In Europe all civic freedoms had come from the city (in early medieval Germany: *Stadtluft macht frei*, "the air of the city makes you free"), long before the French invented the word "citizen" and made it universally applicable to everyone within the national state, including peasants and fishermen living beyond any city. (The origin of *bourgeois*, *Bürger*, *borghese*, etc., was the medieval city too.) I have written about this elsewhere, but it is perhaps especially apposite to Russia, where, unlike in Europe, the cities (except for Novgorod, destroyed by the Muscovites in the fifteenth century) had no walls. In Russia there was no physical separation of the city and the country; the walls were those around the kremlins, separating the quarter of the rulers from the ruled, an oriental tradition and practice. Urbanity, citizenry, civic rights and bourgeoisie are *the* modern Western tradition, going back even to Greece and Rome (*polis*/politics, *urbs*/urbane). The Russian tradition was different.

Nicholas II was a weak and incompetent Tsar. His abdication was a disaster for Russia, and perhaps for the world. Tsar and Tsarism had held that immense empire together. The liberal democrats who succeeded him in March 1917 were incompetent in almost every way. Lenin and the Bolsheviks were more determined; but they, too, lost the western provinces of the empire — which under Nicholas II had been slowly, creakingly moving toward some kind of constitutional monarchy, toward Europe. (Still, there were dreadful obstacles to that, phenomena such as Rasputin, a sinister and powerful "monk," an apparition from the Dark Ages in the second decade of the twentieth century. I have often thought that the true symptom of what went wrong with Russia was the Russian Orthodox Rasputin rather than the atheist Lenin, whose success was but a consequence of the weakness and corruption that allowed for the sordid influence of people such as Rasputin.) In any event, whenever a Tsar was weak, or even somewhat liberal, troubles came. During the century before 1917 Nicholas II and Alexander II were assassinated, and the confused Alexander I disappeared in obscurity; but the martinet Tsars Nicholas I and Alexander III died in their beds, mourned by tens of millions. The long and dreadful Time of Troubles in the early seventeenth century, when Muscovite Russia had shrunk pitifully, was only due to the chaotic confusion and weakness of the throne, when there were years the people did not know who was the real Tsar.

That is a peculiarly Russian problem. France's decline, too, began with the end of the old monarchy; but that was only one of the factors. The French state (and not only under Napoleon) survived. In Russia after 1917 the authority of Lenin and especially of Stalin grew beyond the extent of the authority of a Tsar, but — Stalin may have understood this deep down — it was very vulnerable because of the power they had vested in the party. That was the only cement, the only instrument of the legitimacy of the government. I am not only referring to the fact that had it not been for Communism, Russia would have ended among the victorious Allies in 1918, and — apart from its territorial gains — would have moved swiftly toward the status of a more or less modern Great Power. Communism weakened, not strengthened, Russia. There is a sentence, almost always overlooked, in George Kennan's "X" article in 1947 that has proved to be absolutely correct: "If anything were ever to occur to disrupt the unity and efficacy of the Party as a political instrument, Soviet Russia might be changed overnight from one of the strongest to one of the weakest and most pitiable of national societies."

This is happening now. But there are also Bismarck's wise words: "Russia is never as strong — or as weak — as she seems."

Hereditary and constitutional monarchy can hold peoples together (that is, until the limitations of the monarch's authority decline to such an extent that even the symbolic meaning of his presence is compromised and bereft of respect), perhaps especially in the time of rising democracy. This is true not only of England, as Bagehot observed more than one hundred and twenty years ago. There are many such examples (as, for instance, the return of a monarch, King Juan Carlos, to the throne of Spain). It is particularly true of multinational states. The person of Franz Joseph held the Austro-Hungarian Dual Monarchy together. Russia would profit from the restoration of a constitutional monarchy, though this seems to be out of the question. For Rumania (including its minorities) the best thing might have been if the exiled Michael II had flown to Bucharest on 23 December 1989, the day after Ceauşescu's fall (instead, he waited until it was too late). It would be a good thing for Bulgaria if Simeon II would return as a constitutional king (he left the country when he was a young boy, in 1946). Perhaps even in Yugoslavia, where the son of the sadly forlorn Peter II (the only European monarch who died in the United States) might have prevented the 1991 civil war. If Otto von Habsburg, respected and liked in Austria, Hungary, Czechoslovakia, Slovenia and Croatia, were younger (he is seventy-nine now), more ambitious and shrewd, he would try: he has potential support in these countries; but of course to translate potential into actual political support is another thing. He could be the head of some kind of federation resembling — though only to some extent — the old Danubian empire; something like that at any rate would be more natural, deeper rooted and enduring than those loose economic ties going under the name of a practically nonexistent "European Community."

These are the thoughts of a historian, not the nostalgic musings of a reactionary. A hereditary (as distinct from an electoral) constitutional monarchy is especially suited to modern democracy, when masses of people are not only avid for the symbols of royalty but when, more than ever before, they need the visible presence and consequent authority of a compassionate father (or mother) figure, the presence of a respectable reigning family, with their children. Such authority ensures not fear and perhaps not even power, except that kind of intangible power that is the result of decent, honest human respect. A constitutional and hereditary monarchy in the twentieth century is more than an instrument for continuity and tradition. Its function is historical, but also political and social. It is a guarantee of lawfulness and, yes, even of liberalism. Alas, it will not happen. (Not until centuries from now, when a new feudalism will have formed again, with the rise of new barbarian chieftains, when a future Otto the Great may be an uncultured but extremely intelligent combination of Rock Star and Gang Leader.)

The historical consequences of the retreat and dissolution of empires are enormous. They last through centuries. The bankruptcy and decay of the Spanish empire led to the great Atlantic world wars between France and England. The emergence of the United States was a part of that vast chapter of history. The eighteenth-century world wars between England and France lasted one hundred twenty-six years; the decline and decay of the Spanish empire lasted more than three hundred years, from the defeat of the Armada in 1588 to the Spanish-

American War in 1898. (Eventually the United States inherited much of the Spanish empire, including its naval presence in the Mediterranean, reaching as far as the Philippines — from which it is retreating now, as it will one day retreat from Puerto Rico too.)

On the other edge of Europe the retreat and dissolution of the Turkish empire lasted a quarter millennium, from about 1683 to 1923. It led to what our ancestors called the Eastern Question (more correctly than their present successors who keep calling the Near East the "Middle East"). The retreat and dissolution of the Turks led, among other things, to the outbreak of World War I. In the Balkans the Russians and the Austrians (and by 1914 even the Germans in Turkey) were asserting their interests; their support of their satellites led to many conflicts and small wars, threats of greater wars, assassinations such as that of the Austrian archduke and heir in 1914. Farther to the east, the end of the Turkish empire led to many of the rational and irrational struggles that typify the Near East even now. (Were the Turks still in charge of Mesopotamia, were the Spanish still in charge of Cuba, were the British still in charge of India, wouldn't we be better off? and wouldn't their subject peoples be better off? Now that *is* a historian's nostalgia.)

And now has come the dissolution of the Russian empire. It may be irreversible. What tremendous consequences may follow in that vastest land mass of the world, the Eurasian heartland of the globe about which geopoliticians have been speculating and scribbling since the beginning of the century? Some of their speculations may have been vaporous. Not vaporous was something that, alas, Hitler recognized (and Roosevelt did not): the return of the primacy of land power over sea power after five hundred years. However, the main threat to Russia no longer comes from Europe. Even if the Germans establish their predominance in Eastern Europe, they will not again aspire to conquer Russia. (But a German alliance with a pro-German Russian regime will be possible.)

Meanwhile the faint shadow of a new Islamic or Mongol or Sino-Japanese ambition in portions of Asian Russia is discernible. Whether that shadow will become substance is not certain. Our children and grandchildren will know that. Not for another century will people be able to perceive the lasting consequences of the end of the former Russian empire. And by that time a new age will be upon the world, the texture of history will have changed, it is even possible that the territorial ambitions of large, centrally governed states will no longer be the prime factors of history. (Possible, but far from certain.)

I have been berating Marx for nearly fifty years, to point out that amidst the truly protean evidences of his shortsightedness he never paid attention to nations and to nationalism, the main political force crystallizing already during his lifetime; that he confused the nation with the state. His opposite in the twentieth century was the German Carl Schmitt, whose reputation — perhaps exaggeratedly — is now rising among political theorists, even though he was (at least for some years) what his enemies called him, the Crown Jurist of the Third Reich. Now we are facing a new phenomenon across the globe, including even the United States. Nationalism is as strong as ever, while the authority and efficiency of centralized governments have begun to weaken.

The relationship of nation and state is now variable and uncertain. The modern state is nearly five hundred years old, the ideal of the national state less than two hundred. Among the ruins of the former Soviet Union various states and statelets arise, including even some nationalities whose consciousness of their separate and distinct nationality is very recent, and who had never formed a national state, indeed any state, before. Others (Armenia and Georgia, for example) feed their minds and aspirations from long, and historically often dubious, memories of their medieval or even earlier "kingdoms" that they equate with "independence," "statehood." (Some of these Caucasian peoples had a surprisingly wide range of economic, cultural and even political leeways even under Communist and Stalinist rule. Their tribal habits, including all kinds of illegal trading practices, had been tolerated by the no less corrupt representatives of the Soviet bureaucracy in their midst.)

The great question is that of the Ukrainians. I find it difficult to believe that their full sovereignty would be acceptable to the Russians, that they will let them go entirely. There is the involved problem of millions of Russians living within the Ukraine, as is the case also in the Baltic states. This mixture of nationalities is the main question in Yugoslavia too: were there no Serbs living within "Croatia," there would be no Yugoslav civil war now. One ought to berate the Serbs because of their violent nationalism; but the Croats ought to be berated too, not only because of their horrible misdeeds during World War II, but also because it was they who wanted a Yugoslavia in 1918, just as the Slovaks wanted a Czechoslovakia then. (Both had been better off during the Habsburg Empire and state; but let that go.)

So many various new states and statelets arise before our eyes. They reflect the spontaneous desires of their peoples. But their promoters are ambitious politician-chieftains. While the impulse of nationalism, the desire for one's own independent national state, is one of the results of romanticism (and we are all romantics now, with the classicist rationalism of the eighteenth century gone), its promoters are political practitioners of power, attracted by their prospective emoluments, feeding their personal vanities, the perquisites of high state officialdom: the unexpected obeisances and comforts suddenly at their behest, bloated staffs, salutations, official travel.*

In the case of the Baltic states there was a potential compromise solution that is now gone. When, in October 1939, Stalin and Molotov forced pacts on Estonia, Latvia and Lithuania after they had been assigned by Hitler to the Russian sphere of interest, the Russians got army and navy bases but they did not interfere with the political and social structures of these small countries. Then, in the summer of 1940 after the German conquest of France, Stalin brutally occupied these countries and ordered their incorporation into the Soviet Union. Their status of the first phase, that between October 1939 and June 1940, might have been applicable now: independence and sovereignty for the Baltic states with the acceptance of a limited number of Russian army and navy bases on their territories — the perhaps inevitable reminder that, in the large sense, they are, after all, close to Russia. That condition was a possibility but a month or so ago (I am writing this in September 1991), and I wish that the American government had supported it. It is gone now. The Baltic politicians and many of their peoples would say, "Yes, but that would not have been *complete* independence, *complete* sovereignty." I understand; but little do they consider that complete independence and complete sovereignty in reality do not exist. They are illusions in the life of peoples as they are illusions in the life of individuals.

After everything is said, every nation has the government it deserves. Nowadays all social scientists, most historians, and

---

* I was once told, twenty years ago, that in Soviet Georgia the desired (and achievable) status symbol was a black Cadillac. (Yes, there were Cadillac owners in Georgia, say, in 1972, and not only government officials.) Now it is the black Mercedes, of the more luxurious 300 and S series.

public figures deny the existence of a national character. Yet
— contrary to the American intellectual tradition — the character of a people molds their institutions more than their institutions mold, or influence, their characters. This means
that the lives, including the politics and civil liberties, of the
various peoples of the former Soviet Union (like those of Eastern Europe) will remain very different, even though there may
exist some superficial similarities in their "democratic" constitutions and political institutions.

It is often said (it is, after all, obvious) that Hitler could not
have done what he did without the support of the German
people. This is seldom being said about Stalin and the Russian
people. This is curious because Stalin's victims included millions of Russians, while the vast majority of Hitler's victims
were not Germans. Hitler's only purge that resembles Stalin's
(and Stalin seems to have noticed it) was the June 1934 one,
when Hitler and his minions did away with Röhm and with
the radical leaders of the SA, including a few other convenient
victims besides. Stalin's subsequent purges did not resemble
Hitler's at all, although they had stunning similarities with
the *oprichnina* of Ivan the Terrible. One of the most dreadful
things about Stalin's purges was that he had hordes of willing
collaborators, thousands of denunciators, other thousands of
police personnel torturing people and forcing the most nonsensical confessions out of them. With few exceptions their victims turned abject, groveling, denouncing each other. Most of
them were bereft of dignity, of courage, of true convictions.
(So much for Koestler's phony melodrama about their confess-
ing for the sake of a higher cause: The Party.) Meanwhile the
vast mass of the Soviet peoples remained indifferent to the
spectacle.

There are similarities between Stalin and Hitler (a recent
book by Allan Bullock attempts to describe their "parallel
lives"), though not many. One similarity (ignored, as also

many other things, by Bullock): both lied about their respect
and affection for their fathers. Their fathers beat them; they
loved their mothers. Both fathers, oddly, died in a tavern: Vis-
sarion Djugashvili allegedly in a tavern brawl in Tiflis in 1909;
Alois Hitler sitting at his *Stammtisch* in Leonding in 1903.
There the similarities end. Hitler, as behooves a German, saw
the world according to his ideas. He was fanatical about his
ideas. Stalin had little or no interest in ideas; he was a Caucasian chieftain who thought in terms of power. He was more
suspicious of people than was Hitler. Who was the more cruel
one? No use to compare the numbers of their victims. Cruelty,
as all human characteristics, is a matter of quality, not of
quantity. Hitler's cruelty was cold and mental; Stalin's was
Georgian hot, it was in his blood. Both had learned statesmanship, alas, well — at the expense of their victims and opponents and even allies. There was much in Stalin's foreign policy that resembled that of the Tsars.* Hitler's foreign policy
was very different from that of his predecessors. Hitler was the
more revolutionary of the two. He was the more exceptional
person. He was *sui generis.* There were plenty of other Nazis,
anti-Semites, German nationalists, racialists and demagogues,
but no one like Hitler. We will not see the likes of him again.
He did not accord with any type. Whereas the type of Stalin —
the Caucasian populist-bandit, crafty, cunning, capable of im-

---

* *September 1991.* A book on Stalin by Volkogonov, a former general and
now "Head of the Institute of Military History" in Moscow. He is among the
first to have access to all new material in Soviet archives. Almost every page
has its errors. Is this what we can expect from Russian historical "scholarship"
now that the Communists are gone? It does not fill me with confidence. There
are a few unexpected and potentially interesting bits of information in it, but
none of them are verifiable. The references are Byzantine and shoddy.

There is, however, one very significant item, reproducing Stalin's own
expression and his marginal notes. In July 1940 — the date in itself is significant, the time of Stalin's reconquest of the Baltic states and Bessarabia, which
the Tsars had won and Lenin had lost — *Bolshevik,* the official organ of the
Marx-Engels-Lenin Institute, was preparing the reprint of an article by Engels,

posing his will on people in his surroundings, down to some of his physical characteristics, including his mustachio — is one extant even now, whether in the bazaars of Tiflis or among the peasant-populist figures of the Caucasian and Transcaucasian "republics." We will see the likes of him again in Ossetia or Turkmenistan, though not perhaps in the Kremlin in Moscow.

On the other hand, there is that strange and unexpected element in the Russian character: those conversions springing from a sense of guilt, a willingness to renounce one's possessions, to give things away. Such conversions were exaggerated and mystified by Dostoyevsky in his feverish, heavily panting prose; but they exist nonetheless. There is not much softness in the German character — except for a sentimentality that may be false and cloying in some instances but also genuinely good-hearted in others. Often there is an alternation of a hard, near-blind, barbaric cruelty with an unexpectedly charitable softness in the Russian character. The latter is, alas, rare; but it occurs often within the same person.

There are evidences of this in Gorbachev — and, before him, in Khrushchev. There was something very Russian — stunning, unexpected, impractical — in Khrushchev's decision in February 1956 to go before the entire Party Congress to detail Stalin's crimes. Impractical: because it shook the entire lead-

---

"On the Foreign Policy of Russian Tsarism." Zhdanov and others, unsure about it, submitted it to Stalin for his opinion. Stalin's note in the margin reads: "Aggressive vileness was not a monopoly of the Russian Tsars." Engels "exaggerates them." "In attacking Tsarist foreign policy, he [Engels] resolved to denigrate it in the eyes of European public opinion." Stalin concluded: "It is not worth publishing." Volkogonov cites this as an example of how Stalin interfered with the "scientific" work of Russian academic institutes and literary publications. It is, however, an example of something entirely different. It is much more significant than that. It is a telling indication — among other such evidences discernible through the years — of what Stalin was, or rather, of what he wanted: to restore the greatness of Russia and its empire that the Tsars had made, that Lenin lost and that Marxist dogmatism could only endanger.

ership, and led to the Eastern European risings a few months later. A few subtle statements or references to Stalin's extremes and errors would have done the job. Stunning: because the entire five-hour speech was something like a confession. The theme was Stalin, but he was not the only one culpable. There was a touch of *mea culpa* in it on the part of this Ukrainian peasant whose entire career had been in the service of Stalin; and yet there was no sense of calculation in that belated denial of his former master. Thirty years later Gorbachev, who had risen as Andropov's man, close to the KGB: during the next six years he gave an empire away. He was not pressured to do that; it was not Ronald Reagan's technological bluster that forced his hand, and while the Soviet economy and material conditions of the peoples of the Soviet Union in 1985 were no better than before, they were not worse either. But Gorbachev was not only fully aware of, and deeply exercised by, the corruption of the Communist party. Beneath his more or less conscious dismantling of it was a sense of more than past mistakes; there was probably a Russian sense of guilt. Some sense of guilt may have been instrumental during the retreat of other great empires, but never in that way. Seldom — perhaps never before in history — has anything like this occurred: the abandoning of almost all that had been won in a great war, of an entire sphere of interest, without external or internal threats, without a clear and present danger of material need. And it at least seems that the majority of the Russian people did not care much about giving up Eastern Europe, perhaps not even about letting many of the other "republics" of the Soviet Union go. This, too, is something rare. I think that to attribute all of this to mere materialism or to indifferent stupidity would be wrong. Yes, those elements exist; but that indifference to imperial possessions, indeed to the traditional territorial extent of one's very state, may be a mark — perhaps even one of the spiritual marks — of a great people, after all.

V

GERMANY. THE CENTER.

On a short visit to south Germany in 1982 I first sensed that the presence of an American army there was something that was fading into the past. The German parliament had just voted in favor of the positioning of new American missiles aimed at the Soviet Union. Did that matter in the long run? I thought not. There was a faded quality — sometimes visibly so — in those American signs on the edges of German towns and villages:

> when we drive on the Autobahn in Germany the signs indicating an American military enclave or command post already give the faint impression of anachronism, a leftover impression from the era of the German-American symbiosis, when the principal political reality in West Germany was the American military presence stretching ahead to the iron curtain.

In 1983 I was in Hamburg for a day, a Hamburg

> which was devasted by bombs and a firestorm forty years ago, hardly less than Hiroshima and worse than Nagasaki. Out of her ashes a new and sparkling city has arisen. This includes the poisonous glitter of an entire quarter dedicated by the city fathers to organized sexual excess. But the city includes, too, acres and acres of solid villas, comfortable and cozy, their light behind their thick curtains reflect-

ing the warm fug of German bourgeois family life; patrician houses with a heavy elegance that is traditional and perhaps therefore impressive. In the winter evening they glowed with the interior promise of stability and probity. . . .

On a grey morning I went to Hamburg Dammtor Station, following a curved walkway that goes through the hallways of what was until recently a luxurious hotel on the Esplanade but now is an office building. I had to take a train to Kiel. There was a German punk in a leather jacket painted over with obscenities, shaven bald except for a savage crest of painted hair that was more brutal than military. But he was lost in the milling north German crowd with their severe faces. The buffet was at least fifty years old but spotless, except for the rack of sex magazines bordering it. There were a few smart women, clutching their fur coats. I went up to the platform. . . .

Trains were going through, pulling in, sliding out every two minutes. The city commuter trains, the S-Bahn, were running on the same tracks as the suburban locals and the direct trains and the expresses and the Inter-City trains and the trans-Europe night trains. The indicator rang: the numbers dropped down with the time and the name of the next train. Another indicator rattled. Another sign showed the composition of the trains with the sequence of their coaches. This efficiency was vital, not deadening; its source was the duty of service, of human purpose behind the mechanism. Train from Munich. Train to Altona. Train from Frankfurt. Train to Leipzig — with East German coaches. Train to Amsterdam. Train to Berlin — West and East German carriages on that one. The Mont-Blanc to Geneva. The Prinz Eugen to Vienna. All within fifteen minutes. There, before my eyes, the evolving history of Germany, of the German nation, was going on. Train to Kiel.

(A German professor was sent to meet me at the station in Kiel. Youngish but stiff, he was as humorless as any of his

forebears. I tried some small talk with him while he drove
me to the university. I asked him something about the origins
of the name Kiel, which he explained to me at some length.
"Thank you," I said. "I like to collect all kinds of useless
information." We had stopped at a red light. He turned to
me grimly. "This is not useless information," he said. Had he
not had his huge hands on the wheel, he would have
pointed his finger at me.)

By 1989 the iron curtain had crumbled to bits, the Berlin
Wall not yet. For the last time during the cold war, developments in Germany and Eastern Europe were different, they
ran not apace, including the movements of people. The relatively safe route for an Eastern European who wanted to flee
to the West before 1961 was to make his way to East Berlin,
from where he could slip unobtrusively over to West Berlin
by riding on the subway still operating between the two
halves of the city. By 1989 the reverse was going on: East
Germans wishing to move to West Germany made their way
to Czechoslovakia and Hungary, from where they could proceed to West Germany through Austria. This hegira was as
cumbersome as it was ridiculous. Months before the Berlin
Wall was breached, it was evident to me that the separation
of East and West Germany was over. It happened on 9 November; I was exhilarated by those scenes that flickered on
the television screen. I also thought of yet another coincidence, of those four Ninths of November in the history of
Germany in this century. On 9 November 1918 the Kaiser
abdicated and the German Republic was proclaimed. On 9
November 1923 Hitler tried his Putsch in Munich. On 9 November 1938 occurred the horrid Kristallnacht in Berlin and
throughout Germany: the destruction of Jewish stores, the
burning of synagogues, the cruel mistreatment of many
Jews. Now on 9 November 1989 the breaking not of clean

glass but of ugly concrete, the final crumbling of the Berlin Wall. The reunion of Germany.

🔰

2 December 1990. Today the German people, for the first time since 1933, voted in an all-German election; and the people of all Berlin, for the first time since 1946, voted to elect their own government. I was in Berlin that day. There was something of a Sunday stillness in this great city; but it was not the hush of a great historic occasion. It was the sense of approaching Christmas. There were Advent candles and wreaths, electric and flickering, in many apartment windows, and a few twinkling trees set up this early outside on the balconies — the latter probably an American-inspired custom. But the sense of inwardness prevailed everywhere over outwardness on this day. I hardly saw any people at the voting stations; yet more than 80 percent of the people were voting. There were not many people and billboards. In the evening, when the election results came in (amazingly soon, and amazingly accurately) there was little hoopla, few of the rituals of American elections (except that at the Free Democrats' headquarters there played a — German — Dixieland band). The comments of the German politicians, winners as well as losers, were less rhetorical, less sentimental than what is now customary among American candidates. All in all, this was a dignified election, something that Americans may contemplate with respect.

One of the reasons for this lack of excitement was that the result was known well in advance. The polls had been extraordinarily precise. They predicted that Kohl and his party would get about 43 percent of the vote, and so they did. We ought to pay more attention to what this polling business means. It is one of the incarnations of the Heisenberg discovery — that is, the act of observation affecting the behavior of the object (or that the publicity given to certain acts produces more such acts).

Perhaps this is particularly applicable to the German people, who have a powerful innate desire for respectability. Hitler knew that. In November 1923 he attempted his Putsch in Munich, knowing that in their hearts many elements of the established order shared his German nationalist sentiments; but because he marched that day against the respected barriers of order, he failed. He learned quickly. Less than ten years later he was the chancellor of the Reich, because large masses of otherwise conservative Germans concluded that, unlike the Communists or other extremists on the left, the National Socialists were respectable Germans after all. In this respect the otherwise very reliable and accurate German newspapers are wrong. They now write that this 2 December 1990 was the first free all-German election since 1932. No: the last one was that of 5 March 1933, when Hitler was already chancellor, a democratic election (with one exception: the Communist party had been ordered dissolved). In that election Hitler and the Nazis got 43.9 percent of the all-German vote — to the last percentage point exactly what Kohl and his party got today.

There is nothing really wrong with Kohl. He has nothing of the Nazi in him. He does remind one of those middle-class, Catholic, non-Nazi, Rhineland Germans who (and whose party) in March 1933 chose not to obstruct but to support Hitler, mostly because of his anti-Communism and because of his stressing of a newly found German national unity and national order. But I know that this is an unfair hypothesis. More importantly, a new Hitler, or even a future Hitler-type mass movement, is an impossibility. Hitler and the Nazis *belonged to the twentieth century; and that century is now over.*

Berlin does not belong to the Atlantic sphere but to the continental one. This is evident in many things, including its climate. Not much of a spring, and not much of an autumn. There is a light northern summer, like a pale-blond young woman with milky skin and round watery blue eyes. Berlin is a very large city in circumference, with many lakes, long summer evenings with late lights shining over the smooth stone terraces of the waterfront villas, the trees acid green and never sere. So there is a bit of country on the edges of this city, though that rus in urbe is the opposite of the English ideal of urbs in ruri, meaning an urbane existence amidst country living. I am inclined to think that the most characteristic — and, in many ways, the best — Berlin season is the winter. The sky is uniformly grey. But underneath that grey flannel canopy is a crisp cold, unlike the wet windy chill of Atlantic seaboard winters; and one has the curious and agreeable impression of a city that is both modern and cozy, both upper and lower middle class, both Brandenburg and European, a sprawling northern city away from the stunning wintry darkness of the estranging seas: a western metropolis on the sandy and oft-bloodied eastern plain.

I look up with a certain respect, and perhaps even desire, at the well-lit, large-paned windows of the modern apartment houses in the Budapester Strasse, one of the few chic streets in the middle of the city, aware of their interior atmosphere, the prosperous comforts of all of these Stilmöbel, armchairs and sofas upholstered in brown plush, with a few Biedermeier pieces here and there, and one large and usually dreadful abstract painting on the Salon wall. Unlike a smart French or Swiss haut-bourgeois house, these apartments do not breathe elegance; but they exhale comfort. This is a very prosperous country now, with a people whose aspirations for well-being are solid and reasonable, though their recent acquisition of riches is often crass. But where are they not?

For a long time West German democracy was inseparable from West German Americanization, the evidences of which have been protean, ranging from the admirable to the comic, including the Americanization of much of the Germans' everyday as well as of their business language. But this has begun to ebb, for more than one reason. One of them is the decline of American prestige, including the decline of the dollar, which shows every sign of not being a transitory phenomenon. It is not only that for an American Berlin is very expensive, with a small shot of spirits at a bar costing eight dollars, and breakfast in my hotel seventeen. (Let's stop here. There is more to this than a report on currency rates, and more than a materialist observation. Has it ever happened, since the foundation of the United States, that an American traveling abroad found that he was poorer there than are the natives of his class? Less elegant, less sophisticated, less polished, less worldly — perhaps. But poorer? This is not an ephemeral situation. It is replete with a meaning that has nothing to do with materialism.)

Some of this I find melancholy. On Monday I wander into KaDeWe (Kaufhaus des Westens), the now traditional big department store on the Kurfürstendamm. It is all aglitter, pulsating with bright luxury, full of people and yet without a sense of jostling crowds, with knowledgeable and helpful staff, handsome young women at a myriad of counters. I am sad as I suddenly realize that this is how a great American department store looked thirty years ago.

The German people, by and large, like Americans — for which they have plenty of reasons, one must add. Their political judgment is more realistic than that of the people in Eastern Europe (wherefrom I had flown to Berlin). There even the most intelligent people startle me to a point where I find that arguing with them is impossible. This happens when they tell me that this world-historical change, the end of an epoch, the decline of the Soviet Union and its astonishing retreat from Europe, was due to one man: Ronald Reagan. Reagan, who with his brilliant armament program and his Star Wars, forced the Soviet Union into bankruptcy. Reagan made Gorbachev do what he had to do. I hear this again and again; and, after a few stuttering replies of "Nonsense!" I give up.

The Germans don't believe this. They know the Russians better than that. They know what they owe to Gorbachev, which is to their credit.

It is not pleasant when a German likes America and Americans for the wrong reasons. A German couple, naked and pink in the sauna of the hotel, tell me that they are off to the United States on their annual vacation in Florida in December. They tell me that they love it. They tell me that they also love Las Vegas. They love Atlantic City. But this is not only a matter of questionable taste (of which there is plenty in Germany, though perhaps less in cities such as Berlin or Hamburg than elsewhere). They like America and Americans but they respect America and Americans less and less. They think of Americans as a well meaning, loud, fairly dumb, energetic, adolescent people. It must be a long flight to Miami, I say, and then a three-hour drive to Fort Myers. Do you get jet lag? "I never get jet lag," the German man says.

*"Tomorrow night I will have a Twenty-Ounce Steak for me!"
His naked wife adds: "Cajun style" (she pronounces it
Kä-Dschun).*

I did not have jet lag but I went down to the hotel's splendid
pool and sauna after a three-hour walk across Berlin, to
thaw out before dinner. I put on bathing trunks which I borrowed from the pool director, an attractive young Berlin
woman in a white uniform. Within the sauna women and
men stretch out together, entirely naked. This is not new to
me; I have been in German saunas before; it is their custom
of the past twenty years or so. The Germans have often
prided themselves on their body culture (Nacktkultur) and
on their lack of hypocrisy. However, the absence of hypocrisy does not mean the absence of other kinds of dishones-
ties. Instead of being "free" and "natural," the naked
women cover up their nervousness by affecting an amoral
nonchalance. Their eyes slyly wander; they are more alert
than the men. I noticed these things before, too, but now
comes the ludicrous topping of it: the directress enters and
tells me that while I am supposed to wear my bathing suit in
the pool, I must not wear it in the sauna. I.e., this is Germany, where all regulations must be obeyed. I leave the
sauna, immerse myself in the ice-water dip and wade into
the pool.

Something in this runs against the Nietzschean idea that
has caused the Germans so much harm in the past. For
there is, really, not much difference between immorality and
amorality. (If anything, the former may be preferable to
the latter, as indeed the self-consciousness of hypocrisy
is preferable to the worse dishonesty of self-deceit.)

I walked through the Tiergarten to the Brandenburg Gate, a
good two miles from my hotel. When I first espy it, it looks

smaller than I had imagined it. The ubiquitous greyness of the air, of the pavements, of the roads, is light rather than dark, transparent rather than opaque, clear and not foggy. Long before I reach the Brandenburg Gate I sense that I am walking eastward, away from the Atlantic. About half a mile from the Brandenburg Gate, still on the formerly Western side, there is the Soviet war memorial. I cross that broad avenue (broad enough so that during the last days of the war a few German planes were able to land and take off from there, a few hundred yards from Hitler's bunker head-quarters). The war memorial, inscribed to the heroism of the Soviet soldiers who liberated (if that is the word) Berlin, is neo-classical, in the thirties' monumental style (though built after 1945) and not unimpressive. What is particularly im-pressive is the sight of the two statuesque Russian soldiers, obviously of an elite guards' regiment, in their long great-coats and white gloves, standing motionless before two pil-lars of the memorial. There is a low wire fence separating the memorial from the sidewalk, patrolled by two German policemen. People stop, stare and watch, no one says any-thing, at least not while I am there.

And ten yards away begins the startling scene of a ba-zaar: the scum and froth atop the oceanic ebbing of the great historical tide, of the actual withdrawal and the poten-tial dissolution of the great Russian empire that flooded into Berlin forty-five years ago and settled there for a long time.

There are ten? no, twenty, fifty, one hundred trestle tables in a disorderly row, heaped high with Soviet army fur caps, with the red star embedded in the dark fur. Officers' caps, of all of the Soviet armed services, spanking clean. Soviet mili-tary decorations of all kinds. Service medals. Binoculars. Army belts. Pistols. Canteens. On the pavement, spread out on plastic sheets: Soviet army greatcoats, a variety of uni-forms.

The officers and soldiers of the Soviet army garrisons in East Berlin are selling their equipment for German money. Remnants from an army in dissolution. Many of the vendors have Mongol faces. Some of them are in sweaters, in jeans, tucked into army boots. An American student tries on a Soviet artillery officer's greatcoat in perfect condition.

I am tempted to buy one of those fur hats for thirty-five marks; for a souvenir? because it is warm? Then something stops me from doing so.

The ragged line of the tables with their vendors stretches straight to the Brandenburg Gate itself, and then bends around it, petering out on the other side.

I have never liked the Russians, and I fled them from Hungary more than forty-four years ago; but what I experience now is a sentiment of helpless sadness, as always at the sight of someone or something being humiliated.

I walked a little more in East Berlin. The Unter den Linden was their showcase boulevard. Pas grand'chose. In the side streets the peeling, heavy sights and smells of those dark Whilhelmian apartment houses, Mietkasernen, that somehow survived the war, sheltering countless weary people during forty-five years of Communist rule. They must smell of coal smoke and thick pea soup pot-heated in small dingy kitchens. I am cold and tired. I have been walking for three hours. I find a taxi. Back to the concrete luxury of my hotel in the West.

One more startling sight. We drive along the eastern side of what was The Wall. That Wall was more than one hundred miles long; it consisted, in most places, of two parallel walls with mine fields in between. It was first breached a little more than a year ago, and by now nothing, I mean nothing, of it remains. German working habits, German elbow grease. But as my cab drives along what is still Otto-

Grotewohl-Strasse (named after an East German Communist leader, but surely not for long), another wall blocks the
view to the west. It is a three-block-long row of apartment
houses, where a year ago the no man's land on the eastern
side of The Wall had stood. They are spanking new, well
built, attractive, with large postmodern angular bay windows. They must have been built in eight or ten months, not
more.

All over Berlin are posters: "Help Russia!" — on the television screen, on kiosks in the streets, information about where
to send or deposit money to the funds for Russia. I read that
some German veterans sent a convoy of trucks with food
and clothes for the families of Russian veterans. Another
poster reads: "Ein Herz für Russland." A Heart for Russia.
  I am impressed by this. I know that in so many acts of
public charity there is an element of self-satisfaction, the
pleasure that parvenus or the nouveaux riches take in showing that they are in a position to give. But this is irrelevant
now. As Dr. Johnson said: "Intentions must be judged from
acts." Not to speak of the fact that the Russians conquered
and brutalized Germany forty-five years ago, and whose
presence kept it divided for forty-five years. All of this is
gone, gone with the wind.

I flew out of Berlin in the black December dawn; at seven
A.M. there, it is still completely dark; I was on a Lufthansa
flight to Frankfurt, where I would change to another flight to
Philadelphia. Until the end of The Wall, the West German
Lufthansa was not allowed to fly the Berlin corridor; Pan
American had the Berlin–Frankfurt run. On the flight we had
the dubious blessing of a talkative captain, telling us
through the microphone many things that I was not inter-

*ested in hearing. Among other things: "Meine Damen und
Herren! Please excuse some of the shortcomings of the service on this flight. We are flying with a Pan American crew
whose training has not yet reached Lufthansa standards."*

☙

David Hume in 1748: "Germany is undoubtedly a fine country, full of industrious honest people; and were it united, it
would be the greatest power that ever was in the world." Bismarck united Germany in 1871. It became the greatest power
in Europe. That was enough for Bismarck, who knew that to
want more meant asking for trouble; that to be the greatest
power in Europe meant, too, a world power of considerable
rank. That was not enough for William II. What followed were
the two world wars, for the outbreak of the first of which
Germany was partly responsible, for the second just about entirely so. The two world wars of the twentieth century were
the last attempts of a European power to become the greatest
power in the world. It was Germany's turn, after Spain and
France and England. That will not happen again. Such imperial
ambitions and achievements belong to an age that is now over.
Germany was defeated twice, with the help of extra-European
powers such as the United States, and the half-European Soviet
Union. After her first defeat she rose again. Her second defeat
was more decisive. Her power was gone and she was divided
— in ways different from her divisions before 1871, but divided
still. But in 1989 that division was over. There is a united
Germany again.

The social and political structure as well as the inclinations
and the political rhetoric of the people of this Germany are not
like the united Germany of the past. There is another difference. The German people are more homogeneous than before.

Their society has become more democratic. Her regional differences have been diminishing — substantial changes that had begun during the Hitler era. More important is the fact that the greatest and most enduring change in Europe after the Second World War involved a rearrangement not of the frontiers of states but of their populations. For about eight hundred years Germans in the lands of Eastern Europe were a strong presence. They had a definite influence because of their cohesion, pride, culture and industriousness, well beyond their numbers. In the last months of the Second World War and during the years that followed most of these Germans fled westward to Germany, with hundreds of thousands of them perishing on the way. Millions were expelled later by the new rulers of the Eastern European countries. Ten years after the war every fourth German in West Germany was a German refugee or expellee. Their presence and their resentments should have produced the greatest problem for a Western German democracy. They did not. They, and especially their children, were absorbed successfully within that new, prosperous and — at least on the surface — not pronouncedly nationalist Germany. Their desire to regain their former homelands, to move eastward again, diminished year by year. Among their children it hardly existed at all. Will it revive among their grandchildren and great-grandchildren? One doubts it; though one cannot tell.

In 1945 Europe was divided. In the center of Europe Germany was divided. Within Germany Berlin was divided, as the cold war began. In 1989 the cold war ended, together with the division of Europe and Germany and Berlin. The last vestiges of the iron curtain disappeared with the Berlin Wall. Yet during the cold war the sequence of events separating Eastern Europe from Western Europe and East Germany from West Germany were not synchronized.

The reason for this was that for some years after 1945 neither the Russians nor the Americans were certain what the next German state would, or should, be. It was only after the cold war had definitely begun that the division between West and East Germany and between West and East Berlin hardened. But that division was not total even during the worst of the Stalin years, when the rest of Eastern Europe was sealed off from the West. In 1954 the Russians recognized the West German government, without demanding that the Western powers recognize the East German one. Finally, faced with the steady and increasing trickle of their people moving to the West through West Berlin, the East German rulers, having convinced their reluctant Russian allies, closed down their entire border with West Germany and built the Berlin Wall in 1961 — when travel restrictions between the other Eastern European Communist states and the West were beginning to be eased. Thus the last half-open passageway between West and East Germany was shut at the very time when elsewhere small holes through the iron curtain were beginning to appear.

Before 1961 and The Wall, the West German government and the great majority of the German people had built their hopes on the American card. The German-American alliance would eventually lead to a Russian withdrawal, and to the liberation of East Germany. By 1961 some Germans recognized that this would not happen. The United States and also the other Western powers were not particularly dissatisfied with the division of Germany and Berlin. They would protest against the Berlin Wall, but they would do nothing to change the division of Germany. That monstrous erection stood, after all, within the lines of East German territory.* Yet The Wall

---

* During the involved and unsuccessful negotiations that followed Khrushchev's reopening of the Berlin "problem" in 1958, it was evident that the United States and the Western allies were concerned only with the safety and

was not totally leakproof either, even during the worst years of its existence. Ten years after its construction the Germans began to recognize and take some comfort from the idea that Germany consisted of Two States but One Nation. This was the essence of *Ostpolitik*. There followed, in 1971, the Western and West German recognition of the East German state. The Germans had now learned what Bismarck knew only too well. One-sided alliances, no matter with what powerful states, led them nowhere. They must maintain good relations with the greatest power in the East as well as with that in the West. Still, it was not German diplomacy that led to the end of the division of Germany and to the destruction of the Berlin Wall. The maker of that was Gorbachev — a Gorbachev who not only wanted peaceful relations with the West, who not only knew how weak Communism was, but who knew, too, that the division of Germany could not last.

Many years before 1989 the contacts between West and East Germany were increasing. In its revival of German traditions East Germany was pulling slowly closer to the West. But West Germany, too, was pulling slowly closer to the East. One less and less dependent on Russia, the other less and less on America. Both in West and East Germany the respect for things Prussian rose in the 1980s: for Prussian culture, Prussian order, Prussian self-discipline, Prussian probity. There was nothing very wrong in this. There were many things wrong in the Prussian tradition and in the Prussian image, but there were admirable things in it as well.

The bodies of Frederick the Great and his father were brought back from the south of Germany where Hitler's gov-

---

the status quo of West Berlin. They did not raise the question of East Berlin during these talks, in order to avoid the admittedly slight possibility that the Russians might agree to a mutual revision of the status of both halves of the city, and thus reopen the prospect of a neutral Germany.

ernment had moved them forty-eight years before, to protect them from the bombs raining down on Berlin and Potsdam and from the menace of the approaching Russians. This was done in August 1991, during the very days of the collapse of Communism within Russia itself, at the time of Russian retreat from the Baltics. Great historical coincidences are not only "spiritual puns" (Chesterton); they are the hush of the wings of the angels of destiny.

How strange this was during the cold war: the supposedly pragmatic Americans thinking in terms of Communism, the supposedly abstract Germans thinking in terms of Russia. The cold war is over now, but what continues is the mixture of revulsion and fascination that the Germans feel toward Russia and the European East, together with the emulation mixed with apprehension they have of America and the far west.

If at the end of World War I (that is, at the beginning of the twentieth century) Communism had come to power in Germany, not in Russia, its influence would have been immeasurably greater. Russia and things Russian had no prestige, no attraction among Russia's neighbors. In Russia the Communist revolution succeeded; outside Russia it failed. Many of the social conditions of the peasantry and workers of the Baltic region and Poland were by and large not that different from conditions in the vast tracts of Russia; yet the local Communists, even when supported by the Red Russian armed forces, were routed in all of these countries in 1918–20. The opposite was true of Germany and things German. The German cultural influence was very large, even in those European nations that had been arrayed against Germany in the First World War. That cultural prestige, including the German system of education, was such that anything that was new and revolutionary in Germany — probably including an eventual German

Communist regime — would have been, whether consciously or unconsciously, emulated by ambitious people, radicals, revolutionaries, intellectuals. (That was, after all, what happened with Hitler and German National Socialism. They had plenty of adherents and emulators in other countries — Rumania, for example — where, on occasion, they were able to come to power without the presence of German armed force — something that the Russians could not count on, even at the time of or after their great military triumph in 1945.)

Then there are those differences in national habits: Russians inefficient, Germans efficient, sometimes alarmingly so. Had a Communist system established itself in Germany, some of its achievements would probably have been impressive, especially for the workers in an industrial state. A Communist Germany would have been even more avant-garde than Weimar Germany, in many instances. Much of Germany would have become a Bauhaus, at least for a while. Yet the fatal shortcomings and stupidities of Marxism would have weighed it down in the end: its materialism, its atheism and, most of all, its shallow and insubstantial internationalism. It might have survived a nationalist counterrevolution, for a while. It would not have survived the pull of German nationalism among its adherents and its leadership. Like everywhere else in the Communist world, the nationalists would have triumphed over the "rootless cosmopolitans." Eventually a German nationalist Communist would have arisen, inspiring the masses — a minor variation of Hitler.

Stalin admired the Germans, even after they had invaded Russia and devastated most of it. He admired Hitler, who in turn respected him. (On one occasion Hitler said that when the war against Russia was won, he would install Stalin somewhere comfortably, perhaps in Potsdam.) In December 1944 Stalin told de Gaulle: "That poor Hitler." This after Hitler's people had killed millions of Russians.

Only the Americans surpass the Germans in the esteem of the Russians. (Not to speak of many Ukrainians, who regard their enemies as Poles, Russians, Jews — they have been the natural allies of Germany throughout this century.)

Churchill saw the fate of the world, of his own country, of Europe, as early as 1940: Britain, even with the help of the United States, could not conquer the Germans and reconquer Europe alone. There were only two alternatives. Either all of Europe dominated by Germany, or the eastern half (more precisely, one third) of Europe dominated by Russia; and half of Europe was better than none. To this add something that Churchill knew: that while Russian rule over Europe would not last, no one could know whether a German domination of Europe would not have sufficient power to last for a very long time, changing the history of the entire world. His perhaps most famous speech (the "Finest Hour" speech of 18 June 1940) included this passage: If Hitler wins, "then the whole world, including the United States, including all that we have known and cared for, will sink into the abyss of a new Dark Age made more sinister, and *perhaps more protracted*, by the lights of perverted science." The italics are mine.

The retreat of Russia from Eastern Europe, which is now complete — and the disintegration of the Russian empire, as yet incomplete — leaves a large vacuum of power in the heartland of the world. That vacuum will not be filled by the United States. It will not be filled by a "United Europe," something that, in reality, does not exist. It will most likely be filled by Germany.

The prospect is not that of another Hitler, of a German *Lebensraum*, of a Fourth Reich. But political geography, together with the cultural inclinations of peoples, remains a definite condition of their histories.

Both world wars broke out in Eastern Europe; but the Second

World War broke out *because of* Eastern Europe. Something like a dozen "independent" states came into being in Eastern Europe after World War I, in part because of the dissolution of the Austro-Hungarian Empire (that, too, was inseparable from the then retreat of Germany and Russia). It was predictable that sooner or later either German or Russian power would rise again, at the expense of an independent Eastern Europe. That was what happened: because France and, behind her, Britain were both unable and unwilling to engage in another war for the sake of Eastern Europe; because none of the Eastern European states, including even Poland, were strong enough to defend themselves against Germany, not to speak of a German-Russian alliance; because most of these states, again including Poland, intrigued against each other, unwilling to band together; and because some of them preferred to be allied with Germany, from whose resurgence they would profit. These conditions still exist now, in the 1990s, when the twentieth century is over — though in circumstances and with consequences that are different from what they were before.

Continuity is as important as is change. In the early 1930s the revival of German power had begun even before Hitler. When it came to Russia, we have seen that the retreat of the Russians from the center of Europe had begun long before 1990, from Austria and Finland as early as 1954–55; and that, whether willingly or not, Moscow consented to increasing extents of independence of almost all Eastern European states well before 1989.

The resurgent independence of many of these small countries — not only of the Baltic states but of Croatia and Slovenia in what was lately Yugoslavia, and of Slovakia within Czechoslovakia — makes the prevalence of German influence in these countries increasingly probable, and natural. To this add the factor of their sympathy for Germany (the Poles and the Czechs are perhaps the only exceptions to that). In some of these countries — the Baltic states and the Ukraine, for example — Hitler's army was their liberator from Soviet rule during the Second World War. At least two other states, Croatia and Slovakia, were actually created by Hitler before and during the Second World War. These memories remain strong and attractive even for successive generations who otherwise (whether because of conviction or because of caution) still think it better to disavow Hitler and Hitlerism. To this we must add the overwhelming popular appeal of the ideology of anti-Communism: for elsewhere, too, those who fought Russia and Communism on the side of Germany during the Second World War now appear in a favorable light, while those who had bitterly opposed Germany and Hitler, including the anti-Nazi resistant patriots, conservatives, liberals and democrats, are losing some of their well-deserved respect.

The political structures of the newly independent Eastern European countries are, for the time being, marked by the existence of multiple parties. There can be little doubt, however, that (as happened before the Second World War) some of these parties will be (indeed, some of them already are) increasingly inclined to seek German, rather than American or other, support, not only financially but also ideologically.

On material and economic levels, too, it is German, rather than other Western European, influence of capital, management and joint ownership that will naturally prevail. This tendency had already begun during the decade before the great changes of 1989 — just as the rise of German and the decline of French financial and economic influence in many Eastern European countries had begun years before Hitler came to power, developing quickly even during the worldwide depression years of 1929–1933, which had otherwise affected Germany worse than almost any other country in Europe.

.   .   .

The political prospects of Austria now require more attention than they have been receiving.

Even before World War I, and before the disintegration of the Habsburg Empire, there was a small but significant number of Austrians who wished to regard themselves as Germans, desiring that Austria become a part of the Greater German Empire (the young Hitler was among them). After the end of the Habsburg Empire there remained a small Austria that many of its citizens did not regard as viable. As early as 1919 a majority of them (not at all early Nazis) wanted to be joined with Germany. During the 1930s Austria was the key to Europe. There was an ominous rise of the Nazi movement within Austria, its popular surge was similar to that of the Nazi tide within Germany. But there was no great leader among them; and for a number of reasons, including Mussolini's onetime support of Austrian independence, the Austrian Nazis did not prevail — until 1938, when Hitler marched into Austria, with Mussolini's acquiescence. That was his first territorial conquest. From that moment on his Reich was the greatest power within Europe. The majority of Austrians in 1938 hailed their union with Germany enthusiastically. During the Second World War the number of Austrians within the SS was disproportionately high.

In 1943 Churchill, Roosevelt and Stalin agreed that an independent Austria would be restored after the war, that its union with Germany would be prohibited. That was what happened. The Russians were not particularly interested in subjugating Austria by Communizing it; but they wanted to keep their occupation zone for a while. We have seen that in 1955 they agreed to the Austrian State Treaty, whereby they and the Western powers would evacuate their occupation zones in exchange for a "neutral" Austria that must remain independent of Germany and not join either the Western or the eastern military alliance systems. That corresponded not only with

the then heartfelt wish of all Austrians but also with the diminution of their identity problem. Now it was proper as well
as profitable to be Austrian, and not German. Economically,
too, Austria was evidently much more viable than an earlier
generation of Austrians had thought. Austria was well on its
way to becoming another Switzerland, a neutral and prosperous Alpine republic.

The two political parties of long standing that governed Austria after 1945 were the Social Democratic and the People's
(formerly Catholic-conservative) parties. Now that the Russians were leaving Eastern Europe here, too, in 1989 came
symptoms of change. Some of the Austrian politicians began
to question the neutrality clause of the 1955 State Treaty. This
at least suggested that there were still many Austrians who
had not come around to seeing themselves and their country
as something resembling the Swiss and Switzerland. In Austria
the adjective "national" refers to people who were and are pro-
German. A new nationalist party rose in Austria, calling itself
the Freedom party. Its supporters consisted of people who had
been attracted by the past of the Third Reich and others who
had grown weary and impatient with the restrictions (and occasional corruptions) of the Austrian two-party system. In
1989 and 1990 the Freedom party garnered about 16 percent of
Austrian votes. In November 1991 something happened in Vienna that ought to remind us of what had happened there
exactly one hundred years before. In 1891 in Vienna, as indeed
in many other places in Europe, the opposing forces had been
those of liberals and conservatives; but then and there appeared, rather suddenly, a third force, Lueger's Christian Social
party — anti-liberal and anti-Semitic, nationalist and populist
— overwhelming the others and winning the city in a land-
slide. In 1991 the nationalist Freedom party, including certain
neo-Nazi elements, won 23 percent of the vote in Vienna, at
the expense of the two large and now traditional parties that

had had a near-monopoly in Austrian politics since 1945. On several occasions its attractive youthful leader, Jörg Haider, made favorable references to the era of the Third Reich — aware that there are many Austrians who regard the official and censorious wholesale condemnation of that past as a Big Lie.

What will happen in Austria is, again, significant and perhaps even centrally important for Europe. The ending of the American-Russian division of Europe is reflected in the weakening of the Austrian two-party system and in the rise of the Freedom party. If the latter were to grow to achieve the direct or indirect support of the majority of Austrians, then such a change in the internal political constellation of Austria could be as ominous for the future of Europe as what had happened within Austria in the 1930s. Yet history does not repeat itself. There are virtually no Austrians now who are willing to abandon the independence of their country for the sake of a union with Germany. (But, then, in 1938, too, most Nazi leaders in Austria preferred an Austrian Nazi state rather than its complete absorption by Germany.)

Continuity, yes; but also change. The present Germany is not the Germany of the past. Germany is respectable. Most Germans have been prosperous for more than forty years. Those Germans who have nostalgia for the Third Reich are few. Most Germans reject Hitler, honestly and conscientiously; others because they find some comfort in regarding the entire Hitler era as an unnatural episode in the history of their country. There are other factors at work. There is that earlier mentioned, important factor: the historic German populations east of the Oder no longer exist. There is the other, temporary factor of the difficulties within the former East Germany; economic and other difficulties, whereby the Germans' hands are momentarily full — even though these difficulties, in my opinion, will pass sooner rather than later. This does not mean that their aggressive expansion in Eastern Europe will then necessarily begin. The texture of history and the structure of societies have changed. A German military predominance in Europe, leaning heavily eastward, is most unlikely. More important, the relations of peoples are no longer governed principally by the relations of their governments. Ranke's famous formula, "Das Primat der Aussenpolitik," the primacy of foreign policy, is largely valid still, but no longer categorically so. This has an especial significance for Germans for whom the authority of the state was for so long, and so unquestionably, sacrosanct.

The Germans have much to contribute to Europe and to Western civilization. It may be encouraging that the movement of the "Greens" started in Germany, more than a decade ago. They are questioning the meaning of "progress" — the rethinking of which is the main task of the twenty-first century, everywhere in the world. (By God, do we need more American Greens! — and not merely Wilderness People.) The trouble with the Greens in Germany is the extremism of their behavior, their often unsavory and disrespectful radicalism, whereby they have not succeeded in increasing their popular support; and that is not only a question of impolitic behavior. They are often the self-made prisoners of their leftist and anti-establishment inclinations. They are split-minded: traditionalists and anti-traditionalists at the same time. They want to conserve the land, and they are opposed to the inhuman progress of bureaucracy, automation, technology. In that respect they are conservatives, in the proper, larger than political sense of that word. Yet at the same time they favor abortion, feminism, unlimited immigration, nomadism — at the expense of the traditional family, of traditional patriotism, of traditional humanism, of the traditional respect for rights of property. (They are the reverse of those American "conservatives" who are strident nationalists, enthusiastic proponents of inhuman technology, either indifferent or opposed to the conservation of American land.) I am inclined to think (or rather, hope) that sooner or later Greens will appear on the right, not on the left; but then "right" and "left" are terms that have outlived most of their meaning after two centuries, at the end of the twentieth century.

If German predominance in Central and Eastern Europe remains economic and cultural, there is no harm in that. But there may be no clear line of division between what is cultural and what is political. They may no more be separable than are prestige and power. The collapse of Communism and the weakness of Russia led to the reappearance of German power and German prestige, including some things that Germany represented during the Second World War. "Yes, Hitler was wrong, but we had fought Communism, hadn't we? That, and our army's defense of Central Europe from the Communist hordes, was our main duty and task in that war." In the 1950s there were many Germans who tried to impress this upon Americans, not without success. (They did not impress the British.) In the 1980s, well before the great changes of 1989, respected German historians began to argue something like the above in their scholarly books, with the results of a historians' debate within Germany, the so-called *Historikerstreit*. The quarrel was inconclusive, mostly because neither side expressed itself clearly. Yet the sense that the British (and Roosevelt) were shortsighted because of their dislike of Germany, because they were unwilling to recognize that for the Third Reich the struggle against Communist Russia had the definite priority over an unnecessary war with Great Britain, is still widely current in Germany. It is in Germany that the reputation of Winston Churchill is relatively lowest. The psychic relationship of Germans and British remains uneasy.

German-American relations have turned more complex, in part because of the changing composition of the American people, in part because of the open question of Germany's relationship to "Europe" (the quotation marks are not accidental). Someday the Germans may have to decide whether their alliance with the United States will remain incompatible with their membership in an increasingly independent and non-American Europe (the only raison d'être for a Europe not within quotation marks). For forty years the Germans did not have to choose. They will not be able to avoid that choice forever.

Their other choice concerns Russia: whether their present policy of a benevolent and special relationship with Russia must, or must not, have a priority over their relations with the non-Russian, and often anti-Russian, nations both within the former Soviet Union and in Eastern Europe. *That* choice they will have to confront sooner rather than later.

Surely their strenuous efforts to maintain their good relationship with Russia is to a great extent, though not entirely, due to their wish not to disturb the prospect of the withdrawal of the last Russian garrisons from East Germany, scheduled for 1994. It is possible that withdrawal may be speeded up, occurring even before 1994.

The last Russian troops will leave their cantonments in Germany fifty years after the first Russian troops broke through the East Prussian frontiers and entered the Third German Reich in 1944, and eighty years after their predecessors of the Tsar's Russian army trampled across the frontiers of the Second German Reich in August 1914, in that first blood-soaked month of the real twentieth century.

There is no common frontier between Germany and Russia now. Most of East Prussia was given to Poland by Churchill, Roosevelt and Stalin, who did not see eye to eye about Poland, but about that they agreed. They also agreed — wrongly — to accede to Stalin's wish to incorporate into the Soviet Union the old Prussian city of Königsberg (the birthplace of Kant) and a small slice of land with it, accepting Stalin's argument for an "ice-free port" in the Baltic, a geographical argument that made no sense at all. Note that I am not now referring to the Russians' digestive problems, to their "sphere of interest." The Königsberg region was not merely swallowed by Russia. Those Germans who remained there were boiled away; the entire thing was put in an airtight jar and locked in the Russian larder. It is a desolate port, with an even more desolate and depopulated slip of a hinterland. It is an administrative district, an *oblast* of the great Russian Republic, separated from it by Lithuania.

No foreigners were allowed to visit Königsberg, renamed Kaliningrad, for more than forty years. Leningrad, Kaliningrad, both named after Communist personalities. Leningrad reverts to St. Petersburg. Will Kaliningrad become Königsberg again — and not in name only? If that happens, it will not be done by German armed force but by an agreement between a new Germany and a new Russia. It will be a proof that Germany will have returned to the center of world history.

The Russian-American division of Germany, at the center of Europe, is over.

Its key date — it was the key date of the end of the Second World War, perhaps even more than the day of Hitler's suicide five days later or the official surrender of the German armed forces two weeks later — was 25 April 1945, when advancing units of the American and Russian armies met in the middle of Europe, along the Elbe River near the German town of Torgau. On the banks of that river, carrying the flooded wreckage of spring and war, American and Russian soldiers, fired with sentiments of friendship and with plenty of drink, celebrated late into the night. (That celebration was but a forerunner of the great pro-American celebration in Moscow two weeks later.) Among the soldiers of the 58th Russian Guards Division there were some whose home was Vladivostok, who came to the middle of Europe from the shores of the western Pacific; it is possible that among the soldiers of the U.S. 69th Division there were some whose home was Seattle or San Francisco; they, too, had been sent to conquer halfway around the world. Their meeting took place not only in the middle of Germany, they met in the middle of European history; for Torgau is about midway between Wittenberg, where Luther's fire of great revolutions started, and Leipzig, where Napoleon's course of great victories ended. Less than fifty years have passed since then. Now the Russians are going, and the Americans will be going soon.

Sooner or later Americans will have to make a choice too, a choice that has nothing to do with whether those already useless American garrisons and bases remain in Europe or not. In a few years we will see whether "Europe" becomes more "European" or more and more German-dominated. That is: whether the still largely powerless "European" institutions will develop sufficiently to assume a more definite character capable of inspiring authentic loyalties; or whether the German participation in those institutions in Brussels or Strasbourg will be not much more than formal and secondary, when compared to an increasing reassertion of the primacy of German national and political interests.* In the event of the latter — which, I think, is the more probable one of these two alter-

---

* Thus these alternatives of the future of "Europe" may resemble the alternatives of the future German union one hundred fifty years ago. The Zollverein, the German customs union, and the all-German Reichstag in Frankfurt already existed; but the latter — as Bismarck foresaw — proved incapable of bringing about the union of Germany. That would be accomplished by Prussia.

natives — the United States and the American people may be faced with a choice between Germany and Britain . . .

That choice will reflect something deeper than strategic calculations. It will have emotional, cultural and ethnic elements, as in 1914–1917 and in 1939–1941. Then a decisive element was the presence and influence of a largely Anglo-Saxon, upper-class elite, whose presence and influence have weakened greatly during the second half of the twentieth century. A reflection of that is the present (I am writing this in early 1992) confrontation between the weak, unconvincing and unconvinced representative of that former elite George Bush and the "America Firster" Pat Buchanan. Contrary to the accepted ideas — and to his own assertions — Buchanan is not really an isolationist (consider, for example — and it is a significant example — that this so-called isolationist is a strong advocate of American recognition of and support for Croatia, Slovakia and the Ukraine, as are all German and Austrian nationalists). But many of the America Firsters in 1940 were not really isolationists either. They were bitterly opposed to Roosevelt and to those Republicans who wished to engage the United States against the German Third Reich on the British side. In 1940 Hitler correctly named these Americans "radical nationalists." In that year the Anglophile internationalists among the Republicans were stronger than the radical nationalists; hence they engineered (there were no primaries then) the nomination of the anti-German Willkie. In 1992 Buchanan will not be the Republican nominee; but he and the nationalists may attempt to gain the control of the Republican party. With some luck they may be able to achieve that. If that happens, their success will resound among the nationalists in many parts of the world, especially in Central and Eastern Europe; one consequence of which will be the revision of many of the still accepted ideas about the Second World War.

.   .   .   .   .

During the crucial quarter century of 1920–1945 there was a triangle of forces and powers in the world. Three great forces existed throughout the globe. There was Communism, incarnated and represented by Russia alone. There was Western, capitalist, liberal democracy, represented mostly by the English-speaking nations and by those of northwestern Europe. There was a new kind of radical nationalism, incarnated principally by National Socialist Germany, but also by other nations. Of these three forces the last was the strongest one. National Socialist Germany was so powerful that it took the unnatural alliance of the other two forces to defeat it. These divisions existed not only among states and armies. They existed within almost every country of the world. Still (as Proudhon remarked, more acutely than Marx), people are moved not by ideas about social contracts but by the realities of power. In 1945 the Third Reich lost the war. Not only among Nazis and Germans and Austrians but also among their allies and sympathizers, their empathy and respect for the Third Reich had to disappear, surely in public. Germany had lost, the Russians and the Anglo-Americans had won. In Germany and Austria (and Japan and Italy) the Americans mattered more than the Russians, whose behavior and reputation soon seemed even worse than that of the Nazis — a view that accorded with the views of many Americans soon after the war. But now Communism and the Soviet Union have collapsed; British power is largely gone; and the prestige and power of the United States has begun to decrease. Should we then wonder that the prestige of Germany, past and present, may be rising again?

Are the Germans immune to the revival of their nationalism? Yes and no. Yes: because for most Germans the rejection of the Hitler past is not merely the result of a politic calculation. No: because that rejection is not necessarily identical with a rejection of German nationalism, including its memories. In the event of a surge of a populist nationalist party, people such as Kohl and others of his party will not be immune to the temptation to seek some kind of compromise, to adopt some of the rhetoric and some of the politics of the new nationalists of a younger generation. Again there will be more to that temptation than politic calculation. The official repudiation of the Hitler era will not cease. Nor will the cultivation of good German relations with Israel. But the time may come when at least some of the German memories of the Third Reich and of the Second World War may undergo a deeply felt revision, a matter of memory, which will be more than a matter of quarrel among historians; for, as Kierkegaard once said, "we live forward but we can only think backward" — and there is, of course, an inseparable connection between memory and knowledge, between a view of the past and a view of the future, between thinking and living.

⚓ VI ⚓

BETWEEN TWO WORLDS

Europe is my mother. America is my wife.

⚓

1990. Sometimes after dinner I walk out to the grassy slope beyond our terrace. In those moments the charm of the present is inseparable from a satisfying sense of the past, because it is good to know that nearly everything I now see is still the same landscape that the American ancestors of my children saw 50, 100, 150, 200 years ago. The sense of the future; I am afraid of it.

Will my children inherit this landscape? One hundred or 150 years ago our ancestors hoped that the railroad or the telegraph or the new highway would come close to where they were living, the sooner the better. In our time the news that a new highway or a new pipeline or a new development or a new shopping mall is coming close puts fear and loathing in our hearts.

I am not alone in this. Most of my neighbors feel the same. That is why, for the past twenty years or more, I have served on the Schuylkill Township Planning Commission. Each month my colleagues and I spend a long evening poring over the plans of subdivisions and developers that we may or may not recommend to the supervisors. All of our discussions are constrained by the technical and legal categories of definitions — matters, however, that ever so often are thick cloaks thrown over deeper personal, political divisions, divisions of differing views of the world. Most of us know how often development amounts not to opening but to closing, how it means the eager spreading of cement and the indifferent razing of the land. We know how often construction means destruction — not only of trees and meadows but of certain ways of life. "Are you against progress?" people sometimes ask me. The time has surely come to rethink the meaning of that word.

I have been living in this township and on this piece of land for thirty-seven years. But I am not a native American. I came here from my native country, Hungary, forty-four years ago, fleeing the imposition of a Communist regime by the Russians. I thought then that this would last at least fifty years. But history is unpredictable. I did not know then how its dissolution would happen. That it would happen I began to see many years ago.

I have not been involved in émigré affairs or in Central European academic politics. At the same time I have kept close to a few old, trusted friends. One of them is an old priest, Monsignor Béla Varga, a leader of the prewar democratic Small Holders' party (of which I was a youthful member forty-seven years ago). He was the last chairman of the freely elected Hungarian parliament. He fled Hungary forty-three years ago. He is now eighty-seven years old and in frail health, the chaplain of a convent in New York, where I go to see him every time I am in that city.

And now came another, unpredictable coincidence. Elections were held in Hungary this spring. The largest party would form the new government; their candidate for prime minister is the son of Monsignor Varga's ally and friend during the war, when both of them did a heroic job saving and protecting Polish refugees, escaped French prisoners of war and many Jews from the Nazis; and the candidate for the new foreign minister is a historian friend of mine. The monsignor and I followed developments in Hungary, though not very closely. From more than four thousand miles away we wished them luck.

And then one day in April, the routine of our lives changed. Things were speeding up. I was at the Planning Commission meeting when Béla called my wife. The new, freely elected parliament would meet on the second of May. Its leaders wanted him, and me, to be there. What follows is a necessarily breathless (though perhaps not superficial) account of those days and of my thoughts, in diary form.

April 18, Wednesday. Fairly long Planning Commission meeting. This developer (to whom I spoke on the phone yesterday) is unusually eager to push his development through. Try to pin him down on how much of the woodland he will destroy. This is not easy. Details to be attended to: Trees with a diameter exceeding six inches must be shown on his plan. Two of the building setbacks on each plot missing. Ingress and egress of plotted driveways: PennDOT approval required. Behind these things looms the menacing shadow of Big Brother — i.e., the Valley Forge Sewer Authority — not to speak of the restive steamroller of the Fernley tract. The latter is gathering strength before the bulldozers are ready to roar.

April 19, Thursday. Béla calls from New York. Antall (the incoming prime minister), Géza (the incoming foreign minister) called from Budapest. They implored Béla to come and speak. Béla still reluctant. Doctor says he can go, provided that fatigue is kept to a minimum and all medications properly taken. He asks me to help with his speech. He says that

I must come with him. Am reluctant — have millions of things to do here — but Stephanie says, "If he says so, you must." Details to be attended to: must get airline seat next to him. Hungarian visa (not easy: cannot go up to consulate in New York). Write and xerox circular letter to a few friends in Budapest. Have no idea where I'm going to stay once I'm there.

April 28, Saturday. Wake up with a hangover. Reason: drank a bottle of champagne last night, in order to celebrate first harvest and glorious consumption of white — yes, white — asparagus spears cut last afternoon, something that I tried to grow for nineteen years in vain. (White asparagus is green asparagus, except that it must be planted much deeper. Asparagus expert told me it won't work, white asparagus is a different strain. Expert was wrong.) I talk to R. and T. about coming supervisors' meeting on Wednesday, May 2. I'll be in Budapest then, at the first meeting of the new parliament of Hungary. Plenty of problems at both meetings. Here: Big Brother, i.e., the Sewer Authority, at it again, with its local allies who long to develop the entire township, pouring concrete over what's left of open space. There: Big Brother, i.e. the Soviet Union, largely gone, but plenty of ambitious politicians wishing to pour rhetoric over what's left of open space in Hungarian minds.

First day of historic journey. I take the train to New York, to Béla's convent apartment. Nuns stand on the steps, with tears in their eyes, waving good-bye. Limousine to America's number one concentration camp, Kennedy Airport. Thought occurs to me that I was in a sort of concentration camp in Hungary forty-six years ago. Fellow inmates preferable to mob at Kennedy.

April 29, Sunday. Arrival very moving. Bright windy morning. Béla comes slowly down the steps, leaning heavily on his cane. Government delegation on tarmac, with flowers, also Béla's old sister. His return to his homeland after forty-three years. I keep back, with tears in my eyes. Must say that this way of arriving is agreeable. No customs, no passport examination, limousines waiting for us at the plane. Antall arranged that Béla and I will stay in a Government House. We drive into Budapest, the industrial suburbs giving way to streets lined with those old, sooty apartment buildings with their smoky, vinegary smell. We cross the Danube. Government House is high up in the Buda hills (not far from where my grandparents' villa was). Now my big job begins — fending off people from this old priest after his wearisome journey. I wave a reporter away, unsuccessfully. Turns out to be editor of a newspaper, to whom an interview was promised. So Béla sits on an uncomfortable sofa, answering stupid questions. ("What did you think when you first saw a Hungarian flag?" Plenty of Hungarian flags in the United States.) The township reporter of the Evening Phoenix much more intelligent.

Staff of Government House more than helpful. They are evidently personnel of previous Communist government, probably including former secret policemen, all anxious about their jobs now. After we settle Béla down, I ask them to call a taxi for me. "Sir," they say, "there is a car and a driver and a bodyguard at your disposal here." Car at my disposal is a Lada (Russian Fiat), bodyguard a policeman in civvies for whom proper adjective is "burly." (There are clichés that are true.) Not knowing where I'll stay, I had telephoned I. to get me a hotel room, also told her that I'll come straight to her apartment. The streets leading down to the city are green and gold and all the trees in leaf. I tip the driver and tell him not to bother to come back for me. I'll just take a cab. I.'s small apartment, in which she survived more than three decades of Communism, is a perfect combination of elegance and coziness (not House and Garden stuff).

That *kind* of survival is what is best about Hungary and Hungarians. Later that day I meet an American diplomat. "Tell me one thing," he asks. "Why is it that every Hungarian I meet is deeply pessimistic but at the same time they enjoy life so much?" That is a very intelligent question. Finally I come up with an answer. "I can't tell you why. I can only tell you how."

Back to Government House again. Large, semi-opulent furnishings rather unbeautiful. Béla rests through the long afternoon. Telephone keeps ringing without cease. Staff keeps telling me that they will serve food and drinks for us, whatever and whenever we like. After all, only a few guests in the building. When George Bush came to Budapest last July (for a single day), his staff consisted of at least five hundred people. (Is this what the Republicans mean when they say they are against Big Government?)

At night descend to town again. Dinner with I. and L. We are told about great economic distress in Hungary, but the restaurants are crowded. I fought jet lag all day and now take a sleeping pill and collapse into bed. I address a request to the former secret policeman: breakfast in my room at eight o'clock, please.

April 30, Monday. I am awakened as huge breakfast arrives on huge tray at 7:59:60. I had thrown off all my sheets and find myself naked on top of bed. (It is not always wonderful to have obsequious servants.) I dress and walk out on terrace, heavy smell of lilacs in the air. Between the trees, the roofs and towers of the city, four miles away, scintillating in the sun. Garden not too well kept. Thoughts of all of the mowing I'll have to do when I return home. Staff, who had no idea who I was when I arrived (perhaps American secret policeman, accompanying the main guest?), now have been told by someone to call me Professor. (Well, I've known many an American professor working for the CIA.)

Read Hungarian newspapers, find them quite good. One cartoon worthy of the old New Yorker. Farms in Hungary were collectivized by Communists, but through the years peasants have done rather well, everyone doing his own thing in those collectives. Cartoon shows well-dressed couple in well-furnished apartment with large TV, VCR, lots of furniture. Man reading the paper, turning with a worried face to his wife: "They are returning our land to us. What are we going to do?"

At night, dinner at apartment of my friend the incoming foreign minister. Could not send flowers to his wife, since all shops closed, this being a holiday, the eve of May Day. (Will it remain a holiday?) Dinner party consists of many of his friends, some of them future ambassadors and ambassadresses. I drink less than usual, to E.'s considerable surprise. Am flattered to hear that some of them know me, having read my articles and books published in America and England. Does not happen in Philadelphia or Phoenixville, but perhaps no great loss. Cannot find a taxi, but walk through the warm liquid midnight air to the Intercontinental Hotel, its doorway still crowded with loud — very loud — Germans. I say something to the doorman in Hungarian and get a taxi ahead of the Germans. Great improvement, this: not so long ago it was better to speak English if you wanted to arrange something in Budapest. Suggests a rise of national self-confidence, without which most political changes turn out to be meaningless.

May 1, Tuesday. Hurried call from superintendent of Parliament Building, to look over and arrange Béla's arrival, seating and speech tomorrow. This superintendent is an excellent man. The building is splendidly refurbished. I am touched by a sense of historical continuity: the intaglioed woodwork, the 1900 lettering, the frescoes, the heavy gleaming brass ashtrays set into the windowsills of the corridor for the convenience of the honorable members. The Parliament Building has twenty-four gates. Béla will arrive at Gate Six, from where the walk is shortest and there is an elevator close to the entrance. Then we will rest in a chamber and have coffee and refreshments; and then through the high, Gothic-eaved corridors into the main chamber. Below the rostrum are the red velvet armchairs of the government ministers. Will Béla speak from there? For there is a microphone at that place. Or will he be able to mount the rostrum? Well, yes. It is only eight steps and has a strong brass railing. But there is no place there for him to sit. And now the superintendent produces a standing desktop that will be perfect. Béla can lean on it as he holds his speech in his old, lovable, trembling hands. That is how it will be.

This was the largest parliament building in the world when it was finally completed in 1901. Now I am playing a part in it, as I am playing a small part in the government of Schuylkill Township, which has one of the smallest township buildings in Chester County, surely bereft of intaglio, scagliola, marble and red velvet. Now — without so wanting — I am involved in politics here, too. There are pressures on us to do this or that with the speech, to add this or that to it. The pressures involve the historical prospects of my native country Hungary. It is surely different from my involvement in the Comprehensive Plan of Schuylkill Township, Chester County, Pennsylvania. Now I am involved in the phrasing of summary judgments on previous centuries, on an entire nation's relationship with Europe and with the Russian empire, with allusions to some of the deep differences and fissures within the democratic Hungary now emerging, with suggestions heavy with meaning — not with tree calipers, roadside berms, ultimate rights of way, sideyard setbacks and lot averaging.

Two kinds of politics. Two very different places. Two very

different occasions. And yet — ultimately the essence of these matters is the same.

First and foremost: the history and the essence of politics are a matter of words. This may sound strange in this age of pictorial presentations and numerical computerization, but so it is. In the beginning was the Word, as the Bible says, and so it is still. It is words that move us, hurt us, inspire us, depress us, because we think in words. In this historic speech a change of one word or two, the omission or addition of a single phrase, could make all the difference. It could affect not only the tone but the entire meaning of the message that this old and honorable man addresses to a nation. His words most probably will not change the course of world history. But within my lifetime there were words that did change the course of history: Hitler's words to which an entire nation rose to respond, ready to bear arms; and Churchill's words that made another nation ready to respond, to resist Hitler even when it was largely bereft of arms.

It strikes me that the future of Schuylkill Township also depends on words. Not on "facts," because there is no fact in this world that exists apart from the words with which it is expressed, or thought. It is words — about zoning, about wetlands, about lot lines, about soil configurations — that decide the fate of what may be built and where, and of what may be preserved or where; it is words that a judge will use when he makes a legal ruling, deciding a case for a developer or for a township. The law consists of words.

Right now I am making a great deal of fuss because a friend wants us to change one sentence to be heard tomorrow in the parliament of Hungary. Last year I made a great deal of fuss because the consultants whom the township supervisors had employed to draft the new Comprehensive Plan had chosen to define unbuilt parcels of land in Schuylkill Township as "vacant lands." I rose up against that.

"Vacant," I said, means abandoned, empty, useless. Does this mean that every single plot of land of ten acres or more in this township that is not yet covered with buildings is abandoned, empty, useless? Some people thought that I was making a mountain out of an empty lot; or that perhaps I was only speaking as a professor. No, the matter was not that of the traditions of language. It was the preservation of honesty and decency — in the Schuylkill Township building as well as in the National Assembly of Hungary in Budapest.

Words are inseparable from ideas. Communism is gone in Hungary because for many years no one believed in it, including Communist party members, and now including the present leader of the Russian empire. That is why Hungary — thank God — has gone through a bloodless revolution; not because Reagan and Weinberger forced the Russians into an armament race that the latter could not financially afford. In Schuylkill Township the battle will be won once people's ideas — not merely their feelings, those are already changing — change to the extent that they recognize the outdated vision of technological progress that would make the entire world into one gigantic suburb, with endlessly sprawling shopping malls or airports.

The second essential similarity between these two places is that of the human element in politics. The main political division in Hungary now exists between two large political parties, the Hungarian Democratic Forum and the Association of Free Democrats. The literal sense of these words means nothing, just as in the United States, where there are no monarchists or aristocrats, only Republicans and Democrats. The real divisions go deeper. They exist within the parties, not among them — in Hungary as well as in Schuylkill Township. There are good eggs and bad eggs in both parties. And who are the bad eggs? Well, whether in the Danube basin or in Chester County, Pennsylvania, they are the same kind of people: people who are moved mainly by envy and resentment — envy of other people who are (or who seem to be) more respectable or successful than they are, resentment of people who are (or who seem to be) better off because they seem to know more of the world. Such people exist within the majority party in Hungary, as they exist among the majority party in Chester County. They are a minority, but sometimes a hard minority. That is exactly what is missing in the numerical configurations of the pollsters. A hard minority may — I am not saying that it will — exert an influence beyond its numbers, let alone the quality of its component men and women, because when there is not much more than a soft majority in its way, a hard group of people or a well-organized lobby can give the public impression that it represents the popular and respectable majority. That is the danger of populist democracy in Hungary, between East and West, as well as in Schuylkill Township, between Phoenixville and Valley Forge.

In the history of Hungary, Dr. Johnson's famous phrase has been, alas, often applicable — patriotism having been the last refuge of scoundrels. In America too, to which I must add that free-enterprise patriotism is often the last resort of developers. The danger to democracy is not political extremism. It is the kind of ambition that is fueled by resentment and greed — and greed itself is a consequence rather than a cause, a consequence of a sense of fear. That fear is not really a fear of financial insecurity. It is a fear of personal inadequacy. The father of greed is vanity — in Budapest and Hungary as well as in any American small town or suburb.

May 2, Wednesday. A brilliant May morning, full of promise. I am worried about the arrangement: Has my old friend taken his pills along? Will he bear the strain of stand-

ing up so long? But all goes well, including my secondary
worry: since I am not a former member of parliament, but
only his companion, will there be a seat for me in the gallery
once he is escorted to the parliament floor? But then I am
led to one of the six ceremonial boxes on the floor itself,
each with four red velvet chairs. I sit next to Princess Walburga von Habsburg, daughter of Otto von Habsburg, who
is also here. The son of the last king of Hungary, he is a
well-liked figure in the country now. The princess is handsome and tells me that she has one of my books on her night
table in their house in Bavaria. Before I have a chance to
feel flattered, we all stand. The national anthem is played. It
could not be more appropriate at this moment. (At some of
the supervisors' meetings in Schuylkill Township we recite
the Pledge of Allegiance, which I do not find quite appropriate there; but then here, too, an actor goes to the platform
and recites a poem, "To the National Assembly," written
one hundred and forty years ago, and I find his tone and his
declamation not quite proper.) Finally my old friend Béla
rises and slowly walks to the rostrum. His speech lasts not
more than eight minutes. They fly by. It is a strange experience to hear some of the things that he desired to say as
they are expressed in some of my phrases. At the end is a
passage that is as fitting for Hungary as it is for the United
States — for my native country as well as for my adopted
one. He says that the Nazis and the Communists incarnated
a pagan barbarism from which Hungary is now freed; "but
ahead of us are perhaps the shadows of a new, technologi-
càl paganism, threatening the nature of our homeland, our
continent, our mother earth."

There is a standing ovation. Two other, much longer
speeches follow. Then an intermission. There is a champagne reception in the presidential chambers, above the
Danube. The sunlight pours in. Béla is tired. He will not stay

for the rest of the long first session of parliament; he wants to go back to the house and rest. I will go with him; I say good-bye to some of my friends and acquaintances and to Walburga: "Je vous prie de bien vouloir soumettre mes hommages à Madame votre mère." I wished that my mother had lived to see this day and that my American wife were here, but that was not to be. Back in Pennsylvania dawn is now breaking. It is the second of May, the monthly supervisors' meeting. What is happening in Budapest is the celebration of the end of a long, painful chapter and the beginning of a new chapter in a nation's history. What will be discussed in Schuylkill Township is many petty matters but, after all is said, the preservation of something that means more than a few acres here and there: the preservation of a countryside, of a landscape, of a way of life, of a country.

All of the world's great newspapers are here. I give the correspondent of the Frankfurter Allgemeine my English translation of Monsignor Varga's speech. The next day the paper prints a precise account of it. This never happens in the New York Times or even in the Philadelphia Inquirer, though it does happen sometimes in the Evening Phoenix, not to speak of the Schuylkill Township Civic Association's newsletter, where all the details do count.

1991. Nine months later I am, surprisingly, in Hungary again, teaching in the university, living in a spacious rented apartment. My roots are here — and in America. This is a physical impossibility but (as with many other human phenomena) not a spiritual one. I am not a hybrid. I belong to both places. But America — more precisely, Pennsylvania — is my home now.

I write English better than I write Hungarian. I find it easier to lecture in English than in Hungarian. Now that I am here I can talk Hungarian as well as I can talk English (or I think so). I read Hungarian as fast as I read English. As I read, I find that I am exceptionally sensitive to the nuances in Hungarian journalism, detecting — often without wishing to look for them — the underlying suggestions of animosities and disaffections, the opportunisms latent in so many words — the choice of every word being less a stylistic decision than a moral one.

All day I speak and hear and listen to and read Hungarian. Then, at night, I pick up Trollope or Jane Austen from my night table. Reading Emma at night in Budapest is like drinking cool, pure, clear water in a crystal glass. That purity amounts to more than innocence, the rosy innocence of that wondrous English girl (I mean both Emma and Jane Austen) of nearly two centuries ago. That English prose is full of subtleties and insights, it is elegant and modern. Two hundred years ago it was far ahead of Eastern European prose (probably no longer true of most English prose — this is perhaps sad).

Another night I flip on Hungarian television. A 1942 movie with Fred Astaire. Against his loose-limbed elegance (and the swinging music) the silly script does not matter. Oddly, or perhaps not so oddly, I am moved by it.

28 February 1991. Bush comes on the television. I was against the Gulf War. I thought that it was none of our ("our": I can seldom use that American pronoun with ease) business; that the Near East was, and remains, a quagmire; that Bush's way of speaking is lamentable, it reflects the puerility of his thinking. But now, for once, I am moved by one of his phrases: "This war is now behind us." That simple sentence touches me. For a moment I feel American.

One afternoon *I see a Hungarian flag, on a thin long pole,
flying over the northern bastion of Castle Hill, and I am
moved as I think that this simple national flag has somehow
prevailed. It is 1991 but it might as well be 1848. There is
something so historic as to be almost eternal about it. That
lone banner is not assertive or grandiloquent. I feel no exhil-
aration, no nationalist pride; I feel the presence of the endurance of something decent and modest and good.*

31 March 1991. *Dinner at the familiar apartment of J., the
present foreign minister. I know most of the people but I do
not quite feel at home there now.*

9 April 1991. *Dinner, with Dervla Murphy, at the residence
of the British ambassador. I know few of the people but I
feel at home there because it is a very beautiful house, because it once belonged to the Scitovszkys, an old Hungarian
family, of a world that is now gone.*

*Gone, too, is that large part of the old Hungary of one
thousand years that was torn off and given to other, new
states after World War I. I am sensitive to the evocative
power of certain place names, old American place names
such as Cinnaminson, Christiana, Sumneytown, though not
Wounded Knee. And now of old Hungary: Vihorlát, Gör-
gényi havasok. Something in these names is more than
music. When I read their names in print (or on a map), my
imagination crystallizes. But it is not only imagination. I see
those windswept, morose, lonely mountain ranges in what is
now Slovakia, the other in what is now Rumanian Transylvania. Alone, mysterious, with their largely unvexed forests,
with a few sparse paths trod by poor peasants and paced in
the winter by hunters. So they were, still of a very old world,
that other world, before 1914, they belonged to us, to the
other Hungary, before I was born; but these things are within
me. Forever. "A nation cannot be an object of charity" —*

that is, love — Simone Weil once wrote. "But a country can be such, as an environment bearing traditions which are eternal."

The apartment that I rented in Budapest in the late winter and spring of 1991 was very comfortable and well furnished but of course not beautifully, on the Pest side of the river. (I would have preferred Buda but I was fortunate in having secured this kind of apartment, after all.) It is not more than a half mile away from the sanatorium where I was born, and a quarter of a mile away from a house where my family once lived for a short time. Both buildings no longer exist, they were destroyed by American bombs in the summer of 1944, in a neighborhood that was otherwise largely unharmed by the war.

So often I walked through the streets here on grey winter evenings, with the streetlights spraying a thin misty halo through the pearly fog. This was once an upper-middle-class neighborhood, with most of the houses built between 1890 and 1910, semi-palatial villas having one or two apartments on each floor, with large, high-ceilinged rooms, stuccoed or coffered ceilings, French windows, parquet floors — an atmosphere containing soupçons of pretentious elegance and a solid essence of bourgeois comfort. Some of these houses were impressive, with a limited majesty of their own, a few of them built in the then Parisian style, emulating the nouveau riche villas and apartment houses of the belle époque, of the Bois, Auteuil, Neuilly (unlike elsewhere in Budapest, the Austro-German architecture of private houses was not ubiquitous here).

Then came 1944–45, the last dreadful year of the war, with the bombings and the protracted siege of Budapest; and soon after that, four decades of darkness — literal darkness — of the Communists' rule. The once owners and occupants of these houses and apartments disappeared. They came to be occupied by new, unsure, dark-faced tenants: by newfangled functionaries of the ruling party; by Mongolian or Vietnamese embassies; by head offices of trade unions. About five years ago came another change. The Communist era was fading. Some of these apartments were occupied by new families again. Unlike fifty years ago, the curbs of these streets are now lined with automobiles. The Automobile Century had not fully arrived in Budapest then; it has surely arrived now.

In that wintry fog there are not many lights casting a pleasant glow into the street from the small crystal chandeliers of those second-floor drawing rooms or family rooms. So many of the windows are dark. Perhaps ten years hence much of this will change. A new class rises on the ruins of Communism in Hungary, the latter having been a foreign-imposed episode that was almost unbearably long for those who had to live through it but, really, not so long in the history of a nation.

It snowed again, and I walked through these streets to a restaurant and then back again. Now the evening was beautiful, the snow illuminated through the arcs of the streetlights and then resting on the pavements, the air metallic and clean. There was no breeze, the falling snowflakes had a quiet, unbroken quality of something silent and endless. What was missing was the contrast between the snow and the houses, between the peacefulness of the winter outside and the warm interiority inside.

I love winter because of that contrast, whether in my Pennsylvania country or in a European city. Now, in Budapest in 1991, there is little of that. A few pale curtained windows, a greyish rather than yellowish (is it the flicker of television?) light filtering through. Of the ten, twelve, fifteen French windows opening onto the streets, perhaps two or three are lit here and there, suggesting the impression of private life inside. How different from fifty or sixty years ago, with the then promise of comfort and some impressively beautiful rooms and furnishings, once one had entered the massive front doors and found oneself in a well-lit foyer or vestibule, aware, after the snow-laden silence of the street and the chilly staircase, of the high chatter of people, or of an entirely different warm silence, the muffled breath of well-brushed rugs and tobacco-brown plush.

All I can sense here and now is some kind of restricted living, a huddle under high ceilings, not much of an interior life, not even that of comfort. Yes, "privatization" will come. Some of these buildings will be vacated by the present occupants and institutions and offices; new nouveaux riches will occupy them. That has happened before. And, no matter how one may have disliked the nouveaux riches then, it behooves one to know how quickly (that also is very Hungarian) those then nouveaux riches learned so much about taste and fine things. Within one generation these palatial houses became occupied by families worthy of them. But now this will not happen again. There will be no more haute bourgeoisie — not here, and perhaps nowhere else in the world. The offices, too, will remain — indeed expand, with fluorescent tubes glaring from those high stuccoed ceilings. Computers, large television sets pushed against the now dulled boiserie wainscoting. One kind of bureaucracy replacing another. Elegance, no. Never again.

The great, profound moral shortcoming of anti-Communism — that is, anti-Communism from a safe distance — springs from two sources. The first is a sense of self-satisfaction: knowing that one is on the right side, on the respectable side, together with all of those right-thinking people. The other is the exaggeration of the diabolical powers and machinations of Communism and Communists.

The exaggeration of the powers of someone or something alien is a frequent human shortcoming. It is different from paranoia, which exaggerates the powers of someone or something that is, or that we think is, our determined opponent, someone or something that we know. Most anti-Communists are not paranoid. Paranoids indulge in their fears, an indulgence that is masochistic and not particularly satisfying. Anti-Communism at a safe distance is self-satisfying; it may even be turned to personal and occupational profit. Of course this is not true of people who live under Communism, who are oppressed by Communists or threatened by them. Their opposition to Communism is admirable.

I have criticized the ideology of anti-Communism often, the insidious inclination to consider it as if it were identical with patriotism. I wrote about when and how anti-Communist ideology resulted in a misreading of the intentions of Soviet Russian foreign policy, or when it damaged the essential standards of traditional American institutions. I alluded once, briefly, to the sense of insecurity and inferiority that I saw among so many Communists in Hungary in 1945 when, as a matter of fact, they were either in power or about to come to power. I knew that they would come to full power, which is why I left Hungary in 1946.

A year or so later the Communist regime was cemented into place. Around that time, in 1948 or 1949, the then new residents, with their organizations, institutes, consulates and embassies, moved into these abandoned and sequestered semi-palatial villas allotted to them. They did not enter these buildings in high spirits, with the sureness of self-confidence.

Three years after the war and the sordid tragedies that had befallen Budapest, these buildings were deadeningly dank, empty and cold, their walls peeling, with no sign of human presence except perhaps for a few pieces of furniture left behind. They were not like the Smolny Institute or Kseshinskaya's palace three decades earlier, swarming with excited revolutionaries. It was not like Brest-Litovsk either: these new ambassadors, ministers and council presidents were second- or third-rate former intellectuals, not peasants or workers. And they were not alone. Unlike the revolutionary Communists of the past, they did not bring their own personnel. They were made dependent on a staff assigned to them by the real masters of power, the bosses of the secret police. Those janitors, mechanics, drivers, waiters, telephonists and secretaries were often of working-class or peasant origins, culled from volunteers coming forth from the dregs of the proletariat, satisfied with the stroke of fortune that had come to them, instinctively aware of their power over their present superiors. They were — often with the kind of contempt with which a crude servant watches a weak master — watching the latter as they were sitting and shuffling along beneath those cold high ceilings.

That new ruling class: the men and women whom Americans (including the CIA) saw as idealist fanatics, committed to a world-revolutionary ideal, to be combated with fire and poison, "the Communist totalitarian international revolutionaries of the world." At most, they were ephemeral beneficiaries of power, but not for long. They knew that. Their positions, their dwellings, their titles and their perquisites depended on others whom they could not hope ever to control. They knew something else too — another contribution to their sense of inferiority. They knew (without, of course, ever saying so) that everything that was Russian and Soviet and Communist was second rate. That is why, even around 1950, in the peak years of untrammeled Stalinism and the iron curtain, the high moments of self-satisfaction in their social lives occurred not when they were invited as guests to another Communist embassy reception, say a Bulgarian or even a Soviet one, but when they were allowed to appear at a "Western" one: not American or British, of course, but perhaps a French one; say, a reception given to a fellow-traveling Paris intellectual or filmmaker. They knew that everything in the West was better and richer. They did not for a moment doubt that life (or an assignment) in Moscow or Peking was not preferable to Paris or Brussels, though they hoped (well, perhaps some of them) that sooner or later the Communist part of the world might reach those Western standards or even improve them — once, say, France would become Communist; but I think that deep down they knew that would never happen.

Those thoughts and ambitions and tastes — of an ephemeral new class of Communist bureaucrats, in their urban compounds, run-down and fear-ridden — those evenings in those villas in the 1950s! There will be no Balzac to describe them, and not only because of the decline of literature. There is more to this than my imagination, or the fragments one now knows about life among the Communist high officialdom at that time. Now it is 1991. Almost every day I pass the Albanian embassy as I go to the Andrássy Avenue subway station. The building is locked tight, with one Peugeot at the curb with its diplomatic license plate, covered with dirty snow, looking as abandoned as most of that embassy building behind its forbidding, heavy iron railings. Now there is hardly anyone in sight except for the occasional presence of a couple of unshaven men squatting behind the fence, stubbing out their cigarettes, talking *in an unintelligible language, with their sharp suspicious eyes, their smoky, gap-toothed, stubbled, half-feral faces.*

━━

April 1991. A three-day trip to northeastern Hungary with S. and Dervla. I rent a car, a Lada, the cheapest available. Made in the bowels of Russia in a giant factory planned and constructed by Fiat engineers in the early 1960s, when even Khrushchev had to consent to the mass production of private cars. (He had been against that originally, having seen traffic jams in the United States — in this Automobile Century, had that been one of the reasons for his fall?) This brand-new Lada is about forty years behind Western standards, impractical (the ignition requires poking under the wheel with your left hand), but the frame and steel are much heavier than those of Japan-made cars. (Perhaps that was the key to the success of Russian tanks during World War II: primitive but solid and heavy.)

The Hungarian countryside is better kept than ever before. This was already so twenty years ago, under the Communists, when the human reality (this family is in charge of this field, that yard is yours) was more important than the official categories of collective farming. Now, in Eger, in the beautiful narrow streets beneath the old fortress walls, every second house is being restored, repainted, refurbished. This is the essence of real hope for Hungary, this kind of private ownership and enterprise, that is: enterprise for the purpose of ownership (as is the case of so many Americans who work on their own houses) and not the reverse (as is the case of developers). I can imagine living here when getting old, a cozy existence, ambling in a big sheepskin coat on clear cold evenings on my way to a tavern; expecting in the morn-

ing guests from far away and knowing that I can drive once in a while to Budapest or Vienna, or fly to Kandersteg or Bruges from there; and walking in the town cemetery once in a while, not too deep in thought.

We drive on to Sárospatak. We have an extra two hours, so we drive across the mountains — they are very lonely on this cold April afternoon — to Lillafüred, to the Palace Hotel, where I spent five fantastic days and nights in January 1944. We stop there in the chilly spring twilight. The hotel is fairly intact. The Russians used it as a military hospital during the last months of the war and for some years thereafter. Then it became an official resort for trade unionists. It is still that, but the ownership is now in question, and the hotel takes guests again. It is smaller than I had remembered it — as is everything else from one's youth. The dining room, now empty, with its fake-medieval carvings, is the same. My heart twitches only when I see that curve along the first-floor corridor whereto I hurried down night after night on the back stairs to the room of a woman I was madly in love with then.

There is an exhibit of largely yellowed photographs of the opening of the Palace Hotel in 1927, and guests from the early 1930s. I am surprised how incredibly far away this seems now. The photographs evoke a past, people whom I knew and recognize very well, but — unlike in other places of the world — none of this is recoverable here. In so many other places, with so many other people, fragments of the past are still alive. Here the past is dead.

In Sárospatak we find a good small inn, originally a convent in the seventeenth century. The Rákoczi-Windischgraetz castle next morning, made into an excellent museum (Lajos Windischgraetz, that dubious prince, had turned it over to my mother and stepfather for a week, for their honeymoon in 1932; surely it could not have been the entire castle). Then we drive and stop and find a muddy lane, three miles out of town, leading to the country house where I spent a, perhaps magical, summer at the age of ten, in 1934. Well, I find the house. I walk on its empty porch. Someone must live in one of its back rooms. But it is a dead house.

On the way up, tramping through the mud, I find and talk to a family of workers in the vineyards. In this part of the vineyard the vines are held by wires strung up between concrete posts. (Farther uphill they are still trained on wooden poles.) What they tell me about the conditions, the advantages and disadvantages, of "private" ownership and belonging to the "collective" only confirm how these categories are full of holes; that reality hardly corresponds to these definitions; that ownership, possession, income and profit have now thick and uneven layers of different meanings, and that it will be a long time before these things are newly defined and accepted by those whose lives depend on them. Ten minutes with these workers confirms again my basic optimism about my native people: that they have risen in intelligence and self-confidence; that they are a people with great, perhaps potentially very great, talents.

Next day, after a dreadful and dreary lunch at Nyíregyháza (where I find Krúdy's birthplace and have S. photograph me there), we stop along a ditch of the two-lane highway going east. Dervla and I take down her bicycle from the roof of the car. She tells us to leave, since it will take her at least half an hour to mount her panniers astride the back wheels. She will cross into Rumania at night along a dirt track, avoiding a frontier post, skirting the paved roads. If the Rumanian police or soldiers catch her, she will show them a letter (translated into Rumanian) from her (and before her, Byron's) publisher John Murray, on London office stationery, with a big rubber stamp on it (the latter is very important in Eastern Europe). What is even more risky, she carries in her rucksack the Hungarian videotape I got in

Budapest, a two-hour tape showing the Rumanian mob attacking the Magyars in Marosvásárhely, from a sad and bloody two days of incidents. It is extremely dangerous to travel with such a videotape in Rumania. But she stuck a label on the cassette that now reads La Traviata.

Yet this farsighted and admirable Dervla is not altogether inclined to favor the Magyar side in Transylvania. Only one of her explanations makes sense to me: she says that, being Irish, she has a natural inclination to at least understand and at best sympathize with the underdog — that is, with the people who are often being looked down upon. She says that in some ways the Magyars are the way the English have been, and the Rumanians the Irish. But, Dervla, I say: the Rumanians have ruled the bloody place for more than seventy years now, and they suppress the Magyars! She says that there are two sides to this; the Magyar complaints are often imprecise and exaggerated (perhaps true?); and she finds something about Hungarians, even in Budapest, that she does not quite like. They are unfriendly. Or: less friendly than are Rumanians. I cannot see this, which is why I cannot agree with her. Yet she is so observant, so perceptive, so intelligent and so honest that I am disturbed: there must be something in what she says. But I do not know what, and how much.

Hospitality in Europe, especially in Eastern Europe, and in Hungary. In Eastern Europe people are exceptionally hospitable to foreign visitors. There is an oriental element in this. They want to impress those visitors; and — in most cases not quite consciously — they think that they might benefit from this kind of hearty (and it is hearty; nothing false about it) hospitality, sometime, somehow. At the same time, they will invite you only when they think they can (and must) offer you substantial hospitality. (Of course there is a reason for their anxiety: their cramped apartments and living quarters.) This is now a handicap for foreigners. To come over for a drink, to take potluck with us — that is very American, missing here (but also in Western Europe). This is a pity, since there are few coffeehouses, clubs and taverns where one can otherwise get together in a convivial fashion.

One thing that I miss now: a well-appointed American bar in an American city, downtown, with a serried array of twinkling bottles, plenteous and decorative with the glimmer of dark wood and pleasant lights, around six o'clock in the evening, waiting to meet someone there before dinner — one of the moments of mundane American life at its best, rich and easygoing as the alcohol lifts one's spirits higher, though that is merely incidental.

Budapest has an immense problem that would require literally billions of dollars to fix. This city (especially on the Pest side) rose quickly, it grew out of the earth in an extraordinary burst of energy, with the result that an overwhelming majority of its houses were built almost exactly one hundred years ago, and now in need of the most essential repairs. And this is Europe where space is limited. Unlike in a fast-growing American city, these houses were not abandoned or allowed to become slums in one generation after their first dwellers. People have been living in them, crowded, anxious and jealous to preserve their homes through decades. Had I speculated about their future fifty years ago I would have imagined that by 1990 or 2000 vast tracts of these Mietkasernen would, indeed should, be torn down and a new city of sunlit modernity, replete with glass surfaces, would or should arise. Not now. That is no longer desirable. They must be rebuilt, carefully, made livable and enduring, so that one hundred years from now people and tourists will say: How beautiful this all is, this late-

nineteenth-century city! This is one of those things that I find
to be conceivable as well as imaginable. (I fear it won't
happen, except here and there.)

On the Körönd, the Rond-Point of Budapest. Those magnificent — ugly but magnificent — 1890 palaces of apartment
houses, with their Wilhelmine-German towers. In one of
them, in April 1940, I was at a party of young people, one of
the jours anxious mothers gave for their daughters, inviting
boys and girls from their dancing schools. Now the gigantic
iron railings are rusty, the weeds are rank and high in the
courtyards, it is almost like the ruins of the Altstadt in Dres-
den I saw six years ago. But there are a few lights in the
windows, so people are living in them.

The neighboring, lower-class streets have more life, with
young people and older people, the latter with grim, hard-
bitten mouths and faces, not so different from the past, except perhaps for the poison-sweet ubiquitous smell of diesel
fumes in that otherwise thin and dry continental, eastern air.

What is well preserved in this city is very beautiful, because of the dedication of people in charge of it. The Museum of Fine Arts, for example. That, too, looked
monumental to me fifty years ago. Its interior spaces and its
façade are still impressively large, but now I see and know
that its size and proportions are near-perfect, and smaller.

May 1991. Even if my home and my family were not in Pennsylvania, I do not think that I could live happily in Budapest,
except perhaps in the event of the immense luck of finding a
small apartment on Castle Hill with Biedermeier furniture
and one large French window over the Castle Walk, facing
west. Even then, only for part of the year. The reason is politics. I would become (I already am) too deeply involved,

upset, with the stupidities and the demagoguery and the opportunism of political jostling. I see how, step by step, the
television news and other programs are tightened more and
more, their tone changed degree by small degree by the nationalists, mostly of the governing party. Most people may
not notice this, since the selection of what is and what is not
shown on television is a hidden and technical manipulative
process, difficult to pin down.

Is my telephone being tapped now? I do not find it impossible.

But this native people of mine are a very talented people.
In the long run they were not damaged by the last fifty years.
Of course this is an immense generalization, without accounting for their suffering and their damages, physical and
mental and spiritual. However: just as Gorbachev and Co.
have already proved better than Kerensky and Co. in 1917,
in Hungary, too, Imre Nagy, the once Communist peasant,
martyr and hero of the 1956 rising, was braver and more
manly than Admiral Horthy, the once aide-de-camp of Franz
Joseph, the Regent of Hungary from 1920 to 1944. I have
often (and at the risk of unpopularity) defended Horthy. But
when in 1944 he was forced by the SS and the local National Socialists to abdicate, he signed that paper. (The life
of his son was threatened, though not his.) In 1958 Imre
Nagy went to the gallows, when not only his life but his
private freedom would have been spared by a single signature or statement that he refused to give.

I am not an admirer of athletes as they are interviewed on
television; but as I watch some Hungarian soccer players
answering a reporter, I find that they are intelligent and
fairly modest; they express themselves so much better than
American sports figures before the camera, spitting out a
few inept phrases while chewing gum.

My worst Hungarian students (those who do not do the

readings and who fudge the answers in their written exami-
nation) write better than my best American ones. Here the
reason is simple: despite their evident deterioration, the
Hungarian high schools still require more work and higher
standards than American ones. Still, hordes of young and
even middle-aged Hungarians chew gum, masticating with-
out cease. The worst habits of the "free world" are extant
and spreading. The once most elegant street, Váci-utca, is
now a semi-oriental bazaar.

I had planned, carefully and expressly, a Reconstruction
— more than a Remembrance — of Things Past. Circa 1943,
when I was a student at the university, I would occasionally
stride through that street of the Inner City, meeting my beau-
tiful mother at Gerbeaud's, she fresh from her weekly hair-
dresser's appointment at Femina's (that hairdressing salon
still exists, in the same place), and then sitting with her and
her friends for a short half hour before riding home on the
bus. I told S. and L. about my plan, but somehow the ar-
rangement did not work. I abandoned it. However, instead, I
asked S. to wait for me at a café in Váci Street. We'll meet
there after I finish my class at the university a few hundred
yards away, and then go to dinner. We do this once or
twice, and the knowledge that I am walking down that street
to meet her at a café fills me with an ineffably melancholy
sense of pleasure. One's life is a pilgrimage, not a work of
art (which is why some of the most intelligent aesthetes and
hedonists so often mess up their lives). Still, once in a while
God allows (and inspires) one to add a small bit of penti-
mento to one's life: an overlay (rather than a reconstruction)
of something that is beautiful, sad and nostalgic.

But I cannot end here. There was this episode, a precious
little memorable resurrection of a fragment from my past, an
achievement with a psychic, if not altogether spiritual, pur-
pose. But getting there was different. I do not mean the ob-

vious difference between myself at twenty and at sixty-
seven. I mean: traversing the same street, Váci-utca, then
and now. I must not overemphasize or sentimentalize the
smartness in 1943. Yes, it was a smart place, with well-
dressed men and women in the midst of Europe in the midst
of the horrible Second World War, with all kinds of people
in its espresso bars, and "a fevered undercurrent of social
strivings and snubbings." (It had even then a Central rather
than a Western European look.) Some of this has remained
(or rather, it prevails, again and again): the façades of
some of the buildings, a few superficially elegant shopfronts
of new boutiques, the same florist's shop, and two good
bookstores, though not the wonderful ones where I spent my
(and my father's) money nearly half a century ago. But the
people in the street now consist of unkempt tourists padding
amidst sinister groups of moneychangers and other half-
criminals, hardly disturbed by a few ill-dressed policemen.
Both sides of the street are lined by a chain of poor women
and a few men from Transylvania, or God knows where,
holding up their wares for the tourists: pieces of sheepskin,
gaudily embroidered tablecloths and vests. A semi-oriental
bazaar this once smartest street in the Inner City has be-
come. The café-bar whereto I hurry for my rendezvous with
my pretty cheerful wife is neither pretty nor cheerful, full of
dubious people and groups of tourists sprawling on the low
and uncomfortable modern settees. But then, there is no
longer anything very Eastern about this: soon all Europe, all
of the Western world, will be like this too.

1991. Is Eastern Europe still the Other Europe?

Yes and no. The question is wrongly put. When Lady Mary
Wortley Montagu traveled across Hungary and the Balkans to

Constantinople two hundred and eighty years ago, it never occurred to her that she was going through "Eastern Europe." When Balzac was rattling across Poland on his last sad voyage to Madame Hanska in the Ukraine, I doubt whether the words "Eastern Europe" meant anything to him. Eastern Europe — that indistinct and imprecise term, laden with a kind of odd and strong cultural flavor, became current not much more than one hundred years ago.

How remote were Poland and Hungary from "Western" or even "Central" Europe two hundred years ago! One example: less than one hundred forty miles downriver from Vienna on the Danube there was no such thing as Budapest. There were only Buda and Pest, two dusty and dirty villages, separated by the Danube, unconnected by bridges, with a population perhaps one tenth of Vienna's, among whom Magyars were a minority. But one hundred years later a Budapest had risen, its size almost comparable to Vienna's, urbane, civilized, bursting with self-confidence and vitality, the beauty of its setting, its bridges and buildings and town plan, admired by German, French and American urbanists and architects. Now, at the beginning of the twenty-first century, Vienna and Budapest are, at least in some ways, on the way to becoming twin cities, almost as Buda and Pest had been twin cities two hundred years ago.

The Gypsy Baron was composed and produced a little more than one hundred years ago. Its creation reflected the then emerging Vienna-Budapest symbiosis: the music was written by Johann Strauss the younger, the libretto adapted from a story of Mór Jókai, the Hungarian Dickens. *The Gypsy Baron* takes place in a sparsely populated, feudal and semi-barbaric, fantastic and exotic rural Hungary around 1720. The story involves the Emperor-King's eventually awarding to a Hungarian nobleman a large estate on a vast, empty, flat land from where the Turks had been driven out only recently, the fiefdoms of a millionaire swineherd — that is, the gypsy baron himself. In 1890 that was still a good story, with some of the scenes and the players imaginable to Viennese audiences. Now, one hundred years later, *The Gypsy Baron* is wholly and nicely implausible (despite the ubiquitous and insufferable Gypsy bands in the tourist restaurants of Budapest). To Hungarians now, the world of *The Gypsy Baron* is more remote than is Homer to the Greeks of the present.

Hungarians, Poles and Czechs (and also Slovaks, Slovenes and Croats) argue that they are not of Eastern but of Central Europe. Admittedly the cold war was an anomaly, sundering them from "the West." Admittedly much (though by no means all) of "Eastern Europe" is "Central." But then, there is more to this than "culture" (including cafés, restaurants, theater pieces, novelists, article writers for *Granta* or *The New York Review of Books*). "Eastern Europe" — probably including the European portion of the Russian empire — may have become the *central* theater of the history of the world.

This requires explanation — an explanation of the devolution of empires.

During the entire Modern Age — that is, the last five hundred years — much of the history of the world evolved as a consequence of the dissolution of two empires. The Spanish in the west and the Turkish in the east. The Turks pushed into southeastern Europe at the same time that the last Arabs were driven out from southwestern Europe. The Turks were gathering at the southern rim of Hungary when the fabulous advance of the Spanish empire westward across the globe began. That was an expansion of Europe, of one kind of Europe. A century later the Spanish empire started to decline, while England, Holland and France were rising. Another century later the Atlantic world wars between England and France began. They were world wars of which the birth of an independent United States of America was but a part, wars fought mostly for the inheritance of a bankrupt Spanish empire — bankrupt mostly because it was not seaborne enough. Another century later the remnants of the Spanish empire would be inherited neither by England nor by France but by the United States. When that happened — 1898 and all that — no one (not even the brightest and the best: Admiral Mahan, the young Churchill, Theodore Roosevelt) could imagine that the primacy of sea power would soon be gone, that the primacy of land power was coming back after five hundred years (with the automobilization of the world being its main instrument). Now, another century later, the Atlantic has ceased to be the central sea of history. The British Empire is gone (it was only seaborne); the ports of New York and London are empty of ships save for a few cruise liners, empty of the once swelling traffic of the great Atlantic seas. It is Eastern Europe, the lands over which the giant land powers of the twentieth century, Germany and Russia, have fought, which is again full of history. Full of history, alas. (One of Saki's Englishmen, circa 1912: "The people of Crete unfortunately make more history than they can consume locally." *Vide* Yugoslavia now.)

That history — the retreat of that other empire, the Turkish one, with all of its long-range consequences — also started more than three hundred years ago. At the end of the seventeenth century the recession of the Turkish empire began, having briefly reached its high watermark under the walls of Vienna in 1683. Soon the Austrian and Russian imperial forces would push the Turks farther and farther back into the wilder recesses of southeastern Europe. Elsewhere, too, the Turks were losing their grip, in North Africa and in the eastern Mediterranean, where the British would take their place to secure their passage to India: the Ionian Islands, Malta, Cyprus, Suez; Egypt in the late nineteenth century; Palestine during the early twentieth. For a century the sea-minded British worried about the expansion of the land-minded Russians as the Turkish (and, to some extent, the old Chinese) empire seemed to crumble; but early in the twentieth century both the British and the Russians realized that the most dangerous intruder in the Near East (not yet wrongly named the Middle East) might be neither of them but Germany, with Turkey as its client state. By 1913 — two hundred thirty years after those horrific ululations under the walls of Vienna — Turkey in Europe was reduced to a small sliver of Eastern Thrace, northwest of Constantinople; and less than a year later the Great War began.

The Great War in July 1914 would not have come save for the grim conclusion of the leaders of the Great Powers to the effect that, well, if war had to come, better — for their own countries, they thought — now than later. It was a catastrophic concatenation of calculations — miscalculations, as we now know, and as they had not known at the time. But that chain reaction began in Eastern Europe, and because of Eastern Europe. Unlike all of the previous — Atlantic — world wars, it was there that the First World War began. At the end of it a vast rearrangement occurred. Four monarchs and monarchies — the German, the Austrian, the Russian, the Turkish — were gone. Two of the great multinational empires, the Austro-Hungarian and the Turkish, were largely gone too. The German and Russian empires were reduced, in a state of — as it soon would appear, temporary — retreat. A dozen new "independent" states were formed, or formed themselves, in Eastern Europe, between Germany and Russia. That arrangement did not last, for many reasons. Foremost among them was the rise of Germany again. Even before Hitler came to power, in the midst of the global depression Germany had the greatest economic and cultural influence in Eastern Europe, and her political power was growing fast too. The Second World War, then, broke out in Eastern Europe, and because of Eastern Europe. (For the first, and almost certainly the last, time in her history faraway Britain felt compelled to offer her alliance to an Eastern European country, Poland, solely in order to deter the Germans. It did not work.) The most decisive land battles of the Second World War were fought in Eastern Europe, between the vast German and Russian armies. At the end of the war the Germans were driven out of Eastern Europe by the Russians, dividing Europe (and Germany) in the middle — whence the cold war between the Soviet Union and the United States of America. Fifty years later the cold war ends — because the Russians leave Eastern Europe.

What will happen to Eastern Europe now? The present semblance is this: between a chastened and democratic Germany, and a chastened and diminished Russia, an array of states and statelets of different sizes, a tier stretching from Finland in the north to Greece in the south, all members of a league of nations (now called the United Nations), some of them associated with a few bureaucratic "European" organizations: new parliamentary, constitutional democracies, eager for and seemingly dependent on the approval and the benefices of "the West" (whatever that means) — in sum, a return to something like 1920, by and large. That semblance — I do not believe it.

Twenty years ago I wrote: "Europe is of one piece only when people look at her from outside. There were few Europeans in 1939. The national differences were profound. From Albanians and Andorrans to Serbs and Turks: there were more European nations than there are letters of the alphabet." It is as true in 1991 as it was in 1939, with one important difference. The nations of Europe have become Americanized. Sometime around 1920 something happened in the United States that has had no precedent in the history of mankind. Before that, the structure of every society resembled a pyramid, with the relatively few powerful and rich on the top, the impoverished and mostly powerless masses on the bottom, and the middle class or classes somewhere in between, within the tapering sides of the pyramid. By the 1920s the shape of American society resembled not a pyramid but a huge onion, or a balloon. The bulge in the middle had become enormous. It was a — superficially — homogeneous society, with one vast middle class (to the extent that the very word "middle" began to lose its original meaning), a small upper class (the point of the onion), and the somewhat larger but no longer fundamental root end of the poor (who will be always with us, as Jesus had said). I think — and fear — that such balloons will explode sooner or later and something like a new pyramid shape will reoccur. But that is not my point here.

My point is that the social shapes (but only the shapes) of the nations of Europe — all "democracies" now — resemble that of the United States; and this may be even more true of the "new democracies" of Eastern Europe than of the democratic nations of the West. All *nomenklaturas* (political upper classes) notwithstanding, forty-five years of Communist rule contributed to the homogenization of their societies. The old proletariats have been diminishing. As in the United States, there is no longer any meaningful difference between "workers" and "bourgeois," or between the working class and what we might call a lower middle class. There is some, but not much, difference between a lower middle and an upper middle class; but, as in the United States, that difference is less financial or material than it is cultural, and — in the television age — that is diminishing too. There are a few new rich on the top; but an upper class, not only in a traditional but in the functional sense, hardly exists at all.

This is one of the reasons that the prevalent view of Eastern Europe in the West is wrong. According to this view, the deep crisis in Eastern Europe is economic; and its nations' uneven progress toward liberal democracy is a consequence of that. By and large — I repeat: there are profound differences between, say, Albania and Hungary or, say, Serbia and Poland — the opposite of that *idée reçue* is true. The great and enduring problems are political, not economic. They involve the lust for power, not for money. (But then, this has been true of mankind ever since Adam and Eve, misunderstood by Adam Smith as well as by Karl Marx.)

The material problems (I prefer the word "material" to "economic") *are* serious. The universally accepted idea is that they are the result of forty-five years of Communist mismanagement. There is much truth to that; but it is not the entire truth. The material conditions in the lives of most Eastern European peoples are *less* different from those of the peoples of Western Europe than they were forty-five years ago (Rumania may be the only partial exception). In every Eastern European country the great majority were peasants forty-five years ago, whereas there is no country today (with the possible exception of Albania) where more than a minority are engaged in agricultural work. All over Eastern Europe people to whom such things were beyond the dreams of avarice forty-five years ago now possess their own automobiles, refrigerators, television sets, with electricity at their disposal.

What remains true is that Communist governments delayed — and compromised — these developments considerably. Had there been no Communist regimes in these Eastern European countries, their populations would have reached their present material standards twenty-five or thirty-five years earlier. Yet even in that case they would not have reached the standards of everyday life in Finland or in Austria — the former mutilated and impoverished by the war, and thereafter having had to adjust its ideas of national interests to certain desiderata of Russian foreign policy; the latter partially occupied by Soviet troops until 1955. National conditions and, yes, national character remain as important as before, notwithstanding the uniformities declared by Communism. Yugoslavia pronounced her independence from the Soviet bloc in 1948, opened its borders soon thereafter and began moving toward a mixed economy more than thirty years ago; yet even then Budapest was more of a Western city than Belgrade; and of course so it is now.

This brings me to the anomalies and contradictions in all economic "facts" — or rather, in the categories defined by economists that have scant relevance to the realities of everyday life, including its material realities. In Poland (alone in the Soviet bloc) agriculture was not collectivized; and agriculture in Poland is now worse off than in almost any other Eastern European country. Rumania is the only Eastern European country whose foreign debts were wholly paid off; and material and financial conditions are worse in Rumania than anywhere else in Eastern Europe. In Hungary material conditions are visibly improving, and the Hungarian national currency is now very close to Western standards of international convertibility, meaning worldwide acceptance; yet opinion polls as well as personal conversation show that Hungarians are among the most pessimistic peoples of Eastern Europe — a condition that has nothing to do with the Hungarian gross national product but quite a lot with the prosody of Magyar poetic diction, characterized by its ever falling tone.

This twentieth century is now over; and as we move into the twenty-first, Western and Eastern Europe will become more alike, as far as material conditions go. Foreign investments in Eastern Europe will assist in bringing this about; but — again, contrary to accepted ideas — they will not matter much in the long run, for a number of reasons, one of them being that all foreign investors in Eastern Europe want to gather their profits in the short run. Their present advantage is the still low cost of labor in Eastern Europe which, however, is bound to rise, sooner rather than later.

All over the world people tend to confuse international finance with economics. The first is — at least in the foreseeable future — truly international, with monies flowing rather freely across frontiers (in this respect Russia may remain an exception); but then, capital has become increasingly abstract, and the more abstract money becomes, the less durable it is. Economics, on the other hand — in its proper, old, original meaning — refers to the husbanding of one's household assets, in the Greek and biblical (and also German: *Wirtschaft*) sense of the word. To believe that Slovaks or Bulgarians have now "entered" or "reentered" the capitalist phase of their historical development is nonsense. Capitalism has grown slowly, with difficulty, in Western Europe during three hundred years, coming to its full development in the nineteenth century. That was the result of particular social, political, religious and intellectual conditions that hardly existed in Eastern Europe then, as they do not exist now. Capitalism, as well as parliamentary liberalism, were nineteenth-century phenomena with little relevance to the twenty-first, with its current material realities being obscured by an outdated vocabulary of economists, their definitions meaning less and less.

An example of this is the now current term "privatization." Bloated industries, bloated bureaucracies, inadequate and even fraudulent accounting practices have been the results of the socialist order — or, more correctly, of the party state. At the same time there occurred in much of Eastern Europe a growth of truly private enterprise. In agriculture this involved more than the — in any event, considerable — energy and production within the so-called household plots. It involved the condition that, in more than one way, the collective farms have been collective in name only: particular families have taken charge of particular fields for planting and harvesting or animal husbandry, and a fair portion of the profits have come to them. To parcel up most of the collective farms and to return to an agriculture where the average peasant possesses not more than five or ten acres is largely useless. (But then, is agribusiness, as practiced in the United States, private enterprise? Hardly: it is ruled by corporations and its profitability is entirely dependent on government subsidies.) Meanwhile in Hungary, Czechoslovakia and Poland fewer and fewer people work in agriculture. What is growing, as elsewhere in the West, is the so-called service sector. There private enterprise had come into being decades before the political transformations of 1989–90. Whether for shoe repairmen or television mechanics, for many years now the state has allowed the existence of individual suppliers of services; and even where such official permits had not been issued, people have been paying separate monies to people whose services they need, whether to bricklayers or to doctors.

Of course there is, and there must be, a considerable selling off of state or municipal businesses, which is, almost without exception, a good thing. The question remains, however: who will staff them? In most cases the same people. The services may improve, but not dramatically so. This is because the very words "employment" and "unemployment" are inaccurate (as they are in the West). The question is not whether "work" is available — yes, it is, and plenty of it; but people are less in quest of work than they are in quest of jobs — jobs with an acceptable and secure salary (and pension). Whether these jobs are arranged for them by the state bureaucracy or by a commercial one, by a "public" or a "private" company, is a matter of indifference to them. In cultural life — university salaries, theaters, publishing — the issue is not privatization but the diminution of government subsidies, and that has become a crisis indeed. It is, however, counterbalanced by the fact that under other titles — research and travel grants, for example — such government subsidies continue to exist. The underpaid professor of an Eastern European university finds himself in the same situation as a somewhat underpaid minor business executive in America whose company pays his trip abroad. (That there are two kinds of monies, private money and expense-account money, and that the management and the real value of these may, at best, overlap, while their meaning for their beneficiaries is quite different, is something that has not yet affected the figurations of economists, either in East or West; and I fear that it never will.)

Housing is the great problem in Eastern Europe — and there, too, the question is not what is private or public "ownership" but the sense of possession. Most people in Budapest, Prague and Warsaw (but also in Vienna, Berlin, Paris) are renters of apartments, not the owners of houses (or even of condominiums). The difference is that in Eastern European cities the rents are still low. (That difference is decreasing, too, with the governments having to raise all utility fees.) But we must consider two things. First, that an Eastern European living in the same apartment for many years, often decades, has a far stronger sense of both permanence and possession than a houseowner in America who moves every three years and buys and sells "his" house accordingly. The second is that the number of people in some Eastern European countries who actually *own* real estate — mostly summer houses or condominiums — is much larger than it ever has been, and that people acquired most of these private possessions during the last twenty or twenty-five years of still officially Communist rule.

In Eastern Europe (as also everywhere in the world) the once clear line between what is public and what is private is by no means clear. Much of it has been washed away during this century. The irony is that in Eastern Europe (this is possibly true of Russia as well) people who do have some private property have a much stronger sense of the private character of their possessions than in the West. But this, too, is involved with the corroded and corrupt meanings of our still standard economic vocabulary. What is "private"? What is "public"? What is "property"? What is "possession"? Indeed, what is "money"? (Actual money? Credit allowance? Expense-account money?) In sum, while the economic problems of Eastern European countries in the 1990s are serious, they are not entirely different from those in the West, and these differences are bound to diminish. Where they are very different, the cause of this is not different economic but different political customs and structures and habits. *Those* are the deeper problems, both apparent and latent.

I have a friend who returned to Hungary permanently after forty years in the United States. He was a young lawyer and a member of parliament until 1949 when he fled from the rapidly advancing grasp of Communist terror. He had had a decent career in the United States. He had passed the New York State bar examination, and busied himself with lawyering and with émigré affairs. About a year ago he chose to return to Hungary for good; and because of the then existing (and by now waning) prestige of Hungarian émigrés who had made a name for themselves abroad, he is now a leading personage of one of the smaller political parties that make up the government coalition. In May I read a passage from one of his speeches in the newspapers. "The opposition," he said, "is the enemy of the Hungarian people." Forty years of liberal democracy in the United States had melted away in the heat of Hungarian political rhetoric. Earlier I read another statement by a member — indeed, a government undersecretary of state — of his party, not an extremist one. "The enemy of the Hungarian people," this man said, "is no longer Communism. It is liberalism, atheistic liberalism." I am neither an atheist nor a liberal; but I surely did not like what I read.

The main political reality in Eastern Europe — it is a reality and not a specter haunting it — is nationalism. The principal factor of the two world wars of the twentieth century was nationalism; and both of these wars broke out in Eastern Europe — as did the so-called cold war, which is now over, while nationalism in Eastern Europe is as strong as ever. In Eastern Europe nationalism is the only popular religion, by which I mean the only religion that still possesses a popular rhetoric. (That the traditional Western Christian religions no longer have much of a popular rhetoric may not necessarily be a loss — but only God knows about *that*.) When I say to an American nationalist that being a good American will not necessarily get one into heaven, he may be startled but he will understand, and presumably even agree. When I say to a Hungarian nationalist that just because someone is a good Hungarian he will not necessarily get into heaven, he *is* startled, and may find it difficult to agree. Populist nationalism, as distinct from the now almost extinct variety of the liberal nationalisms of the nineteenth century, is a modern and democratic phenomenon. Populist nationalists are self-conscious rather than self-confident, extroverted, essentially aggressive and humorless, suspicious of other people within the same nation who do not seem to agree with some of their populist and nationalist ideology. Hence they assign them to the status of minorities, suggesting — and at times emphasizing — that such minorities do not and cannot belong within the authentic body of the national people. This is, of course, yet another manifestation of the potential tyranny of a majority — which, as Tocqueville observed, is the great danger of democratic societies in democratic times.

When, in 1931, the king of Spain abdicated and a liberal parliamentary republic was proclaimed in Spain, Mussolini said that "this was going back to oil lamps in the age of electricity." He was right. Parliamentary liberalism belonged to the nineteenth century, not the twentieth. Indeed, in Spain it soon degenerated to a sorry mess, and after five years to civil war. But then came the Second World War and the demise of Hitler and Mussolini, reviving the prestige of Communism (which is now gone) and of American-type democracy, which is not gone yet. For that we must be thankful; and its effects must not be underestimated. It is because of the prestige of the West that populist nationalism and the tyranny of majorities in Eastern Europe will constrain themselves within certain limits, for a foreseeable time. But this does not mean that parliamentary liberalism — including the habits of dialogue, compromise, and the sense of a certain community composed of the kind of people who make up the parliaments — is, or will be, the dominant political reality in Eastern Europe. Parliamentary liberalism, like capitalism, in the nineteenth century was the result not only of certain ideas but of a particular structure of society. That society was semi-aristocratic and bourgeois — bourgeois and not merely middle class — a class with a patrician tinge, a class from which most of its administrators, governors, professionals and parliamentary representatives were drawn. Such societies, especially in Eastern Europe, do not now exist.

The Communists (including Stalin) came to understand the powerful presence of nationalism long ago. Long before 1989 the Communist parties in Eastern Europe had two wings, cordially hating each other: one internationalist, the other nationalist, with the former weakening steadily. Thus there is more than opportunism latent in the fact that many of the populists among the new democratic parties, and even governments, of Eastern Europe are former Communists — of the nationalist wing, of course. For what happened in 1989–90 was more than the end of Communism in Eastern Europe. It was, as I wrote earlier, the end of a century that was characterized by the two world wars and by their consequences. One not unimportant consequence of the end of the Second World War was the anathema pronounced upon Hitler and the Third Reich. Yet in one sense of these terms, nationalist socialism survived Hitler. Every government of this globe has become a welfare state of sorts, and Eastern Europe is no exception to that. International socialism is a mirage. It is finance capitalism that is more international than socialism, which is why Hitler hated it and made it national, answerable to German needs. That was easy: because money succumbs to the pressures of populist nationalism even faster than class consciousness does.

There is a growing nostalgia and appreciation of nationalist Eastern Europe governments before and during the Second World War. This of course differs from country to country. At least two "independent" states in Eastern Europe — Slovakia and Croatia, for example — were created by Hitler. There are other nations, too, whose anti-Communist and nationalist past was inseparable from their alliance with Hitler's Reich during the Second World War. In Rumania, streets and boulevards in town after town are now being renamed in honor of Marshal Antonescu, the Rumanian *Conducator* (*Führer*) whose personality Hitler esteemed very highly. In Slovakia this hero worship involves Father Tiso, the nationalist prelate who was the president of Slovakia appointed by Hitler, and who was unusually eager to deliver his country's Jews to the Germans (meaning Auschwitz), even before Hitler pressured him to do so. In Croatia schools and streets are named after members of the Nazified Croatian government of 1941–45. In Hungary (unlike in Rumania, where the murderous Iron Guard now enjoys a recurrent wave of nostalgic prestige) there is no belated appreciation for the Hungarian National Socialist Arrow-Cross. But there are many people who have come to regard the nationalism before 1945 as something healthy that Hungary should cherish.

Then there is the prospect of returning German power. Not

yet. The Germans have their hands full with the East German mess for some years to come. Also — and this is more important — most of the West German people *have* come to terms with their history, so that the idea of a recurrent German expansion to the east is still alien to them. Yet there is a great political vacuum in Eastern Europe; and it is reasonable to assume that this will be filled eventually by Germany. This applies to the political configurations within each nation, too; there will be (indeed, there already are) certain political parties attracted to and willing to depend on German, rather than on other Western European or American, political support. Keep in mind the prospective fragmentation of Eastern Europe: Slovenia, Croatia, Slovakia, the Baltic states and the Ukraine are natural allies of Germany. What is already happening in Eastern Europe (consider but the Yugoslav crisis as I write this) is not only the dismantling of Yalta — that is, of the results of the Second World War. Here and there we see the dismantling of Versailles, of the results of the First World War. Indeed, the twentieth century is over.

These are worrisome portents. But they are counterbalanced by other large realities. If Tocqueville's prophetic warnings about the tyranny of the majority are applicable, so is that other profound chapter in *Democracy in America:* "Why Great Revolutions Will Become Rare." Revolutions are made by desperate men; and not many people in Eastern Europe are desperate enough to risk their painfully acquired and jealously preserved private possessions. The age of great revolutions and of great wars seems to be over. That great revolutions and great wars between nations are being replaced by protracted guerrilla warfare, not only between different nationalities but also between different sections of a population, is already a fact — not only in, say, Yugoslavia, but in many places in the West, involving such populations and places as Ulster, Basque Spain and portions of the once great cities of the United States. Whether guerrilla warfare, with its protracted uncertainty and its brutalities, is preferable to civil wars is impossible to determine. In the long run the power of the state, of centralized government, will weaken everywhere, including Eastern Europe. This means a profound change in the structure of societies, indeed in the texture of history. Whether it bodes good or ill is, as yet, impossible to tell.

The private aspirations of masses of people in Eastern Europe to middle-class possessions may not be very attractive; but they are obstacles to appeals of demagoguery, including extreme nationalist ones. Add to this the often unreal and illusionist desire of Eastern Europeans to belong to "Europe" — something that means, among other things, the desire to be approved by "the West." How long that will last I do not know. There will not be anything like a united Europe in the foreseeable future. But the differences between Western and Eastern Europe will decrease year by year. And I am sometimes more optimistic about Eastern than about Western Europe, precisely because the former is still behind the latter, because it must catch up with some of the realities of the West — before Eastern Europeans realize the troubling and often corrupting nature of some of those realities. For the West the time has already come to rethink the entire meaning of "progress," while in Eastern Europe the practical applications of that rethinking are still some years away. Not in every way: some of the environmental problems in Eastern Europe are much worse than in the West, precisely because of the stupid and corrupt Communist industrialization programs and production demands. "Greens" in Eastern Europe are still few and far between. I wish there were more of them and fewer of those newfangled "Christian conservatives" whose traditionalism is

nothing more than the kind of nationalism that is a substitute
for religious belief, meaning that they are neither truly conservative nor really Christian — like some American conservatives whose hatred of liberals is stronger than their love of
liberty.

A new kind of democracy is developing in Hungary — and
probably throughout Eastern Europe.

At first the collapse of Communist rule brought the instant
semblance of a Western-type, liberal, parliamentary, multi-
party democracy, with freedom of the press (including pornography, alas). But how long, and in what ways, will this
endure — especially in countries where the traditional experience for that kind of liberal democracy and the structure of
a national society to support it hardly exist, or do not exist at
all?*

Something like this happened in most of Europe after World
War I. The then victory of the Western democracies led, among
other things, to the adoption of French-type (and here and
there of British- and Swiss-type) constitutions and political
structures across Europe. But these foreign-style suits did not
fit the stocky bodies of their temporary customers. The seams
soon broke. The cloth did not last. *That* kind of parliamentary
liberalism belonged to the nineteenth century, not the twentieth. Fourteen years, at the most, after 1920 the majority of
Eastern and Southern European countries — Italy, Portugal,
Spain, Greece, Austria, Hungary, Yugoslavia, Bulgaria, Poland,

---

* Sympathetic and knowledgeable intellectuals, such as Timothy Garton
Ash who wrote interesting and often intelligent articles about the East Euro-
pean "refolutions" (his word) in 1988 and 1989 in *The New York Review of
Books*, saw liberal democracy of the best kind blossoming in Eastern Europe.
In 1991 those articles are entirely outdated. The prospects of his hopes, and of
most of his heroes, were wrong.

Estonia, Latvia, Lithuania — had abandoned parliamentary democracy. (Note that this happened even before Hitler's Third Reich would influence, or force, such a change upon them.)

Things are not the same now. For one thing, the model is not France or Switzerland or Britain but the United States (and sometimes democratic West Germany). More important, unlike in the 1920s and 1930s there will be no dictatorship (whether totalitarian or authoritarian) of a single person. Not only is the era of Stalin gone; so is that of Mussolini and Hitler. (And of Perón. Some intelligent people in Eastern Europe say: We are becoming like Latin America. No: there are long-lasting burdens, weighing heavily on the destinies of Eastern European nations; but the Indian curse on the land is not among them.)

What is about to happen — what is already happening — is the establishment of new one-party states. The governing party (together with its coalition partners) may at first have only a slight majority in the parliament, it may not even be very popular. But it will do everything to stay in power; and it will probably succeed.

There are several factors at work here, on different levels. I shall try to describe them, though not in order of their relative importance.

What has already happened is the replacement of one kind of state bureaucracy by another one: a nominally (but often only nominally) Communist one by a nationalist one, often composed of the same kind of people, and sometimes of the very same ones. (Example: the present minister of the interior in Hungary; his powers are extensive and secret.) The powers of the state, in Eastern Europe, are still very great.

The essence of liberal (or, more precisely, of non–anti-liberal) democracy consists of the toleration of the rights and the respect for the opinions of a minority, including the parliamentary one. This is eroding in Hungary now, two years after the *annus mirabilis* of 1989, the new constitution, the new freely elected parliament. There are myriad examples of this. The opposition is labeled anti-nationalist, anti-Christian, rootless, cosmopolitan, subversive. I hear this from my acquaintances (and even friends) in the government party.*

Many people in the government party in Hungary are not very intelligent, but this does not hurt them very much. (Did Reagan's stupidity really hurt the Republicans' cause in the 1980s?) However: the government knows how the protracted repetition of certain slogans and ideas can, after all, influence the minds of people. Thus they try to increase their control over the newspapers, with varying degrees of success. More important is Magyar television and radio, which became more and more independent during the last years of the nominally Communist regime, and have maintained estimably good standards during the last two years. The government is now attempting to control them. This is important because the influence of the daily newspapers is subtly weakening,† while that of television increases, especially when it comes to the

---

* I know no important people in the opposition party except for one excellent man, a triumph of character (he had served time in prison during the Communist era, he was a brave defender in court of political prisoners, he is respected and even admired by many people). I mention his name to a friend who has a very high position in the government. "Yes," he says, "he is a fine man. As a matter of fact, we were close friends. But his wife is Jewish." He explains that she had made her husband join the other party two years ago. This about that charming, intelligent, modest, self-effacing woman! I am appalled and attempt to say this. It makes no difference. Yet her present accuser is not a convinced anti-Semite. (He certainly does not think so.) He accuses the wife not for being Jewish but for having influenced her husband politically. The "Jewish" adjective is but another political argument.

† The same friend in government, on another occasion: "The press is lying." I should have told him that the government is lying too, and that this is part and parcel of modern democracy, the difference from dictatorship being that the lies are of all kinds, not centrally controlled and broadcast. (Ques-

news. The latter is increasingly government-oriented. (The daily news program, uninterrupted by commercials, runs a half hour, or even more; that is where most of the people get their news — and some of their opinions, too.)

There are occasions when a high government official is caught having done wrong and then lying about it. The opposition makes a great fuss in the parliament; but nothing happens to him. In the past — even under the nondemocratic regime before World War II — that official would have had to resign. Not now. The majority rules, undeterred and uncompromising; the minority does not count; majority people say, and presumably think, that this is what democracy is all about. (I read a Lithuanian spokesman: "*We* are the majority now, the minority better shut up.") With all the respect paid to American democracy and the American Constitution, including the borrowing of some features of it in the new Eastern European constitutions, the checks and balances of the American system are largely inoperative here. I can imagine — alas, easily — a situation where the minority party becomes more powerless than almost anywhere in the West; where the government rules not only parliament but, more and more, public opinion; where the constitutional and diplomatic and civil service of the state is hardly more than a bureaucracy composed of the governing party and its partners. Yes, an opposition will continue to exist. But it will be increasingly restricted to a few newspapers, periodicals, groups of artists and intellectuals; it will be less and less influential because of the mutation in the structure of what was once, in the dear old nineteenth century, called public opinion (something that, among other things, was not necessarily the same as popular sentiment).

---

tion: will people, including Americans, arrive at a stage of perspicacity when they will say, "TV is lying"? — more precisely, "I do not believe what I see on TV"?)

A new kind of dictatorship? No, Tocqueville's tyranny of the majority — or, more accurately, of those who think and say that they represent the majority, and whose practices the actual majority may not be inclined to challenge.

Anti-Semitism is a problem in Hungary, for the main reason that many people see Jews (including Christians of Jewish descent) as a non-Magyar minority. There may be an interesting difference between that and the anti-Semitism of the past. There are people now who agree with the legal protection of minority rights, while they are less willing to agree that Jews — including Jews from families who have lived in Hungary for more than a century — are *not* a definite non-Hungarian group. (Complicating this issue further is the fact that there are Jews in Hungary, especially the Orthodox, Zionists and community officials, who argue that Jews *are* a definite ethnic minority.)

Hungary and France are now the only European states where Jews amount to as much as about 1 percent of the population. (Before World War II, in several states of Eastern Europe Jews amounted to 5, 6, and in Poland even 10 percent of the inhabitants.) The survival of about one third of Hungarian Jews in 1944–45 is a more complicated story than it has been hitherto treated. (Even more complicated are Hungarian memories of that period, and its meaning.) Now it seems that more than nine out of every ten Jews in Hungary live in Budapest. It is perhaps significant that there may be more anti-Semitism in some of the provinces where there are no Jews than in Budapest, where they still form between 5 and 10 percent of the population.

But the present extent of anti-Semitism in Hungary is often exaggerated. Its scope and essence are complex; but it is not remotely comparable to the climate of opinion that had contributed to the humiliations and crimes visited upon the Jews fifty years ago by some, though surely not all, Hungarians.

One perhaps profound difference between Hungarians and Americans (more precisely, Americans at the end of the twentieth century). In Hungary a man who is, or who inclines to be, opposed to your opinions (and, perhaps, to your provenance, social status or political affiliations) will listen to your exposition of your ideas or opinions carefully, even when these might seem, perhaps surprisingly, in agreement with his — while he keeps looking for anything that will confirm his existing political or social prejudices. In America, no one really listens to your exposition of your ideas. The American practice may be better.

What is lamentable and miserable in the United States is the search for and the cultivation of the lowest common denominator when it comes to the merchandising of certain goods, of entertainment, of films, of television, yes, even of education: the principle of their marketeers. On the other hand, certain taboos remain in force (some of which may even be unduly sacrosanct): in society, in intellectual life, in politics. What is lamentable in Eastern Europe is the inclination to appeal to the lowest common denominator in politics.

I read G. W. Russell (AE), the Irish writer, in *Co-operation and Nationality* (1912): "lives filled with everlasting littleness fill one with deep despair and madness of heart." He was thinking of the lower-middle-class mentality in Ireland then. I am thinking of some academics in America as well as in Hungary; but they do not fill me with "madness of heart." At worst, I feel closer to Swift's phrase: *ubi saeva indignatio cor lacerare nequit* (where savage indignation can no longer lacerate the heart).

Same AE: "men pass each other with cold eyes, with no thrill of pleasure in looking on a fellow being." * This is not true of democracy, either in Budapest or in New York, where people's eyes are nervously flickering, rapidly observant (because they are nervous and flickering they are not sufficiently observant).

The same AE, 1912, his ideal (and he went on to pass the last years of his life deeply disillusioned): "A vast network of living, progressive organizations will cover rural Ireland, democratic in constitution and governed by the aristocracy of intellect and character." A beautiful illusion, especially about character. Alas, Wilde was closer to the truth: "High hopes were once formed of democracy; but democracy simply means the bludgeoning of the people, by the people, for the people." Only: not simply. Complicatedly.

I have always recognized the importance of ideas, but I see their importance, contrary to Dostoyevsky et al.: that it is much more important, and telling, what men do with ideas than what ideas do to men; that they will adjust their ideas to circumstances rather than attempt to adjust circumstances to their ideas. (I read a sentence from Robert Musil — a Viennese, quite appropriate here: "He went through life burdened with his ideas, and that is a burden dangerous to the very life of him who bears it, so long as people have not realized that there is something in it that they can turn to their own advantage.")

🙰

Dinner at the H.'s in Budapest. We see many things alike, and we have many things in common. I am happy to see

---

* This is interesting because it may have something to do with the mysterious and unexplained phrase that Yeats chose for his tombstone: "Cast a cold eye . . . Horseman, pass by." Has anyone noticed this?

that these people, members of the old, dispossessed and often persecuted gentry, perhaps the class that suffered the most under the first decades of Communist rule, are living rather well; as a matter of fact, the atmosphere, the ambiance and the furnishings (and the excellent dinner) in their villa apartment are much as they would have been fifty years ago. A very Hungarian achievement, amounting to a near-miracle.

H.'s wife is pleased with my appreciation of their fine paintings. (Paintings in families survived the Communist expropriations more often than had other possessions.) Then, as we talk about politics (not very much, and not at all emphatically) she sees that I am not an unreserved partisan of the government party. She turns a bit cooler. She recognizes that I am not quite the kind of person she had thought. This would not happen in America or England or Ireland, this small poison of politics.

Another example, perhaps more expectable because it happens among academics. Every Wednesday, for a few minutes before my class, I chat with my colleagues at the university. In this particular department (cultural history) most of them are populist nationalists. But they are agreeable fellows, and we have some historical and intellectual interests in common. However, the great brouhaha about the Budapest World Expo has just burst forth. The government approved plans for a 1995 or 1996 World's Fair in Budapest (at first a Twin Expo with Vienna; but in a referendum the Viennese refused it). The opposition, including the municipal government of the city of Budapest, questions these priorities and expenses. My colleagues ask my view about this. I say that I am against the Expo, because world's fairs are things of the past — I mention the 1939 New York World's Fair, a success, and the 1964 one, a failure — because now, in the age of quick air travel, world's fairs no longer bring

important investors while they bring hordes of tourists, inun-
dating a city already choked by masses of them, whereby
the financial gain will be ephemeral, not enough to offset
the enormous cost of the investment. This is an argument dif-
ferent from that made by the opposition, but my colleagues
are unconvinced. One of them says: "I didn't know that you
agreed with them."

This is particularly telling, because the promotion of a
World's Fair, involving foreigners, international capitalism,
etc., is not something naturally preferred by nationalists and
populists. It would more naturally fit in the program of the
internationalist liberals of the opposition party. Were the lat-
ter pushing for the Expo, my colleagues would be vocal
against it. But nothing matters except that we are we, and
they are they.

Because I am a historian (and because my formative years were
those of the Second World War), I am saddened by one thing.
We are — perhaps especially in Eastern Europe — about to see
a new kind of historical revisionism involving the memories
and meaning of the Second World War. There will be no rehabilitation of Hitler (except in a few instances, disguised within
certain phrases). But there will be — there already is — a rehabilitation of some of his allies, men and women who fought
the Communists and the Russians (and including those who
would have fought, or had fought, the British and the Americans). The danger here is not merely a renewed twisting of the
historical record; it is, rather, that of the eroding of traditional
values and standards — a result of the nationalist tendency to
see all enemies on the left, none on the right. (And I have been
a "rightist" all my life . . .) There is virtually no one in Europe
who still believes in Communism or Marxism, less than two

years after the end of the Communist regimes. But fifty years after its demise there are still admirers of the Third Reich. I wrote in *The Duel* that the Second World War remains the key to our historical perspective, a war "which was a catastrophe for millions of people but whose outcome spared the world an even worse one."

Yet those dangers must not be exaggerated. Fifty years have passed; new generations have come forth; the ideas, the concerns, the inclinations, the virtues and the vices of these new generations are different. I dare to say that they are better people. The Communist experience gave them a certain taste for freedom. This is the positive element in Hungary now, the negative one being that it is more difficult to be free than not to be free.

　　　　　　　　　　▲

July 1992. Now that I have been back in the United States for a year, I am aware of something that I had thought about before but not in this way. America and Eastern Europe (indeed, America and all of Europe) are more distant from each other than they have been throughout the historical twentieth century. To begin with, there is practically nothing about Hungary in the American newspapers, and hardly anything in any of the periodicals. (The New York Times, for some years, had a resident Eastern European correspondent stationed in Budapest, but no longer.) Even the tragic and horrid events in Bosnia and Yugoslavia receive less attention than they would have in the past (and, perhaps, than they deserve). This reflects the present lack of interest, if not the indifference, of Americans about Europe now that the cold war is over. It reflects, too, the slow but massive tilt of the American population westward, away from Europe; together with the insufficiency of their geographic education and their dependence on the lamentable insufficiency of television news; and with the gradual disappearance of an educated class, mostly from the Eastern seaboard, whose interests, surely in this now past century, were oriented toward Europe. That this increasing separation — for it is a separation — of the United States from Europe exists at a time when a million people fly back and forth across the Atlantic in a few hours, and when "the world community" and "interdependence" are accepted slogans, is but another proof that the real movements of history, including the relations of entire states and nations, have little to do with technology, that they are the results of something other than technical and even material conditions.

Not all of this decline of interest is bad. It suggests the ending of the American Century, meaning the wish of the American people to act (and not merely to regard themselves) as the leaders of the world. This is already evident in the present presidential contest. George Bush doesn't see this, of course — which may be turning to his disadvantage. Something is beginning in this presidential contest that suggests the main question of the twenty-first century, the main problem, perhaps especially for Americans: the necessity to rethink the entire meaning of "progress." Bush and the Republicans are all in favor of spending money (and creating unneeded "jobs") for the construction of vast technological boondoggles such as Star Wars (now fading) and super-colliders in Texas. The Democrats seem to be more environmentalist, though it is not certain whether they will see that as a principal issue and stick to it. Yet that is perhaps the principal issue. Our "conservatives" care not for the conservation of the country, and of the American land. Yet: more than tax policy, more than education policy, more than national security policy, more even than the painful abortion issue, this is where the main division is beginning to occur.

So it is in my township. It is the division between people who want to develop, to build up, to pour more concrete and cement on the land, and those who wish to protect the landscape (and the cityscape) where they live. (Landscape, not wilderness. The propagation of wilderness, the exaltation of "nature" against all human presence, is the fatal shortcoming of many American environmentalists.) Beneath that division I sometimes detect the division between a true love of one's country and the rhetorical love of symbols such as the flag, in the name of a mythical people; between the ideals of American domesticity and those of a near-nomadic life; between privacy and publicity; between the ideals of stability and those of endless "growth." Yes, nationalism is still rampant in Eastern Europe — and, in many ways, in the United States. It is more than a wave of the past; it is still the tide of the present; but perhaps not of the future. Or so I think — and hope.

ᴥ VII ᴥ

EUROPE . . . EUROPE?

June 1991. As I leave Hungary now, there is none of that feeling of relief as at the end of past visits, when the plane began to move and the sight of the last uniform of the police state disappeared.

Still, when at the end of this Budapest chapter of my life I land at Zurich, about to transfer to a transatlantic plane, my heart and mind respond in a way that other Hungarians had felt (and recorded: Sándor Márai, László Cs. Szabó) in the past. That arrival — or return — to Western Europe exhilarates. We have left Eastern, perhaps even Central, Europe behind.

Zurich. I belong to this Europe, too: to the bourgeois and patrician remnants of a world for which I have an aching longing in Pennsylvania as much as in Hungary, an atmosphere where I am at home. Europe . . . Europe . . . I am Hungarian and American. But: I am a European American, and a European Hungarian.

Europe. Arriving in Switzerland, I find myself in a certain Europe. This is not the first time that I think and feel this. There is more to this than coming West from East. I felt it thirty years ago when I arrived in Geneva from Madrid. Not that Budapest and Madrid do not belong to Europe. Still, the civilization of Switzerland, with all of its narrowness and rigidity, is a civilization of bourgeois Europe. A bourgeois civilization, that is: the civilization of at least two or three *centuries, before which there had been wondrous achieve-ments, and Europe had been the center of the universe, but when the very words "Europe" and "civilization" hardly ex-isted at all.*

⚡

For the eventual united states of Europe (the lowercase here is intentional) the model is Switzerland, not the United States of America. And that uniting of Europe will take a very long time, if it will happen at all.

The three Swiss *ur-Kantons* (Uri, Schwyz, Unterwalden, even now in the deep valleys of German Switzerland) fought out their "independence" from a Habsburg in 1291. A united Switzerland did not come about until 1847 (after a small civil war between two groups of cantons). Before that, Switzerland had neither a federal capital nor a constitution (the latter came only in 1874), not even a national flag. From William Tell to a united federal Switzerland took more than five and a half centuries.

By the end of the nineteenth century Switzerland was neutral, pacifist and prosperous. That, too, had taken a long time. The Swiss had been no pacifists but mercenary soldiers: consider but the Swiss Guards, chosen by a beleaguered Pope in the sixteenth century. (Even now Switzerland is a military democracy — consider the exceptional character of its army, including the obligation of every Swiss male to serve for many years, including his duty to keep his equipment and firearm in readiness in his home — unique among all democracies of the earth.) The Swiss were not altogether neutral: as late as during the First World War most of the German-Swiss preferred a German victory, most of the French-Swiss a French one. The Swiss had been poor; until about two hundred years ago they were one of the poorest nations of Western Europe. Then they discovered their talents for disciplined fine work, ranging from chocolate making to watches and mechanical instruments. They also recognized the profit inherent in service, the capital advantages of solid and creditable innkeeping. All of these things depended on the quality of their work — that is, on something nonmaterial. Nonmaterial, too, was the changing image of Switzerland. Owen Barfield put it profoundly: "The economic and social structure of Switzerland is noticeably affected by its tourist industry, and that is due only in part to increased facilities of travel. It is due not less to the [condition] that . . . the *mountains* which twentieth-century man sees are not the mountains which eighteenth-century man saw."

At the end of the twentieth century many other European nations are prosperous and pacific and dependent on mass tourism. But they have a long way to go before they confederate or federate. The Swiss are still reluctant to join the European political, or even economic, organizations; and the Swiss, who were hospitable to all kinds of political refugees during the nineteenth century, during the twentieth have been doing their best — or rather, worst — to keep most immigrants out.

The essence of the difference is this: the Swiss know (and they are proud of the fact) that they are Swiss. Most Europeans know that they are European, but only faintly so; and they are rarely proud of the fact — if fact it is.

The consciousness of being European is neither widespread nor old. The very idea of "Europe" is much more recent than we are accustomed to think. Five hundred years ago, when men from Europe sailed out to find new continents, "Asia" and "Africa" were in common usage ("America" and "Australia" would thereafter follow). The noun "Europe" was not current at all. The common word was "Christendom." In 1496 Henry VII, the first Tudor king of England, gave a charter to John Cabot to explore lands hitherto "unknown to all Christians"; in 1764 King George III commissioned John Byron to explore "lands hitherto unvisited by any European Power." Five or six centuries ago none of our ancestors knew that they were Europeans. The adjective "European," referring to a particular inhabitant of a particular continent, appears in the Western European languages only in the seventeenth century, in the Eastern European languages later. The eastern boundary of "Europe" (the Ural Mountains and the Caucasus separating "Europe" from "Asian" Russia) was designated as late as 1833 by a German geographer, Volger. In sum, the idea of "Europe" was a product of the Modern Age. Now, when the Modern Age (that incorrect term) is passing, there are many reasons to keep that in mind.

Even more recent than the "modern" idea of Europe is the development of a European consciousness. Its intellectual forerunners — Grotius, Sully, Kant, among others — were utopian thinkers in that regard, without consequences to their ideas. The recognition that Europe is but a small peninsula of Asia, and about to be overshadowed by the rise of great powers elsewhere on the globe, began to occur only in the early twentieth century, to such different thinkers as Paul Valéry and, perhaps, Oswald Spengler. Only after World War I did the desideratum for a kind of united Europe begin to attract some people. Only after World War II did it begin to spread — very unevenly and inadequately at that.

Still, in one sense elements of "Europeanness" existed before that recognition would swim up to the surface of consciousness. "European" is both newer and older than we think. This was expressed by Ortega y Gasset when he wrote that "European man" has not only been "democratic" and "liberal" but also "absolutist" and "feudal" (and we may add "Christian") — which he no longer is. "This does not mean that he does not in some way continue being all these things; he does so in the 'form of having been them.'" Hence the condition that the United States was born in the middle of the Modern Age is not an indubitable asset, as so many people (including Europeans) think. At the end of the Modern Age Americans may be less immune to certain dangers than is much of Europe, since they may be exposed to dangerous consequences of the decay of their established institutions and even of some of their accustomed ways of thought.

Unquestionable is the existence of three obvious conditions. Europe is the only continent entirely within the temperate zone, the only continent without deserts. It is the only continent inhabited almost entirely by the white race. Moreover, it is from Europe that the now emerging, and unprecedented, unitary civilization of the world (a unitary civilization only on certain levels) has gone out to cover the globe, and whose features, both good and bad, survived the retreat of the European powers and of European colonization. (This includes the fact that the predominant global language is English, or more precisely American English, followed by Spanish — even though the total number of the English-speaking and Spanish-speaking peoples is less than that of the Chinese.)

The First World War led to the end of the predominance of European powers, including Great Britain, in the world. That happened despite the American and Russian withdrawal from Europe after that war. (The American isolationism of that time was selective; and the United States had already become the greatest power in the world. Had there been no Communist revolution in Russia in 1917 — that is, had Russia not withdrawn from the war and Europe — Russia would have extended her influence over Eastern Europe then; but, unlike after the Second World War, she would also have become more European.)

In any event, this recognition of the decline of Europe led to a rise of a "European" consciousness among some people, and to the first organized movement toward some kind of a united Europe. That was the "Pan-Europe" movement, begun by Count Richard Coudenhove-Kalergi (a highly cultured man with an Austrian father, Greek grandparents and a Japanese mother) in 1923. This aspiration for a European confederation corresponded with the ideas of important and respectable thinkers such as the Spanish Salvador de Madariaga and Miguel de Unamuno, for example, and the German Hermann Keyserling. During the 1920s appreciation of the pan-European movement was expressed by such personages as Aristide Briand, Gustav Stresemann, even Winston Churchill. All that was washed away by the radical nationalist movements of the 1930s, with their leading example Hitler. To nationalists — and not only in Germany — both the "European" adjective and the designation of someone as "a European" were pejorative; to them they meant something or someone cosmopolitan, anti-national, decadent. Only after (and, to some extent, during) the Second World War did this pejorative connotation vanish.

The two protagonists of the last European war — of that first, decisive phase of the Second World War — were Hitler and Churchill. Both of them were Europe-minded, though in very different ways. Hitler, unlike the Kaiser, thought principally in terms of land, not sea, power; of the German domination of Europe and of European Russia. (That was not due to his modesty but to his calculation: he knew that with the achievement of his rule over most of Europe and Russia, Germany would become the greatest power in the world.) But his idea of "Europe" was that of a German-ruled Europe. When in 1940 he spoke of his own version of a "European" Monroe Doctrine — "Europe for Europeans; America for Americans" — this was only meant to impress Americans, to keep them out of the war, to keep them from engaging themselves on the side of Britain. That did not happen. Then, as he began to lose his great gamble in Russia, he and Goebbels thought it useful to talk up "Europe," posing as its defenders. After Stalingrad Goebbels started to exclaim: "The West is in danger! *Das Abendland ist in Gefahr!*" Other, vague statements about a "New European Order" appeared. Once, one month or so before Germany's capitulation and his suicide, Hitler said: "I was Europe's last hope." (Some Europe. Some hope. Did he believe what he was saying?) There are people even today who, recalling their comradeship in arms, mostly in various formations of the Waffen-SS (a French SS "Charlemagne" brigade fought in the streets of Berlin through the last days of the war), assert that in 1944 and 1945 they were defending "Europe" together. But the Europe of the various National Socialists meant nothing other than their desperate willingness to prevail in a barbarian kind of Europe under German rule, secured for them by German military might.

Churchill fought the war less because of the British Empire than because of Europe. This may sound surprising; it is insufficiently understood by Europeans, by historians, and even by his admirers; yet so it was. Churchill was convinced from the beginning, and probably earlier than anyone else, that Hitler represented a deadly danger to Britain — not because Hitler wished to conquer Britain but because of his purpose to conquer and rule Europe. Even after his stunning conquest of Western Europe, in July 1940 Hitler repeated his "peace offer": Britain should stop fighting him; he would leave the British Empire untouched. Churchill did not deign to respond. He would have portions of the Empire transferred to the United States rather than make peace with Hitler — that is, allow him to rule Europe. Other British leaders may have considered Hitler's proposal seriously — not because they sympathized with Hitler or with Nazism but because they had little of that traditional and historic appreciation of Europe and of Britain's place within its civilization than what the half-American Churchill possessed. The Battle of Britain was, then, fought for Britain's survival, and for that of Europe. During the hard years of the war London was the capital of a free Europe, housing entire governments-in-exile, the remnants and regroupings of their armies and navies. This was the time when free men and women in Europe learned to depend on the British Broadcasting Corporation, which radiated news, and hope, in every European language; whose broadcasts began with a symbolic traditional sound of European (indeed German) civilization, the first bar of Beethoven's Fifth Symphony. Even after the war it was Churchill who in a remarkable speech in Zurich in 1946 proposed a new kind of European unity, around a France and a Germany getting together.

When Churchill returned to the prime ministership in 1951 an eventual political, or even economic, British association with European organizations was not on his agenda. Thirty years later Margaret Thatcher's Toryism was much more like the middle-class Toryism of Chamberlain than that of Churchill. She was more insular than Churchill had been; she was, by and large, in accord with her people who do not want any part in a European confederation or in a European army independent of the United States. If the British have to choose between "Europe" and the United States, they will choose the latter — at least in the foreseeable future. They may be right — though perhaps for other reasons than they think. They may be right not because the present projects of a united Europe are too strong, but because they are too weak. The projects (and, behind them, the ideas) of the planners and the bureaucratic leaders of Brussels are antiquated and uninspiring. The ideas of a Europe espoused by men such as MM. Delors or Attali are a continuation of eighteenth-century thinking, governed by economics and an often abstract rationalism, by the Cartesian *esprit de la géometrie*. They (like, alas, many Frenchmen) do

not understand that at the end of the Modern Age the Cartesian view of reality is outdated and often useless; and that it is
surely useless when it comes to the making of a new Europe.

It was in London during the war that the first attempts at
confederation were made by exile governments. There was a
Polish-Czechoslovak agreement of that nature, made in 1942.
It melted away within a year, because of the Czechs' desire
to incur the benevolence of Stalin; they were opportunistic
enough to disassociate themselves from the Poles. In 1944,
shortly before their return to a liberated Western Europe, came
the Benelux agreement, meaning an economic confederation
of Belgium, Holland and Luxembourg. That, too, disappeared
after a few years, becoming absorbed in the first phase of
the Common Market. In 1950 arose the so-called Schuman
Plan, the first step toward a Western European economic community. "Western European Union," "European Parliament,"
"Common Market," "European Economic Community," "European Free Trade Association" — all of these followed during
the next ten years. Eventually the British, the Irish, the Spanish, the Portuguese and the Greeks joined these largely economic associations. They had certain political consequences,
but not many. We heard a lot about a united Europe coming
into being on 1 January 1992. As I wrote the first draft of these
pages, in October 1991, much of that had become meaningless;
as I write this second draft, in April 1992, my skepticism has
been confirmed, alas. The intervention of European organizations in order to stop the civil war in Yugoslavia have failed,
again and again — a lamentable failure that helps to open the
eyes of many Eastern Europeans, who are beginning to see that
"Europe" is a chimerical term. Meanwhile it is Germany and
not "Europe" that takes the lead (and a questionable lead it is)
in recognizing and supporting new Eastern European statelets.
As late as a year ago there was some talk, in Paris and Bonn,

about a small "European" military or security force; that, too, has disappeared — and not only because the British are against it. There remains the problem of NATO. NATO and a European army are irreconcilable. The Germans have been assiduous in trying to paper over the differences between NATO and "Europe"; soon they will no longer care.

Charles de Gaulle almost alone understood that as early as thirty years ago. He knew that economics and bureaucracy follow politics and power, not the reverse. A "European" bureaucracy in Brussels, comfortably ensconced (and paid), lodged in hideous technocratic buildings (whose mere style and shape suggest the outdated character of a now past century), will not a Europe make.

History does not repeat itself; but there are worrisome resemblances between the declining political authority of European institutions now and that of the League of Nations in, say, 1935.

Yes: there are more and more "European" institutions; some of them even work, including the easier movement of goods and people across the softening frontiers of the Western European states. Yet the enthusiasm — and therefore the real movement — toward a European unity has not been increasing but decreasing; weakening, not strengthening. The desire for some kind of Western European union or unity, especially among the young, was at its peak immediately after the war. But thirty, forty, forty-five years later this youthful enthusiasm has declined, if not altogether disappeared. The reasons for this are many, and complicated. At least one of them should be apparent. The economic and bureaucratic "European" institutions lack character and meaning. Whatever their material results, they fall short not only of a functioning political reality but of a conscious (and therefore historical) ideal.

So there is this difference between the piecemeal establishment of the economic and bureaucratic institutions of "Europe" on the one hand, and the ups and downs of the realization of a European consciousness on the other. These two developments have been not only different but often contradictory.

The source of this contradiction (if contradiction it is) is the difference between two kinds of internationalism. One — the largely accepted and predominant — idea of internationalism is economic and progressive, materialist and abstract at the same time. It is abstract because of the current meaning of the word "international." That is a misnomer, because it refers to institutions and relationships connecting not nations but states. "International," in this sense, means only "interstate." This is not merely a linguistic imprecision. We live at a time when the relations of states involve the relations of entire nations, involving the relations of their governments but also much more than those. "Internationalism," as that term is employed today, is a mirage. Both Marxists and capitalists have ignored this. Marx ignored the powerful attraction of nationalism in the age of the masses, its appeal to the workingmen and -women of nations. He also confused the state with the nation, regarding them as synonymous, which they are not. The capitalists, depending on the abstract myth of Economic Man, mistake the interstate movements of capital as a supreme reality; they believe that these things determine the everyday lives and desires of different peoples. They ignore the condition that, especially in the democratic age, economic transactions, indeed the material realities in the lives of men and women, depend on what they believe and on what they think.

What has been, and what still is, disastrous for Europe is not the existence of different nations but the existence of nationalism. For Europe the true alternative to nationalism is not some kind of bureaucratic, materialist and abstract internationalism, but the kind of internationalism that develops from an increasing understanding (and, consequently, from an increasing cultural symbiosis) of its different nations. There is an important principle latent here. A key ingredient of nationalism is xenophobia, the dislike and fear of foreigners. But the proper and desirable opposite of xenophobia is not an undiscriminating xenophilia, a thoughtless and abstract kind of broadmindedness. It is, rather, a discriminating *xenologia*, a comprehensive and compassionate understanding of others, of foreigners.

Sixty years ago, in 1933, a debate between these two kinds of internationalism took place on a high level. The French intellectual Julien Benda, in a celebrated book (*Le trahison des clercs, The Treason of the Intellectuals*), denounced the very existence of different national cultures. The great Dutch historian Johan Huizinga answered Benda in a trenchant essay. Why not the harmony of a potential Europe "in which the different nations will continue to live? . . . Why this deep distrust of a multinational accord? . . . It may be that thought has no nationality; but its expression does." (It may be telling that Huizinga foresaw Hitlerism, while Benda did not.) Benda was, or he thought he was, an internationalist, meaning the very opposite of a nationalist. But the true opposite of a nationalist was Huizinga, who was both a Dutch patriot and a true European.

Huizinga would have understood the differences of the American and the Swiss models, the applicability of the American model to America and of the Swiss model to Europe. Europeans speak, and think, in different languages. That will continue for a long time. Not only the American Constitution but the very existence of the United States depended (and probably still depends) on the condition that the prevalent majority of its inhabitants spoke, and speak, English.

There is another factor: that the American concept of internationalism has been, by and large, the Wilsonian kind — abstract, legalistic and mechanical — whereas the Swiss experience has been organic and historical.

The flag is a symbol not of a nation but of a state. There is no (and for a long time there will be no) European nation. But even though the existence of a people precedes the existence of a state, the idea of some kind of a state, and of its symbols, must be there from the beginning. This is why the question of a European flag is more than an aesthetic consideration. It must be symbolic of something that is particular. The present European flag is inadequate. It does not differ from the "flag" of NATO. Its twelve stars arranged in a circle on a blue background are uninspiring. They will have to be rearranged again and again, if and when other European states become members of the "community." The banner of the European movement of the late 1940s, a green E on a white field, was more inspiring, specific, and apposite. Among other things, its essential feature was a letter: and the culture of Europe is inseparable from a culture of the letter.

The idea of Europe does not merely require, it *depends on* the defense of a certain culture; and that European culture is nothing if not the defense of a certain conception of human nature. This is why the composition of "Europe" must be inclusive as well as exclusive: inclusive of those nations whose political and civil structures represent that conception of human nature, and exclusive of those who do not — or not yet.*

It is telling that the desire — often inchoate and not truly thought out; but isn't that the condition of most desires? — to belong to "Europe" is most apparent among some of the intellectuals of the recently freed Eastern European peoples. The reason for this is simple. Those who are still outside wish to

---

* One of the reasons why the present tendency of the hasty recognitions — suggesting the approval — of most nationalist statelets is shortsighted and inexcusable.

belong, while those who are now inside are no longer much inspired by the idea of Europe. The latter, at best, take those now present institutions of "Europe" for granted. At worst, they know that a "Europe" without power and without inspiring symbols is not much more than a platitude — perhaps a broadminded platitude; but it is a condition of platitudes to be so broadminded that they are flat.

The difference between the two German ideals, that of Goethe vs. Wagner, of German civilization vs. German power, of the old Germany composed of small states vs. the Greater German Reich, may have been the great German problem once. But history should teach us that problems are seldom solved; instead, they are outgrown. These once fatal alternatives may no longer mean much. There is a united and homogeneous Germany now, and it is part of "Europe" in more than one way. But it is Europe that must now incarnate all of the virtues, without the vices, of a composition of small states. We may be at the threshold of a world historical development where, in the twenty-first century, the function of Europe within the world may resemble, on a larger scale, what Switzerland has been within Europe during the last one hundred years. We may be approaching an age perhaps devoid of great wars and great revolutions, but with plenty of new and grave problems, including ghoulish threats created by technology, and a new variety of the migration of peoples — at a time when culture and tradition, when standards of morality and civility may be more important than political power; when they become not only intellectual and spiritual but tangible patriotic assets. This is because — all superficial appearances to the contrary — near the end of the Modern Age the abstract (yes, the abstract) philosophy of materialism is no longer as workable as it seems, or as it was in the past. We live in a time of the increasing spiritualization of matter, of the increasing intrusion of mind into matter. Of this — of its promises and also of its dangers — Europe (and Germany in its center) must be particularly aware, together with a consciousness of inherited qualities that it must not only protect but represent.

There *was* something of a Europe in the eighteenth century, when in St. Petersburg the Tsarina Catherine read and listened to Diderot, when in Potsdam Frederick the Great read and listened to Voltaire, when the diplomatic dispatches even of English ambassadors were often composed in French. But this was only an aristocratic and intellectual conglomeration of spirits; and it was, in reality, more French than European. The twilight of a semi-aristocratic Europe lasted until 1914 when, untouched by the fever of the boiling and heaving nationalist passions of entire peoples, a few aristocratic ambassadors almost alone understood the terrible tragedy inherent in the coming great war. About them the French conservative historian Henry Contamine wrote a nervous and beautiful book in 1953 entitled *L'Europe est derrière nous*, Europe Is Behind Us. But in 1914 Frenchmen and Frenchwomen did not think that they were "Europeans"; and I am not sure that they think so now.

That Englishmen and Englishwomen do not think that they are "European" is natural. For four hundred years, during the entire Modern Age, the Channel has been wider than the Atlantic, with the English having more in common with Americans than with their neighbors on the continent. In many ways the Atlantic, too, has been an estranging sea; but the choppy waters of the English Channel even more so. This has now begun to change, but very, very slowly. General de Gaulle knew that. That is why, more than thirty years ago, during the peak phase of the cold war, he spoke of a Europe "from the Atlantic to the Urals." He foresaw a Russia bereft of her non-Russian peoples and their lands. (He should have said "Caucasus" instead of "Urals." He may have been geographically imprecise but his meaning was clear: a European Russia.) He knew that if faced with a choice, the British, for many years yet to come, would never choose an association with "Europe" at the expense of their association with the United States of America.

I understand: but the British may have missed their chance twice. In the 1770s they ignored and misunderstood their American relatives, whereby they lost their opportunity for a new kind of confederated English-speaking empire. They acquired and achieved great imperial possessions instead, in Asia and Africa; but that did not last. Their second chance came in 1945 immediately after the Second World War. Their prestige — mainly, and only in Europe — was still such that they could have had the leadership of a more or less united Western Europe for a song. But the music of such a song was foreign to them, not something to which they would respond. They were not accustomed to that kind of music. I am not saying that Clement Attlee or Margaret Thatcher was anything like Lord North. I am even inclined to sympathize with the unwillingness of the English to subordinate their characteristic ways and liberties to the rulings and regulations cobbled together by a bureaucracy in Brussels. They might as well stay outside that kind of Europe. Europe and the United States need an independent Britain. Yet that independence must not mean indifference and a bloodless nonparticipation — especially because of what is happening in Eastern Europe and in the Russias. There the British presence and influence have been feeble. But that influence — in every sense of a presence: political, financial, economic, cultural, intellectual — is needed there for many reasons, including a need to balance the German one, both in the short and the long run.

·   ·   ·

It is absurd to believe (as many people do, including some in Eastern Europe) that NATO and an eventual confederation of Europe are compatible. NATO existed simply because of the danger of an eventual Russian move beyond the then iron curtain. Questionable as that eventuality might have been, that purpose of NATO has been, by and large, fulfilled. But that danger has gone, indeed long ago (if in reality it existed at all). Consequently the American military presence in Europe is bound to diminish, if not disappear altogether. A NATO without America would amount to nothing. It was an American alliance system with many shortcomings that, fortunately, was never put to any serious test. (One example: Acheson's idea to include Greece and Turkey within NATO. What did these Eastern countries have to do with the North Atlantic?) More important: NATO had contributed to the division of Europe. The purpose of Washington was to keep Russian and Communist power away from Western Europe, not to challenge it in Eastern Europe, certainly not at the risk of armed conflict. That was evident as early as the 1950s; it went along with Washington's rigid (and often carefully hidden) opposition to any extension of an "unaligned" Europe in the middle of the continent, meaning the mutual withdrawal of Russian and American forces from there. But this is happening now: a Russian and American withdrawal from Europe, for reasons different from those after the First World War, a withdrawal that is not necessarily simultaneous, but a mutual withdrawal nonetheless.

Many people in the United States and some in Western, though not in Eastern, Europe do not want this American withdrawal. Their reasons are complex. They range from inexcusable selfishness to excusable anxieties. But it is going to happen.

.   .   .

Great open questions — for Europe perhaps more than for other parts of the world — are latent in a new structure of history, emerging now. What will matter most in the twenty-first century? The conflicts of classes? of states? of nations? of races? In other terms: revolutions? wars? tribal warfare? mass migrations?

Well, it seems that the era of great revolutions is over, and probably that of great wars between states too. The latter is a more recent development than the former. During the last three hundred years, at least in the history of both Western and Eastern Europe, wars and their results were more decisive than were revolutions and their results.

The word "revolution" was not applied to politics until the eighteenth century. Yes, the principal events of that Age of Reason, or Enlightenment, were the three great Western revolutions that set in motion the movement toward democracy: the so-called Glorious Revolution in England and then the American and the French revolutions. Their inspiration and their effect lasted long. But it is at least arguable whether these revolutions had changed the relations of classes radically. Was not the democratic development of England, America and France well-nigh inevitable in the long run?

There was, at any rate, another important reality in Western Europe in the eighteenth and even the nineteenth century. That was the political geography of Western Europe, evident on the map. From 1689 to 1789, during that century of great revolutions, the extent of France, Spain, Portugal and the Netherlands, including their frontiers, changed hardly at all.

But the opposite was true of Eastern Europe. There the ideas and the consequences of the Western European and American revolutions had hardly penetrated. Yet there *was* an enormous revolution in the political order of Eastern Europe, on the map. In 1700 the largest states, the principal powers in Eastern Europe, were Sweden, Poland and Turkey. By 1800 (surely by

1815) they were replaced by Russia, Prussia and Austria. Sweden had been made to retreat to the western shores of the Baltic; she became a middle-sized kingdom of sorts. Turkey had been pushed back into the Balkans, on the way to what Turkey would soon be called: "the sick man of Europe." Poland disappeared altogether, partitioned as she had become by Russia, Prussia and Austria. That was a revolution of the political geography of Europe, of immense portents.

It is arguable that the rise of Prussia and Russia may have been at least as, if not more, important for the then future of Europe than was the French Revolution. During the nineteenth century the three great waves of European revolutions, those of 1820 and 1830 and 1848 (the last, for a moment, seemed to encompass the entire continent), successors of the French Revolution as they were, proved to be less important than the creation of a unified Italy and especially of a united Germany. The latter changed the map of Europe decisively in the 1860s and, indeed, led to the First World War.

After 1848 wars were more decisive than revolutions, and in our short twentieth century too: its two great world wars were far more important than any of the revolutions, including the Russian Communist one — the main meaning and consequence of which was not Communism but Russia's political and cultural withdrawal from Europe after the First World War, and her reappearance in Eastern Europe — though resting only on military power — during the Second.

Still, the change in the texture of history, leading to a democratic age, had already had its consequences in statecraft two hundred years ago. Those partitions of Poland at the end of the eighteenth century had been decreed and executed by the rulers and the cabinets of states, composed of aristocratic statesmen indifferent to the mass of Polish peasants — just as that peasantry was, as yet, largely indifferent to who their faraway kings and queens were. But there came a change nonetheless. An independent Polish state had, by and large, disappeared but the Polish nation remained; and, as Talleyrand consoled the Poles at Vienna, if it were to maintain its national consciousness, with its language and religion and culture, at a future time Poland would rise to become a state again. Which is what happened in 1918, when the conditions were ripe for that, with both Russia and Germany defeated and in retreat. Then, in 1939, Hitler and Stalin divided Poland again. But this would not last, and not only because of Hitler's defeat. Not even Stalin dared to incorporate Poland within the Soviet Union. He was satisfied by making it a Communist satellite state, with symbols and a few segments of Polish sovereignty still extant. Two hundred years ago the old Polish state could be made to disappear; but a national state could no longer disappear entirely.

The reverse of this is also true. In 1939 Britain and France declared war on Germany because of the German invasion of Poland. They would, or could, do nothing to help the Poles from being swiftly conquered by the Germans and then partitioned by Hitler and Stalin. Six years later the Western democracies had won the war. Hitler was gone. Again they could or would do little to keep Stalin from doing with Poland what he wanted. Yet a Polish state remained. Thirty or thirty-five years later it began to throw off Communism and its dependence on the Soviet Union; another nine years later it was free of both.

In 1991, two years after that, some of the characteristics and traditional weaknesses of Polish politics — those weaknesses that two hundred years ago had contributed to the ease with which Poland was partitioned by its neighbors — have reappeared again. The hero Walesa has some of the marks of a workingman's Pilsudski. There is disorder, corruption, mismanagement, the political parties tearing at each other, unable to agree on national essentials. The Russians have retreated, the Germans have solemnly accepted the existence of Polish frontiers that incorporate vast territories that had belonged to Germans for centuries. Still, whatever their governments may have acceded to, neither Russians nor Germans have much liking for Poles. Poland is again alone, without powerful allies, certainly unable to count on the military support of a France or a Britain in the West. Another partition of Poland, between Russia and Germany, is now unthinkable (though "unthinkable" is something that sometimes must be thought about). The structure of history has changed, because nations have become as important as, maybe even more important than, states.

Two hundred years ago the national content had begun to fill up the framework of states. This was both good and bad — good because of democracy and the evolution of consciousness, bad because it led to brutal wars and hatreds, to entire nations rushing at each other. Now, here and there, the national content has begun to burst such frames — not only in Yugoslavia and Czechoslovakia but perhaps in Canada too. (Not in Switzerland, whose component peoples are Swiss-Germans rather than German-Swiss, Swiss-French rather than French-Swiss, Swiss-Italians rather than Italian-Swiss. But that took a long time, and perhaps that was unique and will remain unique — until and unless Europe learns from it.)

At the end of the twentieth century, for the first time in four centuries, France can find no ally against a predominant Germanic power, surely not in the east. During the seventeenth century her royal and Catholic kings and statesmen felt no compunction about assisting the infidel Turks against the Habsburgs. Before and during World War I republican France was allied with Tsarist Russia against Germany. After World War I she made alliances with a motley group of the new Eastern European states, including Poland; after Hitler rose to power, France signed a military pact with Soviet Russia. Once the German Third Reich was powerful, most of France's allies, including Stalin's Russia, deserted her, preferring to be friendly with Germany. In 1944 de Gaulle tried to revive the Franco-Russian alliance. That became meaningless because of the cold war. Thereafter — in order to balance an overwhelming American domination and, for a while, the possibility of an overwhelming American-German alliance — the French, including de Gaulle, sought an alliance with West Germany, hoping to assume the character of an alliance of equals. After the Berlin Wall came down in late 1989, President Mitterrand made a few feeble gestures and statements hoping to prevent the complete reunification of East and West Germany. That illusion disappeared instantly. German national feeling was a reality stronger than any possible diplomatic move by the Elysée or the Quai d'Orsay.

French governments in the twentieth century still think in terms of states. The trouble with the French is that they cannot easily come to terms with the post–Modern Age. Much of the Modern Age was a French age, and not only culturally. De Gaulle understood that.* He was a solitary genius. He knew, too, that while World War II was a continuation of World War I, it was more than that. Nineteen forty was a catastrophe for France from which the French have not yet recovered. De Gaulle resurrected the French state, which was no mean or easy thing. But 1940 meant a deep wound — not only militarily or politically but culturally and mentally. After 1815 the intellectual, artistic, cultural, individualist confidence of the French survived the defeat of Napoleon. In 1945 de Gaulle succeeded in ranging the French state among the victors, but

---

* His mind and his character hearkened back to the French seventeenth century, not the eighteenth. He was no Talleyrand (and no Clemenceau); with all of his acid wit, there was no trace of Voltaire (let alone Rousseau) in de Gaulle, whose spirit (and prose) were Corneillean, Racinean.

the deep and often hidden wound of French confidence had not healed after the shock of 1940 — not even now.

In 1940 the unity of France was shattered, and badly. That unity had been broken in the past, temporarily, through social hatreds, political infighting, revolutions; but what happened in 1940 was something different, and perhaps deeper. Their very national feeling was broken. Evidences of that were already present before their awful humiliation in June 1940. The French armistice party, Pétainists and their followers, was in the wings (and active in parliament) well before June 1940; and I do not mean only the small conventicles of French Fascists or even Laval. Such different men as de Monzie, Montigny, Bergéry, Flandin, Fabre-Luce, Baudouin, Martin du Gard, Meaulnier, Montherlant, Morand, members of *tout Paris*, all in their elegant English suits, were not fanatics or revolutionaries: they were well-mannered haut bourgeois and intellectuals. They were against the war, against resisting Hitler, against an alliance with the British. They were willing to see a France, to live in a France, to be Frenchmen, in a Europe dominated and governed by Hitler's Germany. They thought that they were French patriots, and in a way they were; memories of the tremendous loss of French blood twenty years before were in their minds, as that was in the minds of an entire people. But even the most defensive or pacific patriot, anxious about the dangers of war for his country, ought to think twice (and the French, once they are satisfied with the logic of their ideas, do not like to think twice) whether peace is worth the price of a great nation's sinking to a level of powerlessness, where it must adjust itself abjectly to the wishes of its powerful neighbor — of an ancient enemy who would not only profit from France's indifference to (that is, her abandonment of) the rest of Europe but who would have nothing but contempt for a nation whose selfishness is but the shortsighted egotism of cowardice, amounting to the abandonment of its self-defense at the expense of honor.*

And besides and apart from the Pétainists were the real French revolutionaries, intellectuals who admired Germany and Hitler — again a varied slew of brilliant and combative French intellects such as Brasillach, Béraud, Drieu, Céline. They, too, had been the beneficiaries of the liberties of speech and of life during the Third Republic. They thought that they were the real nationalists; yet they tied their hopes to the victory of Germany — not only in 1940; in 1944 during the Battle of the Bulge they hoped that the Germans would come back, and defeat the liberation of France. Brasillach wrote in prison: "We slept with the Germans; and, admit it, we liked some of it." By "we" did he mean the pro-German collaborationists or the French people at large? I cannot tell; but I cannot exclude the possibility that Brasillach may have meant both, in which case this was his Parthian shot, the desire of this courageous hater to strike pain into the hearts of his own people.

In any event, these French radicals understood that the Enlightenment was over. They represented a French radical populism that in our day Le Pen represents.

The French did not really find their place in the twentieth century. Perhaps in music they recovered the gigantic German lead of the nineteenth century: Debussy, Ravel, Poulenc, Duruflé; but none of their painters were first rate after the Great War; and French modern architecture is the worst in Western Europe. Yes, much of Speer's architecture was better than, say,

---

* While these French "conservatives" despised — and not without reason — the political and parliamentary corruption of the Third Republic, in 1939 they opposed a war that would endanger the continued existence of that corrupt sweet life whose beneficiaries they were.

Le Corbusier's. What has been done in Paris after de Gaulle was gone — the Pompidou-Beaubourg, the new Bastille Opéra, the La Défense monstrosity, the pyramid at the Louvre — they are ridiculous, at times horrid.

But what makes Paris still beautiful is that Paris is one of the few European capitals the landscape of whose buildings has changed little since about 1910. Its restorations are beautiful; they are more than merely antiquarian, they are imaginative. This happens because the French have great spiritual, intellectual and artistic capital to draw on, and that is far from having been exhausted, so that when they draw upon it intelligently, dividends still accrue. What is most exhausted is their spiritual capital from the eighteenth century, from an atheistic or agnostic Age of Reason. Hence the extraordinary creations of French religious writers in this century, of such different people as Péguy, Simone Weil, Bernanos.

The French are a conservative people — sometimes in the best, sometimes in the worst ways of conservatism. They are very bourgeois too, in the best and the worst of ways. One should hope that the best is more enduring than the worst. Their inner balance was ruptured during the twentieth century. They will, I think, find a new kind of balance in the future, when the best of them will know — they will have learned — where their true assets are.

The nineteenth and early twentieth centuries were marked by the great consolidations of the peoples of Europe. While the national populations began to fill up the great framework of the old regimes of the states, very few people in Europe moved from one country to another, despite the developments of transportation, of communications, of social mobility, both vertically and horizontally, sideward and upward. Most people moved within their countries, from the countryside into the cities. (Before 1800 many people in Europe still lived less than thirty miles from where their direct ancestors had lived centuries before them.) Between 1820 and 1920 perhaps as many as sixty million people left Europe and the British Isles for other continents; but, I repeat, very few people left one European country for another. (The only significant exception to this were Jews, about 90 percent of whom in 1820 lived within the confines of the then Russian empire. During the next century millions of them moved westward.)

At the very end of the Second World War, and for a few years after that, another great migration began. This was the movement of many millions of Germans, partly refugees, partly expellees, into what remained of Germany proper — together with another million or two "displaced persons." Most of the latter left for other continents a few years later. Those who did not were successfully absorbed, as were the German refugees, into the West German Republic. Ten, fifteen years after the war the new phenomenon of "guest workers" began to appear. The Western European governments, first among them West Germany, were in need of cheap labor. They also congratulated themselves on their liberal immigration policies, as borders in Western Europe had become more porous and less definite. At the end of the twentieth century, a reaction has come. Its potential consequences are profound, and as yet unforeseeable. The peoples of Europe are worried at the increasingly ominous evidences of a new migration of peoples from the east and the south. There is more to this than xenophobia. As the Modern Age began five hundred years ago, the danger of invasions of Europe (a recurrent danger that had existed for more than a thousand years) began to vanish. At the end of the Modern Age that prospect, though in different forms, appears again.

One thing is certain. The absolute sovereignty of states, including national states, has been declining. But no state can ever exist without some kind of control of its geographic limits. "Europe" may have arrived at a new stage of its history, when the main threat may no longer be that of great wars among its national states but of invasion from without (whether armed, unarmed, or half armed). One state after another will have (some of them have already begun) to tighten the control of its frontiers, restricting immigration, while the frontiers between the member states of the "European Economic Community" have been dissolving. But what happens when one state restricts immigration while a neighboring state does not? And what will happen — fortunately this prospect is not certain — if, gradually or suddenly, one state becomes altogether incapable of halting a flooding tide of migrants?

Without an all-European policy on immigration, involving the eventual necessity of its physical enforcement, there can be and there will be no "Europe" worth anything. No reality, no "fact" in this world, has any meaning except by its contrast with other facts. If there is a "Europe," it must be different from any other place in this world that is not Europe. That includes the United States too; and it involves not only the immigration of peoples but the importation of goods — not only material goods but even nonmaterial, intellectual ones. (One example: what happens if one member state of the European community decides to proscribe the viler kind of pornography while another does not, at a time when there are no frontiers or trade controls?) Let us not have illusions about those "European" institutions — at least, not yet.

Let us not idealize "Europe." In both Eastern and Western Europe the Pope warns the youth against an uncritical emulation of "the West," against untrammeled greed, materialism, the cult of consumption, sexual license, abortions, pornography. He is right. Two generations ago Belloc said that "Europe is The Faith." Belloc was wrong then, and he is wrong now. Europe is no longer Christian. (Let us not idealize about that, either: in some ways it never truly was.) But Christianity was once a European substance. The question now is not whether Europeans have become less Christian than in the past. That may be arguable, and not an absolute loss (so many people and nations in Europe, while proclaiming themselves Christian, acted so often in non-Christian ways). The question is whether the nations of Europe have become less Christian than some of those in the Americas, and perhaps even than some African ones. It was Waugh, rather than Belloc, a novelist rather than a publicist, who once had it exactly right when he said, in 1932: "I am perfectly confident that in my life-time, if I live as long as you, sir, that I shall see the beginning of a vast recession of the white races from all over the world — a withdrawal of the legions to defend what remains of European standards, European grounds. I am less confident of how much will remain to be defended." *

In some ways — on one level — the world is becoming closer, smaller, more uniform. But that involves only the movements of materials and of images, the ephemeral business of impermanent matter and money and pictures and sounds. (Movements of money are abstractions, entirely dependent on people's confidence in the processes of such transactions.) Meanwhile something very different is happening in the world and in Europe. The governing ideas of a Parliament of Man, the League of Nations, the United Nations, the European Economic Community, the Council of Europe, etc., are antiquated. Fifty years ago such different men as Molotov, Wendell Willkie, E. H. Carr proclaimed that the age of the small states was over, that this century meant the conglomeration of bigger and bigger units and organizations, whether under the

---

* Talk on BBC, cited in Martin Stannard, *Evelyn Waugh: The Early Years, 1903–1929*. New York, 1987, p. 294.

aegis of a few superpowers or not. But now Yugoslavia and perhaps Czechoslovakia and the Soviet Union are breaking up (not to speak of the "independence" movements of Basques, Catalans, Flamands, Walloons, Corsicans). Their principal motive is tribal nationalism, of course. But there is the recognition, too, that large units are neither efficient nor authentically democratic — that is, self-governing.

Yugoslavia is a crucial example. The "European Community" has shown neither the will nor the ability to intervene there, let alone the energy and the authority to impose any settlement. Because of such examples the respect for the Europe of Brussels is melting away perhaps even faster than the respect for the League of Nations had before the Second World War. That respect, too, had melted away in the heat of powerful nationalisms. But the present tribal nationalisms are not quite the same as were those of two generations ago. Nationalism will not remain the principal force in Europe forever. Yes, the present sentiments of "Europeanness" are insufficient for the formation of a united Europe. The representation of that idea by bureaucratic institutions is insufficient. Yet *insufficient* does not mean *nonexistent*. Sometime in the twenty-first century a new recognition of what Europe is, or ought to be — of what being European is, or ought to be — will arise.

April 1991. *The duality of Europe.*

Lombardy disfigured. *Driving from Como to Bergamo, I see how much of the softness of the Lombardy landscape is now compromised by the congelations of concrete and cement, huge long factory buildings, huge apartment buildings, more American than French in their style (meaning that*

*they are not quite as ugly as are modern French buildings,
but almost), huge cement pylons, huge trucks spewing their
fumes in the air. Those older, yellow-stuccoed Lombardy
buildings are visible only here and there. The hills are still
beautiful in the distance, with the village churches and
wheeled bells in their campaniles. But they are in retreat.
Northern Italy is prosperous, Milan expensive and rich; but
there, too, urban and urbane life has been draining away.
For the most part, the center of Milan is startlingly empty at
night. More and more of the wealthy Milanese having chosen to abandon the city, they live in their estate villas outside it, behind high wrought-iron gates wired with electric
alarm systems.*

    *Unlike thirty, even twenty years ago, there is not one Com-
munist poster to be seen. Instead, one sees posters of the
new party of the Lombard League, Lega Lombarda, the historic origins of which go back to the twelfth (yes, the twelfth)
century. It is now a strong and appealing party led by intelligent people. They want to keep foreigners, Arabs, even
southern Italians (Neapolitans, Calabrians, Sicilians) away
from the north. They are opposed to the centralized, inefficient, corrupt maladministration in Rome. They want self-
government. We are different, they suggest and say. Sup-
pose they prevail: will the industrialists of Lega Lombarda
build different apartment houses and factories? Simone
Weil: "Nothing can have a destination which is not its origin. The contrary idea, the idea of progress — poison."*

    *Along Lake Como.   Prosperity and beauty. The first has
not yet disfigured the second. The contained luxuriousness of
the private villas above the lake, on their minuscule
grounds, tiny private lots each. Their prices, their sites, are
now beyond the dreams of avarice. Forty years ago not one
of a hundred thousand Italians could afford a penthouse*

apartment on the East Side of New York. Today not one of a million Americans can afford a restored 1900-style villa above Lake Como.

Isola Comecina. The only island on that deep lake. No one lives there. A boat calls only twice a day. We walk around the ruins of two small churches, destroyed by a jealous bishop of Como (and, they say, Barbarossa) eight hundred years ago. A simple tavern perched over the shore. We are the only two people sitting down on the terrace for lunch. Presently a large motor launch arrives with one hundred businessmen and businesswomen, Americans, Canadians, Frenchmen. Now we see a large dining room opening up behind us. The waiter puts on a Lombard beret, gives them a big spiel about the history of the island while the coffee is set aflame with a thin stream of grappa poured smartly into a huge brass urn. When we leave, in the foyer I find the wall covered by fifty framed photographs, signed by people who had eaten here: Sylvester Stallone, Arnold Schwarzenegger, Henry Kissinger, Elizabeth Taylor, Oscar de la Renta. We laugh. We had congratulated ourselves for having found an out-of-the way place such as this, for not being commonplace tourists.

But that evening I go for a little walk after dinner, a high mile above Cernobbio. The village cemetery with a low wall. The small iron gate is unlocked. There was a funeral earlier that day. Tiny lights flicker here and there on the graves, one behind a great mound of piled-up flowers and wreaths. There, in the shadow, I see a young girl standing with bent shoulders and head. She is softly crying. She had come back to this grave, at night, after the funeral. It is a dark velvety spring evening, a silent fusion of day and night. Down the other side of the hill, below the cemetery, are the lights of the one hundred houses of Cernobbio. This cemetery is not removed from that, it is not a dead place of the past, of what is gone forever. It is not abandoned, bereft of life. It is a piece of ground that breathes together with the soft slow throbbing of life, with the sad immortal music of humanity, with the old world of Cernobbio, Como, Italy, Europe — breathing that limited immortality that certain human beings can confer on certain places where they and their forebears have been living. Limited immortality, limited but immortal nonetheless, and not a contradiction in terms.

Immortal mortal Europe. Where do I feel (more accurately, when am I most conscious of the feeling) that I am really in Europe? In the nave of Notre-Dame? Along a canal in Venice or Bruges? In a country restaurant in the Aveyron? Under the glass dome of Frankfurt Hauptbahnhof? In the shining alley of small shops in Lugano? In the Old Town of Stockholm or Rothenburg or Lucca or Prague? In Tuscan gardens? Yes, but seldom more so than in the Cz.'s flat in Brugg.

Brugg is an indifferent small town on the rail line between Zurich and Basle. The Cz.'s have built their modest existence there. They fled from Hungary a quarter century ago. They live in a modern concrete apartment house. The Swiss Alps are far, hardly visible in the foggy distance. A cement staircase leads to their three-room apartment, like the stairs of innumerable such apartment houses in the second half of the twentieth century, from Los Angeles to Warsaw. Inside, beyond the concrete and steel and glass, it is a jewelry box of sorts. There is that peculiar Magyar (Buda, rather than Pest) Biedermeier air, tangible and inhalable. A few pieces of inlaid early-nineteenth-century furniture, a few small cut-glass goblets in a cabinet, old velvet runners on the little tables, one or two old family portraits on the walls, the portraits of mustachioed ancestors in Hungarian small-gentry uniforms or clothes, from a time when they and their country were on the very edge of Europe, if not beyond. But: this flat

202 / THE END OF THE TWENTIETH CENTURY

now is Europe. Those veneered chests and those cracked
and smoky portraits were somehow brought out from Hungary, moved for the sake of family piety. (And how many
angry quarrels, instead of piety, had been behind those portraits when they had been painted; how many crimson-faced
apoplexies, how many bitter yellow teeth, how many stony-
faced deaths!) And now these pieces and portraits live, re-
vived, in this middle-class flat in Switzerland, in something
like a carefully tended bowl of bourgeois comfort: a bowl in
which a few dried flowers have come alive. They have risen
from abandoned mortal matter, from the dead — at least for
another lifetime. There is more to this than interior decora-
tion. (Or than that promise of superb smells wafting out
from the modern kitchen.) These two dear people have
brought something to life again. They may not know this.
They will be gone someday. They have no children. But no
matter.

◄ VIII ►

NATIONALISM, NATIONALITY,
NATIVISM, NATIONAL FEELING,
NATIONAL CHURCHES,
NATIONAL RELIGION

IF "history is philosophy, teaching by example" (as Dionysius Halicarnassus wrote and Bolingbroke repeated two thousand years later), here is one recent and telling example, not a very promising one.

Near the center of Europe, in the great Danubian valley live the Slovaks, a people who did not achieve a state until 1939, when Hitler allowed them one — because they were instrumental in destroying what was left of Czechoslovakia. That "independent" Slovakia was wholly dependent on the wishes and orders of its masters in Berlin. The majority of Slovaks evidently preferred to be dependent on Germany rather than to remain allied with their Czech cousins or brethren. So do some of them now, more than fifty years after 1939. There is a lesson in this, a lesson of what nationalism can (or cannot) do.

For one thousand years the Slovaks belonged to Hungary. The kingdom of Hungary, with all of its shortcomings, was a natural geographical unit, with three fourths of its frontiers being formed by the great mountain range of the Carpathians. The Hungarians did not treat their non-Magyar inhabitants very well, but they treated the Slovaks probably better than they treated most of the others. The Slovaks were a poor and simple people of woodsmen and peasants. A particular affection for their innocent simplicity is apparent through much of Magyar literature. In the last quarter of the nineteenth century Slovak nationalism began to rise. It was suppressed by the Magyar government but there were few violent troubles. The Hungarian attitude was that of a patronizing restriction of the putative rights of what the Magyars saw as a politically and culturally somewhat backward people. (Bratislava, the present capital of Slovakia, had been Pozsony [Pressburg], seat of the Hungarian Diet for centuries. The very word "Bratislava" was coined by Slovaks only as late as 1837; as late as 1918 most of its inhabitants were not Slovaks.) During World War I Czechs would, on occasion, desert from the ranks of the Austro-Hungarian army; Slovaks seldom, if ever.

From across the low hillocks of the western Carpathians beckoned their brethren and cousins the Czechs, speaking a language that is almost identical with the Slovak. The Czechs were cunning, astute and lucky. By 1918 they succeeded in convincing the French, the British and, above all, President Wilson that the Austro-Hungarian monarchy must be dismembered and that there should be a new and independent Czechoslovak state. A declaration of the creation of Czechoslovakia was signed in 1918 by Czech and Slovak émigré politicians in Pittsburgh, supported by their ward leaders and politicians in western Pennsylvania who had emigrated there during the previous thirty years and were treated as second-class citizens by the native American owners and foremen of the mines and factories. Never mind: that Pittsburgh Declaration was for Czechoslovakia what the Declaration of Independence was for Americans in 1776.

Czechoslovakia lasted for twenty years. That state had many weaknesses, including the condition that it was multinational. In 1938 Hitler took a portion of Czechoslovakia and reduced the independence of the remainder, with the pained tacit consent of the Western democracies, who were not ready or willing to go to war to defend Czechoslovakia. Thereafter it became Czecho-Slovakia, with the Slovak nationalists agitating for their complete "independence," eventually to the extent of near-revolt in March 1939. Hitler knew how to profit from that. He drove into Prague, incorporating "Czechia" into the Third Reich, while an "independent" Slovakia came into being, for the first time in history. So twenty years after Slovak nationalism had helped to destroy the Austro-Hungarian Empire and helped to create Czechoslovakia with its capital in Prague, Slovak nationalism destroyed Czechoslovakia in favor of a new dependence on Berlin.

The record of this new Slovak republic was not inspiring. Its president was a Catholic priest, Monsignor Tiso, who among other things was willing to hand over the Jews of Slovakia to the Germans when (and sometimes even before) the latter insisted on that. He was execrated by the papal nuncio, who as late as 1944 wrote to the Vatican that he could not find in Tiso "any sign of comprehension, not even one word of compassion, for the persecuted. . . . The Slovak government and the President of the Republic are servile followers [*esecutori servili*] of the Germans." The most damning evidence against Tiso is there in his own words in a letter to the Pope (composed in Latin) as late as November 1944, after just about all of the Jews in Slovakia had been gassed in Auschwitz: he explained that he was grateful to the Germans, since the Jews and the Czechs were still the sources of evil in Slovakia * — a sad and, alas, typical evidence of the nationalist and German-

---

* Tiso's letter to the Pope, 8 November 1944, in *Actes et Documents du Saint Siège Relatifs à la Seconde Guerre Mondiale*, vol. 10. Vatican City, 1980, p. 476. The nuncio (Monsignor Burzio) on Tiso, ibid., p. 461.

ophile populism marking the political and ideological preferences of this prelate. (He was tried and executed in 1947.)

Not every Slovak was a Nazi sympathizer or a Fascist. There
were excellent Slovak democrats and conservatives, among
them Milan Hodža, the prime minister of the Czechoslovak
government-in-exile — or Alexander Dubček, the mild and
modest hero of the Prague Spring of 1968. After World War II
the twilight semi-democratic independence of a resurrected
Czechoslovakia lasted less than three years. Under the subsequent Communist tyranny Czechs and Slovaks suffered alike.
This lasted about forty years. Some of the best humane patriots under Communism were Slovaks such as Dubček; so
were some of the most vulgar satraps, such as Bilak. The
movement liberating Czechoslovakia from Communism developed and culminated in Prague in 1989. The new hero was
Václav Havel, whose reputation of intellectual integrity has
impressed the West. Soon Slovak nationalists reappeared —
celebrating the memory of the unfortunate Monsignor Tiso,
among others. Havel announced that his government would
confer on the Slovaks all of the cultural and governmental
autonomy they would want. That was not enough. When
Havel came to the Slovak capital he was shouted down and
pelted with rotten vegetables; he had to cut his speech short.
In October 1991 Havel thought of a gesture that would be both
politic and symbolic, historic and moving. He made the American government agree to relinquish the original document of
the 1918 Pittsburgh Declaration. He chose to fly home with
it, landing not in Prague but in the Slovak capital of Bratislava.
He held the precious document in his hands. But the gesture
was a failure. Again he could not finish his speech; he was
pelted with eggs and shouted down by howling Slovaks. His
bodyguards had to bundle him up and trundle him back to
Prague. As I am writing this (November 1991), the breakup of
Czechoslovakia may not be imminent; but it is probable, like

that of Yugoslavia.* Unlike the Serbs in Yugoslavia, the Czechs will let this happen without fighting. But the result will be the same: among other things, a partial vindication of Hitler.

There *are* many people in Slovakia (as there are in Croatia) who are not hard nationalists, and who do not like the latter. But there are not many people, especially in Eastern Europe, who dare, or even find it easy, to speak out in public against nationalism. The non-nationalists may even be a majority. But they are a soft and perhaps inchoate majority, which may or may not be a real match against hard minorities, united by nationalist hatreds.

There is no first-rate book about the history of nationalism. (There are a few, though not many, usable books about its ingredients.) There are reasons for this. One of them is that nationalism may differ from country to country more than internationalism or socialism do. (That is how and why the very phenomena, including histories, of the right are more interesting than those of the left.) This is not simply attributable to the different national characters of different peoples. Those characteristics, by themselves, have changed through history. Slovak nationalism differs from American nationalism, Latvian nationalism differs from Swedish nationalism, not only because Slovaks and Americans et al. are different, but because the nationalisms of the former are newer than those of the latter. An overall history of nationalism must necessarily proceed chapter by chapter, dealing with one country after another, which makes for dull reading. And while national feelings may be and indeed often are very old, nationalism as a political force is new. (The simple Slovak peasant of two hundred years ago may have been the ancestor of the half-

---

* *July 1992.* Alas, so it happened.

baked Slovak nationalist intellectual of the twentieth century;
yet their circumstances and their very characters, including
not only the subjects but the functioning of their minds, have
become different.)

To think that nationalism is a reactionary phenomenon is a
grave error. Now, at the beginning of the twenty-first century
(and at the end of the Modern Age) the most powerful political
force in the world is nationalism still. So it was in the beginning of the twentieth century, culminating in the two world
wars. That, too, should make those who think that this century was dominated by the confrontation of Democracy and
Communism think twice. (They won't.) The twentieth century was marked not by the strength of classes and not even
by a struggle of ideas. It was marked by the struggle of nations.
Here and there it seems that wars among races might now
succeed the wars of nations; but that awful prospect has not
yet crystallized worldwide, and one hopes that it won't.

At this point we must realize that Hitler himself was an
extreme nationalist rather than a racist.* He had no compunction or hesitation about allying himself with Japanese, Chinese, Rumanians, Arabs, against Nordic Aryan peoples: Nor-
wegians, Dutch, English. There *was* a racist element in his
thinking (as there is in that of almost every nationalist), but
his governing obsession, the one against Jews, was something
other than biological. (On one occasion he referred to Jews as
less a physical than a "spiritual race.") We have seen that early
in his youth, as he put it in *Mein Kampf*, "I was a nationalist;
but not a patriot." He desired to unite himself and the people

---

* He himself expressed this in one of his least-known, yet most telling, long
speeches to a group of generals and officers on 26 May 1944: "We have a *Volk*
that should not be seen as identical with race . . . the [bourgeois] kept telling
me: '*Volk* and Race are one and the same.' No! *Volk* and Race are not the
same. Race is an ingredient of the blood, the kernel, but the *Volk* is formed
not by one race, it is formed by 2, 3, 4 or 5 different racial kernels."

of Austria with Germany, at the expense of the multinational Habsburg monarchy that he wished to see broken up. Patriotism is defensive, nationalism is aggressive; patriotism is the love of a particular land, with its particular traditions; nationalism is the love of something less tangible, of the myth of a "people," justifying everything, a political and ideological substitute religion.

Because it appeals to tribal and racial ties, nationalism seems to be deeply and atavistically human. Yet the trouble with nationalism is not only that it can be anti-humanist and often inhuman but that it also proceeds from an abstract assumption about human nature itself. The love for one's people is natural, but it is also categorical; it is less charitable and less deeply human than the love for one's country, a love that cannot be separated from traditions, akin to a love of one's family. Nationalism is both self-centered and selfish — because human love is not the love of oneself; it is the love of *another*. Patriotism is always more (and deeper) than being merely biological — because charitable love is human and not merely "natural." * Nature has, and shows, no charity. Thus the dignity of human life must proceed from a denial of Darwinism, from the recognition that, no matter how biologically small, there is an essential difference between humans and all other living beings. Both Christianity and Western civilization are humanist in that sense, in the sense of their requisite denial of the survival of the fittest as if that were a principle governing humanity.

Nationalism is both modern and populist. Just as a patriot is not necessarily a nationalist, a democrat is not necessarily a

---

*The sentiments and allegiances of nationalism are masculine — categorical, intellectual, or at least mental. The intuitive essence of women is less categorical, less exclusive, more human and potentially more universal.

populist. It is a historical commonplace to connect the first appearance of modern nationalism to the French Revolution. That is true in the sense that the French Revolution devolved into a kind of democratic totalitarianism because of its unreserved cult of "the people," and that it was the first to institute something like a universal military service, "a nation at arms." (I leave aside the argument that some such features were there in the English Puritan revolution 150 years earlier, and that the rhetorical exaltation of "the people" was there in America twenty years earlier.) Yet throughout the rhetoric of the French Revolution the word "nation" appears seldom. It is all *"peuple"* and *"patrie,"* as in the "Marseillaise," too, just as it is all *"république,"* with only scattered references to *"démocratie."* The French Revolution was anti-monarchist (and anti-aristocratic); but an early prototype of a nationalist populism was the anti-French guerrilla rising in 1808 in Spain.

An aristocratic nationalism is an oxymoron, a contradiction in terms, surely since the late seventeenth century, after which most European aristocracies were at least as cosmopolitan as they were national. Democratic nationalism is an early-nineteenth-century phenomenon. There was nothing very wrong with that. It won great revolutions and battles, it produced some fine examples of national cohesion, including some English-speaking countries. One hundred and fifty years ago my (and Orwell's 1943) distinction between nationalism and patriotism would have been labored, it would have made relatively little sense. Even now nationalism and patriotism often overlap within the mind and heart of the same person. Yet we must be aware of their differences — because of the phenomenon of populism, which, unlike old-fashioned patriotism, is inseparable from the myth of a people. Populism is folkish, patriotism is not. One can be a patriot and a cosmopolitan. But a populist is inevitably a nationalist of sorts.

Patriotism, too, is less racist than is populism. A patriot will not exclude a person of another nationality from the community where they have lived side by side and whom he has known for many years; but a populist will always remain suspicious of someone who does not seem to belong to his tribe.

A patriot is not necessarily a conservative; he may even be a liberal — of sorts, though not an abstract one. In the twentieth century a nationalist can hardly be a liberal. The nineteenth century was full of liberal nationalists, some of them inspiring and noble figures.* The accepted belief is that liberalism faded and declined because of the appearance of socialism; that the liberals who originally had reservations about overall democracy and universal suffrage became democrats and then socialists, embracing the progressive ideas of state intervention in the economy, education, welfare. This is true but not true enough. It is nationalism, not socialism, that killed the liberal appeal. The ground slipped out from under the late-nineteenth- and early-twentieth-century liberals not because they were not sufficiently socialist but because they were, or at least seemed to be, not sufficiently nationalist. (Much the same happened with the socialists, especially in the United States: the working masses found them unappealing not because their economic advocacies were unappealing nor because the American worker was a believer in Free Enterprise or whatnot; socialists in the United States were unpopular

---

* "Mazzini imagined that there was no conflict between nationalism and internationalism, or between nationalism and liberalism. They represented facets of the same thing. Nationalism, representing the freedom of the peoples, was the macrocosm of liberty, whilst liberalism, representing the freedom of individuals, was the microcosm. . . . [But the] true message of 1848 was that liberalism and nationalism were distinct entities and that people tended to put their nationalism before their liberalism." John Clarke, *British Diplomacy and Foreign Policy, 1782–1865.* London, 1989, pp. 226, 238.

because they were, or had the reputation of being, not nationalist enough.)

The history of words: but, then, the history of politics *is* the history of words. Three examples:

1. Jane Austen in *Emma*: "The Coles had been settled in Highbury and were a very good sort of people, friendly, liberal, and unpretending; but, on the other hand, they were of low origin, in trade, and only moderately genteel." In the 1810s, and for some time thereafter, "liberal" was a very positive word, which may be even more telling than the fact that "Liberal," in England, began to appear as a political party designation only about a decade after *Emma* had been published.

2. Of course the broader and nonpolitical meaning of "liberal in spirit" still lingers on, but probably not for long. In the United States as late as 1950 even Republican nationalists such as Senator Taft shied away from the adjective "conservative," saying that he was an "old-fashioned liberal." Ten years later Eisenhower, the supreme opportunist, called himself a "conservative." Thirty years later Reagan, the Hollywood actor, won over the great majority of the American people as a "conservative." By then, for the first time in their history, many more Americans considered themselves as "conservatives" than as "liberals." "Liberal" had become something of a bad word, to be avoided in almost every sense. In Eastern Europe a "liberal" Communist was a good sort of Communist before 1989; but within two years, from 1989 to 1991, among Eastern European nationalists "liberal" has become as negative a designation as was "Communist" before.

3. "People," "popular," even "populism," were leftist words throughout the nineteenth century. (Some of this lived on in the antiquated Socialist and Communist vocabularies during the twentieth.) But already around 1900 in the Germanies (and

in Austria and also elsewhere in Eastern Europe) the new "people's parties" were often rightist, anti-Semitic, nationalist. This was most evident in Germany because of the cult of the *Volk* (the name of Hitler's newspaper later: the *Völkischer Beobachter*). In Italy, too, when in 1914 Mussolini broke with the Italian Socialist party, his newspaper (and later the official Fascist newspaper) bore the name *Popolo d'Italia*. The National Socialist movements throughout Europe in the 1930s and early 1940s often had "the people" for the name of their parties and newspapers. (A last small example: one hundred and fifty years after Marat's rabblerousing *L'Ami du Peuple*, it was the name of an extreme rightist sheet in France.)

That was in the 1930s. It is even more telling how in our time (during the last fifty years) the anxieties of political observers, intellectuals, journalists, indeed of many people by and large, are constantly exercised not by the potential rise of mass movements of the left but by those of the right. (That "left" and "right" have become imprecise and nearly outdated terms is in itself telling, but let that go.) Everywhere there are people who fear the danger of nationalist extremism (whether unduly so or not), because of its potential appeal to masses of people — an appeal that the left no longer has.*

The cult of the state and of the people are essential features of nationalism; but these two cults are not always the same. That was one difference between Fascism and National Socialism. Mussolini tried to elevate the cult of the state above the cult of individualism. Hitler subordinated the state to the people;

---

* The only places where leftists are still in control (more precisely, where their pressures are still prevalent) are those within certain departments of colleges and universities, especially in the United States — represented by academics who, in this democratic age, are possibly more remote from the people than they have ever been.

as he said in a speech in 1938, in Salzburg: "First came the *Volk*. Only then came the *Reich*.*

"Fascism" is an imprecise and illegitimate term when it is used to cover all rightist dictatorships. The more universal reality was National Socialism. Consider but the three great dictators of that bloodiest quarter of the twentieth century: Hitler, Mussolini, Stalin. The Fascist label is not applicable to Stalin, and not even to Hitler. The Communist label is not applicable to Mussolini or Hitler. Yet, in more than one way, all three of them were nationalist socialists, of sorts. Their evolution is telling. As time went on, both Mussolini and Stalin borrowed from Hitler, whether consciously or not. More and more they became nationalist socialists: the first, the Italian nationalist, more and more socialist toward the end; the second, the Communist, more and more nationalist through and after the war.

Nationalism destroyed the Habsburg Empire and monarchy. Twenty, fifty, seventy years later many among its once component peoples look back nostalgically at the life and freedom their ancestors enjoyed under Franz Joseph. Nationalism, too, helped to end the Soviet domination of Eastern Europe. That was all to the good, except that, for instance, the Hungarian minority in Transylvania had been better off — meaning that it had been less oppressed and discriminated against — during the short period when Transylvania was administered by the Soviet army in 1944–45 than when it reverted to Rumanian rule. Tito was a Balkan bandit, but it is not inconceivable that

---

* And in his confidential speech of 26 May 1944: In 1918 "the bourgeois politician only saw the state in front of him; I saw the *Volk*, the substance. For me the state was then nothing but a purely external, a restrictive framework [*Zwangsform*]."

"*Volk*," in German, means "people" as well as "nation." But the *Volk* had not only preceded the state; it had also preceded national feeling.

one day Croats and Serbs will look back and think that even Tito's corrupt multinational Communism may have been preferable to the protracted civil war between Croats and Serbs that is raging even now.

But from Franz Joseph to Stalin and Tito — what a difference!

It is a mistake to think, as many historians and sociologists of immigration do, that nationalism and nativism are identical. They have many things, including a dislike of foreigners, in common. But not every nativist is a nationalist. (A nativist is more likely to be traditionalist than modern.) A radical nationalist is often someone who does not live in the city, the county or the state (and sometimes not even the country) where he was born.

An old-fashioned patriot will dislike a nationalist not only because of the latter's low manners and the shrillness of his tone, but because he senses that the radicalism of the nationalist is superficial (yes, a *superficial* radicalism is not necessarily an oxymoron). The emotionalism of the nationalist grates against the privacy of a patriot's own finer-fibered but also deeper-rooted feelings. A patriot may dislike foreigners because of their intrusion into something that is deeply felt and private. The nationalist is suspicious not only of foreigners but of anyone within his own nation (including even patriots) who, he suspects, does not think in the way he does. Thus the nationalist is both a physical and a spiritual racist of sorts.

Patriotism is not a substitute for a religious faith, whereas nationalism often is; it may fill the emotional — and at least superficially spiritual — needs of many people.

Neither patriots nor nationalists are necessarily anti-Semites (though the latter more often so than the former).

During the twentieth century the essence of anti-Semitism has been xenophobia: suspicion, fear, dislike, envy, on occa-

sion hatred of supposed foreigners. This has been a relatively
— but only relatively — recent phenomenon, and another outcome of populist nationalism. The relationship of Jews and
Christians (note that at this point I write "Christians" rather
than "non-Jews") is a profound, sad and occasionally inspiring
story of two thousand years' duration. For a long time — aware
as we must be of this gross oversimplification — when Jews
were persecuted and discriminated against, the reason (and the
pretext) was religious — that is, by "Christians" rather than
by nationalists. The very word "anti-Semitism" (another imprecise term, at that) appeared, in Germany first, only around
1870, together with populist nationalism. It was a somewhat
novel version of xenophobia: suspicion and contempt directed
not only at foreigners and not even mostly against a new breed
of immigrants but at a certain kind of people who seem
to have adjusted themselves, in some cases and in many
ways successfully, to the civilization and the culture of the
nation.

To dislike certain people may be regrettable, but it is
not identical with the evil of their condemnation. The evil of
anti-Semitism depends on its quality, as does everything else
in the human world: not the "why" or the "what" but the
"how." In the 1930s there were many people in, say, Britain
and the United States and Sweden who did not particularly
like Jews. Yet they were appalled at the treatment of Jews in
Germany, which was not only to be condemned but something to be actively opposed — because of its quality, in which
these British and Americans and Swedes saw something
evil (and so did not a few people in Germany or Hungary or
Poland).

We know how Hitler was obsessed with Jews and with the
"Jewish problem" (though we shall never really know why. He
was no run-of-the-mill anti-Semite). He convinced himself

that Jews were the key to history, surely to European history. In the end he not only lost his war against the rest of the world; he also lost his war against the Jews, in two ways. His extermination of Jews in Europe and Russia, while appallingly extensive, could not be completed; and the realization of those horrors made anti-Semitism unacceptable and unavowable nearly everywhere in the civilized world. But it is possible that fifty years after the war, after the end of the twentieth century, this condition may be passing.

The creation of an independent state of Israel, too, would not have occurred in the way it had except as a reaction to what had happened to Jews during the reign of Hitler. By 1967, twenty years after its creation, most people, including Jews outside Israel, had come to regard anti-Semitism and anti-Zionism as identical. Yet they are not necessarily the same. I am not thinking only of the problems of identity and loyalty of Jews who are citizens of states other than Israel. We are facing ever newer forms of nationalism, and perhaps of anti-Semitism. We must keep in mind that until about 1937 Hitler and his governments were, at least in one sense of that word, pro-Zionist. Had the British permitted and encouraged the emigration of all German Jews to Palestine, Hitler would have welcomed that; Eichmann, for one, had gone to Palestine to study such possibilities.*

Fifty years later there are nationalist governments, especially in Eastern Europe, that prefer to have good, or at least acceptable, relations with the government of Israel while they remain suspicious, and perhaps even hostile, to assimilated Jews in their own countries who wish to play a part in their

---

* Prime Minister Shamir of Israel was a member of Zionist terrorist groups that as late as *1941* (!) tried to approach the Nazi government to cooperate against the British. (See the article by Avishai Margalit in *The New York Review of Books*, May 14, 1992, pp. 18–24.)

national political and cultural life. There are evidences of this in Eastern Europe now.

Here is a German soldier in a World War II film who says that he believes in Hitler: we automatically condemn him, he is a bad sort. There is an American soldier who says that he believes in democracy and that he hates Nazis: we think that he is a good sort. That is too simple. That German soldier may treat an enemy civilian or a prisoner kindly. The American soldier may not. What matters is what they do, how they behave. The ideas of the German and the ideas of the American are not inconsequential; but let me insist, again and again, that what people do with their ideas is more important than what their ideas do to them.

From the end of World War I to the end of World War II there were three great political forces across the globe: Communism, liberal democracy, and the new phenomenon inadequately and imprecisely called Fascism — "radical nationalism," also imprecise, is a better term for it. Until 1945 Communism was embodied by the Soviet Union alone. Democracy was embodied by the English-speaking, and by other Western and Northern European, countries. Radical nationalism had protean incarnations, of which the most radical and powerful was the Germany of the Third Reich. But in addition to their "incarnations" by states, this triangular configuration of forces was repeated *within* every country of the globe, including such faraway ones as, say, Argentina and China. Every country had its radical nationalists (and most of them were, if not pro-German, then anti-British and anti-Russian), including the United States. There were conservatives and liberals within the Third Reich itself, wishing for Hitler's defeat. There were conventicles of Communists in every country, too, though usually not very effectual (as, for example, in the

United States, where Roosevelt's strongest opponents came not from the left but from the nationalist right).

On the global scale, as we have seen, the Third Reich was so powerful that it could not be conquered either by the Soviet Union or by the American-British alliance alone; to achieve Germany's defeat, the alliance of Democracy and Communism — more precisely, of the United States, Britain and the Soviet Union — was needed. Then, in 1945, near the middle of the chronological twentieth century, that alliance necessarily fell apart. The United States and the Soviet Union seemed to have become the only two Great Powers in the world. Thereafter most nationalists and anti-Communists became pro-American. And now, at the end of the century has come the collapse of Communism, and of the prestige of the Soviet Union. One of the triangular forces is largely gone. In various places radical nationalism rises again — and there are some reasons to believe that it will no longer be pro-American.

Until very recently the nationalists depended, if not on the United States, then on the goodwill of the United States. This seems to be less and less so. Two factors are involved here. One is the image of the prestige and power of a dominant nation. The other is the political and social order that it seems to embody. In 1945 the power and prestige of the United States (and, to some extent, of Britain) were enormous. Forty or fifty years later that image has become weaker, if not altogether gone. On the lowest levels of popular "culture" America is still emulated, and will continue being so for a long time, but for reasons that have nothing to do with the virtues of American political traditions. On other, more important levels more and more people are uneasily aware of America's own troubles, inherent in institutions and practices that they no longer wish to emulate. Before and during World War II a respect and affection for England was a latent but powerful common denominator among most opponents of the radical nationalist dictatorships; but that Anglophilia is gone. In sum, the rise of radical and populist nationalism is inseparable not only from the collapse of Communism and the former Russian empire, but also from the decline of Britain and the United States.

The phenomenon of the growth and decline of American influence is of course more complex than was that of British influence. In 1945, and perhaps in 1989, too, it seemed that American-style democracy, with its liberal and capitalist practices and principles, was the triumphant force, emulated * and about to be emulated all over the world. But, then, the ingredients of American democracy are not only liberal but also populist, and nationalist as well as internationalist. And at the end of the twentieth century liberalism is, by and large, in retreat. Capitalism (whatever *that* means at a time when every state in the world is a welfare state, governed by enormous bureaucracies) may have proved more efficient than Marxism; but liberalism has not proved itself against nationalism. Across the globe we can see the rise of all kinds of nationalisms, including the Japanese one — another sign that the legacy of World War II is over. Even within the United States there is ample evidence that the radical nationalism exemplified by able men such as Patrick Buchanan does not need Communism as its target in order to appeal and potentially prosper among people. For the radical nationalist is even more anti-liberal than he is anti-Communist (as indeed was Hitler). The main source of his appeal is his nationalism, not his radicalism. It is his nationalism that makes him respectable at a time when not only political and parliamentary liberalism but also many of its traditional institutions have become sclerotic,

---

* Perhaps it is worthy of note that among the different designations of neo-Nazi parties in Germany the recent and relatively strongest one (and fortunately none of them are very strong) chose the name Republikaner in the 1980s, possibly emulating the name of the Reaganite Republican party in the United States.

breaking down, and when its beliefs governing and binding society together are in varying stages of dissolution.

Nationalism involves language. Important as language is, it does not explain the nationalist sentiment sufficiently. The Slovak and the Czech languages are almost identical; so are the Croatian and the Serbian ones. A nationalist is pleased when a foreign visitor attempts to say something in his language, but he finds it distasteful when a fellow citizen of a race other than his speaks his national language incorrectly, with a jarring slang or intonation. The umbrage that Nirad Chaudhuri observed among certain Englishmen in India ("[he] resented our devotion to English literature as a sort of illicit attention to his wife"*) is a subtle but not uncommon reaction. In one of his novels Evelyn Waugh mentions a foreigner who speaks English impeccably; someone says: "yes, but we must not encourage him." There are millions of German-Swiss and Austrians who, besides their dialects, speak High German perfectly and yet do not wish to consider themselves as Germans. In Quebec the hard minority of radical nationalists are not necessarily those who speak only French, and in Ireland most radical nationalists do not know Gaelic at all. The relationship of nationalism and language is as profound as it is complicated.

At the end of the twentieth century a new phenomenon arises, one virtually without precedent: the coexistence of two languages, indeed of two cultures, across the world. The universal language is American English (the language, for instance, of all airports and airlines). There was a time when Roman Latin was near-universal, or when French was the language of all of the educated and upper classes in Europe. But what is happening now is different. The more or less universal

---

* From his article in *The American Scholar*, Spring 1991, p. 246.

American *lingua franca* is not restricted to an upper class or to a bureaucracy. Living alone in the midst of an isolated Soviet Russia, largely cut off from the rest of the world, the great Russian linguist and philosopher M. M. Bakhtin wrote:

> The new cultural and creative consciousness lives in an actively polyglot world. The world becomes polyglot, once and for all and irreversibly. The period of national languages, coexisting but closed and deaf to each other, comes to an end. Languages throw light on each other: one language can, after all, see itself only in the light of another language. The naive and stubborn coexistence of "languages" within a given national language also comes to an end — that is, there is no more peaceful coexistence between territorial dialects and jargons, literary language, generic language with literary language, epochs in language and so forth.*

Bakhtin is both right and wrong. He is right because he sees, Job-like, the evidences and dangers of a mass culture that is becoming more and more visual and pictorial and less and less verbal. He is wrong because he underestimates the continuing endurance of national languages, not only in everyday life but on high levels. While many of the great writers of two or three hundred years ago hoped to achieve universality, the few great writers of the twentieth century have been increasingly obsessed with their own languages. That is, they have been more *national* than *nationalistic*, because of their respect for the traditions of language, because of their patriotic affection for the Old Language. (Note this among the Bloomsburyites, twentieth-century English intellectuals with all of their weaknesses — and some of those weaknesses were fatal† — but

---

* Bakhtin, "Epic and Novel," in *The Dialogic Imagination: Four Essays by M. M. Bakhtin.* Michael Holquist, ed. Austin, Texas, 1990, p. 12.

† Example. Harold Nicolson on Samuel Johnson: "To Johnson, untruthfulness was not a moral blemish only, but an intellectual defect." The opposite is true. The "only" suggests that to Nicolson "intellectual" was — at least —

when it came to language, a Virginia Woolf or a Harold Nicolson had so much more knowledge of and affection for the traditions of the English language than the anti-liberal Wyndham Lewis or the "conservative" Kingsley Amis. In the United States, too: a champion of traditional language was the self-proclaimed anarchist Dwight Macdonald, not the self-proclaimed "conservative" and nationalist Tom Wolfe.)

Bakhtin wrote the above around 1960, when C. P. Snow published his celebrated *Two Cultures*. Unlike Bakhtin, Snow was wholly wrong. There are no two cultures. There is only one culture, because culture and thought are inseparable. If there is a division, it is not that between the "culture" of the scientist and that of the humanist. It is between the bureaucratic language people employ and the everyday language people still largely use. There *are*, however, two languages now. One is the airline, American English, computerized, scientific, business language employed from nine to five, in Tokyo and Singapore as well as in London and New York. But it is not this language that the Japanese or English businessman speaks after five, when he is at home at the kitchen table. Ultimately it is the latter that counts. Leisure (including some of its superficial forms) is the basis of culture, not the other way around. And language is both older and newer than is written language, or than the printed word. Consider, for one thing, the novel, which is a relatively recent phenomenon, a product of the Modern Age. It is now dissolving in two directions: one tends toward history (which shows signs of eventually absorbing its genre), the other toward poetry, of a sort. All other literary genres are much older than the novel, most of them older than the printed word, and some of them even older than written language. And that is why national

---

the equivalent of "moral." (But that was then an English intellectual reaction against the excesses of Victorian and puritanical moralizing.)

languages will not only survive but grow stronger — indeed, perhaps especially in such places where nationalism is not increasing but weakening. And when that happens it will not be internationalism, it will be patriotism that buds forth again.

The decline of religion and the decreasing influence of the churches became more and more evident during the eighteenth century, at the end of which it seemed as if that decline were irreversible and perhaps even complete. (In two thousand years the power and prestige of the papacy was never as low as it was in 1799.) Then there came an unexpected Catholic and Ultramontane revival, but the decline, by and large, went on during the nineteenth century and continued during the twentieth. Even some atheists and agnostics regretted this on occasion; Orwell, for example, who once wrote that the greatest loss for Western civilization was the vanishing of the belief in the immortality of the soul. That is a difficult subject, because it is not as ascertainable how men and women (how, rather than how much) two hundred and fifty years ago believed in the immortality of the soul. But Orwell was right when he wrote that faith and credulity are different things.

Most people (including intellectuals, theologians, ecclesiastical historians) think that the decline of religious belief has been due to the rise of the belief in science. That may have been true in the nineteenth century, but even so the evidence is not clear. The rise and decline of religious belief did not necessarily correspond to the decline and rise of belief in science. Samuel Butler's vehement rejection of Darwin did not lead to his acceptance or to the recovery of his religion. Henry Adams's discovery of the faith in the Virgin did not lead to his rejection of his own mechanistic-deterministic view of history. Now, at the end of the twentieth century, many people respect religion as well as science, together; but that respect is faint. (This has something to do with the fact that we have descended to a stage lower than hypocrisy, the problem being no longer the difference between what people say and what they believe; now the difference seems to be between what people think they believe and what they really believe.)

The great threat to religious faith in our time (more precisely, to the quality and meaning of faith) is populist nationalism. The democratization of the churches has led to that; but that is only a secondary consequence, inseparable from the democratization of entire societies. The primary element is simpler, and more important. It is that the religion of the nation, the sentimental symbols of the nation, are more powerful than religious faith, especially when they are commingled. Nationalism, I repeat, is the only popular *religio* (*religio*: binding belief) in our times. That won't last forever; but there it is.

In 1870 Jakob Burckhardt gave his great historical lectures to the citizens of Basle, speaking, among other profound themes, of the great, grave, long relationships of churches and states. But he did not yet speak much of the then already rising problem, the relationship of churches to nations, rather than to states. When in the 1950s I asked my then orthodox and rigidly catechized American Catholic students, "Are you an American who happens to be a Catholic, or are you a Catholic who happens to be an American?" all of them chose the former, not the latter. That is a spiritual and mental phenomenon Burckhardt would have instantly understood, as he would have understood that this now means something other than the problematic relationship of churches to states.

The decline of state churches in the Protestant countries of the world does not negate this phenomenon. To the contrary: there the mix of loyalties to church and state in England led to the crumbling of religious faith, especially after World War I — while patriotism (and nationalism) crumbled less, because they were the stronger sentiments.* In the United States most of the fundamentalist Protestant churches are populist and nationalist. So are the rising Islamic movements, from Afghanistan to Morocco. Among Jews, too, the revival of the assertion of their Judaism, beginning about thirty years ago, was inseparable from, indeed it was stimulated by, their newly found pride and loyalty to the cause of the state of Israel. And (*corruptio optimi pessima*) populist nationalism has entered the bloodstream, and often eaten into the marrow, of the supranational Holy Roman Catholic and Apostolic Church, if not at the expense of the supranationality of its message, then surely at the expense of its spiritual essence.

⚜

I am dipping into the writings and speeches of a Hungarian bishop in the early quarter of this century, a very intelligent churchman touched with greatness. They are troubling and also typical of certain political, religious and ideological currents of his period. Unfortunately there is more to them than a period piece.

Ottokár Prohászka has been and still is regarded as a "reactionary" by some Hungarians. The opposite is true. He was a social-minded, modern, in many ways a progressive figure. He did not belong to the nineteenth century, even though he was born then, and began his career during its last, transitional decade. (He died in 1926 while preaching a sermon in the University Church in Budapest.) Prohászka disdained and rejected the older, aristocratic and nobilitarian character of the Church hierarchy in the Habsburg monarchy. Here and there he wrote about the French Revolution,

---

* Note that in England the loyalty (and the solemn oath) is to "King and Country," not to "King and People."

that anathema of the Church in the nineteenth century; he thought that it had been inevitable because of the corruptions of the old royal and aristocratic order. He was ahead of his time in his social-mindedness, in his concern for the people and for the education of their youth. He was an anti-aristocratic democrat, critical of socialism as well as of liberalism, and of untrammeled capitalism. (That was in line with much of Catholic teaching at the end of the nineteenth century, partly exemplified by Leo XIII's Rerum Novarum; elsewhere, too, bishops who were opposed to liberal politics were proponents of social justice.) When Prohászka was made bishop of Székesfehérvár, he made a bella figura by refusing to enter his see in the customary old horse-drawn and crystal-paned episcopal carriage; he walked to his palace from the railway station, carrying an umbrella. He had some trouble with older members of the Austro-Hungarian hierarchy, but that would eventually pass. He traveled widely, he was an eagle-eyed observer and an unusually effective public speaker, with an exceptional talent for writing, extant in a handful of short stories he wrote and that were published.

Prohászka was a nationalist of a very pronounced kind. He was born a Slovak, when Slovakia belonged to Hungary; he spoke Slovak and German before he learned Hungarian. Then he wanted to identify himself as a Hungarian, to associate himself with Hungarian nationalism, implicitly critical of the ruling classes and explicitly critical of Hungarian Jews. Within the fiery excoriation of a godless liberal and capitalist materialism that burned through Bishop Prohászka's speeches, letters and writings were traces of his contempt and a sometimes chortling sarcasm directed at Jews. They marked the self-assurance of a nationalist demagogue rather than the anguished rhetoric of a Demosthenes of the Church. The language, including even some of the "Chris-

tian Socialist" terminology of the early Prohászka, is a fore-runner of the coming National Socialists. Prohászka was also pro-German, as were indeed many other Central and Eastern European nationalists, well before the time of Hitler. In one of his essays about the racial characteristics of different European peoples Prohászka wrote that the most valuable asset in their various biological and spiritual components was the Germanic, not the Latin, cultural and racial element.

There is a saving grace in Prohászka's words and in his character. He belonged, after all, to a supranational church, and he knew that. Had he lived into the 1930s, I believe that he would have condemned Hitlerism, and not only because of the Nazis' sporadic attacks on the Church. His national-ism, too, was not exclusionary: he wanted to see the unity of a "Christian" nation but not at the expense of subject peo-ples. But that saving grace may not have been enough. Of course only God knows this bishop's heart, the matter of His ultimate judgment. What we can tell is that this bishop's contempt for what he saw as his political and national op-ponents may have compromised the goodness of his heart, his impulse for a Catholic Christian charity. The mix (and that was a frequent mix) of his nationalism and his Chris-tianity was a dangerous one, fraught with regrettable conse-quences. He did not see this, I think; he believed in their complementarity, in the identity of being a good Hungarian and a good Christian. He found all kinds of allies and fol-lowers, rejoicing in his nationalism, but it is doubtful that he made them into better Christians. As Chesterton once said, it is not love but hate that unites people, that often brings oth-erwise disparate people together.

There were many churchmen like Prohászka before and during World War II. (In some ways he was a Central Euro-pean forerunner of Father Coughlin.) There are many of

*them even now, at the end of the twentieth century, when
nationalism is still the only popular faith with a popular rhetoric. The temptations of Communism or of an agnostic and
atheistic liberalism are gone, while the temptation of nationalism still exists, because of its respectability — including
among believing Christians. Hence the tendency to national
churches and national religions, even when and where, as in
the case of the Roman Catholic Church, those tendencies
are not wholly conscious.*

The differences between the churches in Eastern and Western Europe are less liturgical and perhaps even less theological
than they are historical and national. Among many peoples in
Eastern Europe the designation "Christian" refers not only to
religion but also to nationality; indeed, among some people
the two designations do not merely overlap, they are identical.
In Russian, "Christian" is the near-equivalent of the noun
"peasant." Because of the national Eastern Christian churches
in the Balkans, in the Ukraine, in the Caucasus, in Russia,
"Christian" has often meant something exclusionary: non-
Russian, non-Greek, non-Rumanian, etc. The root of this is
Constantinism, about which I wrote in Chapter IV. The unity
of church and state was the fatal bane of Russia, where the
Orthodox Church was neither supranational nor independent.
It was not an intermediary institution, limiting absolutism; it
was an instrument created, governed and protected by the central state itself. So it was under Peter the Great (another *fornicator immensis et crudelis*), who resurrected its powers; so
it was under Stalin and his followers.

"In every religion," Christopher Dawson once wrote, "the
religious aim of a culture is determined by the mission and the
inspiration of its prophets and by the vision and spiritual ex-

perience of its mystics. Where these vital organs fail, religion becomes secularized and is absorbed in the cultural [I would say "national"] tradition to a point at which it becomes identified with it, until it finally becomes nothing more than a form of social activity, perhaps even a servant or accomplice of the powers of this world." In Hungary Mihály Babits, a great Catholic poet, thinker and writer, wrote in 1939: "A national church is a great peril to our soul."

In the twentieth century the West has not been immune to such dangers. The Eastern usage of "Christian" had not taken root in the West; but around 1890, with the rise of nationalism in Central Europe "Christian" began to acquire a new meaning: non-Jewish, non-liberal, non-socialist, non-cosmopolitan — the transformation of the spiritual "Christian" adjective into something negative. It was adopted and employed by many people who were not churchgoers, and hardly religious at all. In a different way Constantinism, the identification of the cause of the church with the state and with the nation, has been apparent in the United States, too, including in the American Catholic Church (consider the Pledge of Allegiance often repeated in our Catholic churches, the placing of the Stars and Stripes next to the altar, the ideal of the Fighting Marine Chaplain, etc.). When Church and people are oppressed together, by alien powers, the Church may be an ally and instrument of the people and their national existence. This is salutary and even admirable: consider Poland or Ireland in crucial periods of their histories. Yet Catholicism should be conscious of its independence not only from the state but from populist nationalism. Often it is not. The Catholic Church has performed its greatest spiritual tasks in times of its suppression and persecution. But its greatest temptations and spiritual challenges have always occurred in times of its unquestioned support by the secular powers of the state — and, in the democratic age, in times of its unquestioned and unquestionable nationalist respectability.

That respectability of nationalism — allied, in Germany, with a deeply embedded tradition of obedience to the state — was a potent element from which Hitler knew how to profit. He rose to power because of that respectability. We saw that he also knew how to use the argument of the dangers of Communism. During the Second World War Pius XII, that often and unjustly maligned Pope, was not immune to that argument (in part because of his experiences while in Munich in 1919). In many ways a saintly man, he was not a nationalist, not a Nazi or a Fascist sympathizer. He did have a deep sympathy for Germany and things German (his favorite music was Wagner). More important, politically, too, he saw the existence of Germany as a bulwark against Communism. Even more important was his great affection for German Catholics. His record in not wishing to suggest even the slightest approval of Hitlerism was unexceptionable. He could have perhaps done more by speaking out against it; but when he refrained from doing so, at least directly, that restraint was due to his prudence.

What is not arguable is that Pius XII overestimated the danger of Communism while he underestimated the perhaps less obvious and more insidious dangers of nationalism. He was not alone in this. In 1933 the Zentrum, the German Catholic party, voted to give Hitler the powers he wanted in the Enabling Act. The main reason among its party leaders was their anxious wish to avoid the impression that they were not sufficiently nationalist. Of all the churches in the Third Reich the record of the Catholic Church was the least compromised; but — save for its lonely martyrs and heroes — altogether that record was not inspiring. One inspiring example was the sermon that the aristocratic bishop of Münster preached in his cathedral in August 1941. From his pulpit he openly attacked the National Socialist practice of euthanasia, the programmatic killing of tens of thousands of mentally damaged people in special institutions, including early types of gas chambers. Yet at the same time Bishop von Galen welcomed and praised the fact of the German invasion of Soviet Russia, the war of the fatherland against atheistic Communism. Hitler chose not to move against von Galen; and at the same time he told a Gauleiter in Bavaria to restore the crucifixes in the schoolrooms that the latter — in Hitler's words, foolishly — had ordered removed. He understood how religion and nationalism existed side by side (if not altogether commingled) in the hearts and minds of the German Catholic masses. He knew how to rely on, and profit from, their nationalism. He and many leading figures of the Third Reich were ex-Catholics (and there were practicing Catholics even in the SS). He did not want to affect the loyalty of German Catholics, surely not in time of war.

Earlier in this book I wrote that in April 1938 only 5 out of 3,600 voted against Hitler in the Catholic Austrian town of Braunau, his birthplace; and that twenty miles to the south, in the small village of St. Radegund, only one man voted against him. This was Franz Jägerstätter, a Catholic peasant, the father of a young family. More than fifty years later few people in Braunau wish to remember Hitler. Few among them know anything about Jägerstätter. But the number of those who know about him seems to grow every year. Earlier I said that Hitler may have been the greatest revolutionary of the twentieth century. But Jägerstätter was a revolutionary too — in the prophetic sense in which the great French Catholic poet and visionary Charles Péguy wrote, even before the First World War: "The true revolutionaries of the twentieth century will be the fathers of Christian families."

In this sense the true revolutionary was Jägerstätter, not Hitler.

⩗

The village of St. Radegund is on the ledge of a low hill, away from the road running from Braunau to Salzburg. I drove there on a cold spring day. When the clouds tore away from the sun, the fields glistened in the cool green colors of a northern spring. Except for a small tractor here and there and the distant shapes of modern factories toward the horizon, the scene was reminiscent of a Europe fifty or more years ago. I saw a few women working in the fields, some of them (this is very rare in Europe now) in their traditional peasant clothes. Because of an enforced detour at Ostermiething where a crew was laying pipes, St. Radegund was not easy to find. Half an hour later I felt the errant motorist's customary sensation of relief as I saw the road sign for St. Radegund, below which I was pleased to see another marker: GRAB JÄGERSTÄTTER — Jägerstätter's grave.

St. Radegund was empty. There was silence everywhere. From somewhere I heard the lowing of an energetic cow. After a few hapless minutes, across the road I espied a man who showed me the way to the little church in a hollow, against the wall of which lies Jägerstätter's grave. He was guillotined in Brandenburg Prison on August 9, 1943.

He had refused to serve in the German army; not because he was a pacifist, not because he was an Austrian patriot, but because of his Catholic convictions. This war, Hitler and National Socialism were causes of evil; he said as much to the military court, and in what he wrote both before and during his imprisonment. That was the last station in the pilgrimage of his otherwise unremarkable life. Franz Jäger-

stätter was the son of a servant girl who could not marry his father. Both were too poor for that — the unwritten law among the Upper Austrian peasantry at that time. His grandmother cared for the boy. Two years later a better situated peasant married his mother. He adopted Franz, giving him his name, Jägerstätter. That was near the end of the First World War. Franz Jägerstätter's formative years followed in a poverty-stricken land. He was a hard worker, respected in the village where he was the first to acquire a motorcycle, a handsome young peasant, rambunctious and tough, with a taste for merrymaking. At the age of twenty-six he sired an illegitimate daughter. Three years later he married another young woman. They had three daughters. It was a happy marriage. But trouble came between them in the spring of 1938 when he said that he would not vote for the Anschluss. Afraid of the consequences, his wife turned against him. He was deeply hurt. In time she learned not to question his convictions again.

The faith and goodness of his grandmother had left an impression on him; but he had not been very religious in his early youth. Sometime between 1933 and 1936 his religion had deepened. After his twenty-sixth year the meaning of his faith became a growing concern in his mind. The evidence is in some of his letters to his godson and in some of his own notes from his reading of the Gospels, recently published by his biographer. They are extraordinary because of their simplicity, purity and insight. They are untouched by the neo-baroque language and the otherworldly spirituality of much of the Austrian religious literature of his time. They concern the responsibilities of a believing Catholic in this world. For Franz Jägerstätter these responsibilities included his recognition of the dangers of National Socialism, and the consequent duty to oppose it.

This was not easy for him. In an important sense he was alone among his people. In 1931 the Nazi votes in Braunau had doubled. In 1933 an entry in the parish chronicle of Ostermiething reads: "Our people are devoured [ganz durchfressen] by their enthusiasm for National Socialism, their inspiration for Austria about zero." In 1935 Braunau declared Adolf Hitler its honorary citizen, which was then countermanded by the government of Austria. Political parties had been outlawed but there were many illegal Nazi party members (though not in St. Radegund, where Jägerstätter was offered the post of mayor in March 1938, which he refused).

His loneliness weighed upon him in another important way. The guidance that he received from his Church was often neither clear nor strong. He could draw sustenance from certain allocutions: until 1938 the Austrian hierarchy supported the Catholic Dollfuss and Schuschnigg governments against the Nazis; there was Pope Pius XI's encyclical Mit brennender Sorge in 1937 condemning Nazi racism, which Jägerstätter would often reread and cite; and the bishop of his diocese, Gföllner of Linz, was an old traditionalist who said that a Catholic cannot be a Nazi and that was that. But on March 27, 1938, a pastoral letter issued by the entire Austrian hierarchy and read at every Mass welcomed the union with Germany, praised National Socialism and told the Catholic people of Austria that it was their duty to vote for Hitler. There were Austrian bishops (not Gföllner) who had been sympathetic to the nationalist-folkish persuasion; many others were unwilling to stand in the way of enthusiastic popular sentiment; and perhaps especially significant, in retrospect, are those passages of that pastoral letter which declared the bishops' trust in the compatibility of Catholicism and National Socialism: "We joyfully recognize what the National Socialist movement has achieved . . . [and] that through the National Socialist movement the danger of destructive and godless Bolshevism is being defeated." Jägerstätter came back to this pastoral often. "The Church in Austria allowed itself to become a prisoner," he wrote. Nor could he have gained sustenance from the allocutions of the bishops of Germany. In 1939 Cardinal Bertram of Breslau said: "Heil Hitler: that is valid for this world. Praised be Jesus Christ: that is the tie between earth and heaven." No neater formula could be imagined. In April 1940 Hitler answered the congratulations tendered him by the German Bishops' Conference on his fifty-first birthday: "I am especially pleased by your expression of your conviction that the efforts of the Catholic Church to maintain the Christian character of the German people are not opposed to the program of the National Socialist party."

Jägerstätter was not completely alone. In St. Radegund the priest, Father Karobath, was Jägerstätter's close friend. He was arrested briefly in 1940. Several of the priests of the Ostermiething parish were taken away by the Gestapo. In the Innviertel, indeed in Upper Austria, more priests were imprisoned or executed during the war than in any of the other provinces of Austria. In 1939 a Gestapo official told the pastor of the Braunau cathedral church: "In the Braunau district [to which St. Radegund belonged] we're getting nowhere." There was only one convinced Nazi sympathizer among the clergy, Father Weeser-Krell, a native of Germany, who tried everything to become the pastor of that church in Hitler's birthplace; but Bishop Gföllner refused to appoint him. In 1941 the resident pastor, Father Ludwig (in 1989 he was still alive, in his late eighties), was arrested by the police. When Germany invaded Russia, Hitler and his government expected Catholics to support his "crusade" against atheistic Bolshevism. No matter how wrong the ideas and practices of Communism, Jägerstätter said, this was but another invasion wrought upon innocent people. There was nothing in the practices and doctrines of National Socialism that was preferable to those of Communism.

He wrote down his thoughts in copybooks at home, and spoke about them when the occasion arose, among his family and friends. It is to the credit of the St. Radegunders that he was never denounced to the police. Yet many of his neighbors were of two minds about him. The village men were doing their duty to the fatherland, serving in the army; Jägerstätter was not and said that he would not do so. His wife no longer questioned his convictions and his choice. His mother did, and was bitter against her daughter-in-law for failing to support her. His parish priest told him that he was not wrong when following his convictions. The two of them asked for an audience with the new bishop of Linz, Fliesser (Gföllner had died in 1941). He tried to dissuade Jägerstätter: it would be better for everyone concerned if he obeyed the order to serve in the army, he said.

In March 1943 Jägerstätter was called up. He went to the provincial military center and stated his refusal to serve. He knew where this would lead in the end. But in the prison in Linz doubts beset him. There was his responsibility to his family, to his wife — even though she did not ask him not to follow his conscience. There was the temptation to convince himself that what he was doing amounted to a choice of suicide, a mortal sin for a Catholic. By the time he was moved to a military prison in Berlin these tormenting thoughts had left him. His faith, his serenity, his concern for those other prisoners with whom he had some contact, impressed them. He wrote many letters to his wife, who was allowed to visit him once. He kept writing notes to himself

Among other things he wrote: "It is not given to the powers of this world to suppress the conscience of a single human being." And: "Whoever is ashamed of his faith shows that he knows not Jesus Christ." Jägerstätter was far from being a religious fanatic. It is natural for a true believer, and especially for a man condemned to death, to direct his thoughts to the world to come. Jägerstätter believed, and hoped, in the world to come; but even more he believed in a Christian's duties in this world. Many of his statements remind me of another of Hitler's martyrs, the Protestant pastor Dietrich Bonhoeffer, who wrote, also in prison and before his execution: "The way of Christ goes not from this world to God but from God to this world." Or of Simone Weil: "The object of our concern should not be the supernatural but the world. The supernatural is light itself: if we make an object of it we lower it." (She died in the same month Jägerstätter died.) Jägerstätter was beheaded on the ninth of August. That night the prison chaplain told two Austrian nuns that they must be proud of their countryman. "For the only time in my life I had met a saint," he said.

One year after the war Franziska Jägerstätter brought her husband's ashes back to St. Radegund. Father Karobath had returned to his pastorate. Some of the villagers did not know what to make of Jägerstätter's story. Many of their husbands and sons had fallen in faraway Russia; many of them returned wounded or maimed. Centuries of tradition and custom had made them obey the call of their country's rulers. Why was Jägerstätter a special case? For some time the Austrian government rejected Franziska Jägerstätter's application for the standard pension of war widows: some bureaucrat declared that her husband had not been a soldier. For many years the widow and the priest were criticized by veterans and their relatives for honoring a man who had "abandoned" his fellow Austrians. Some of them said that Jägerstätter had "betrayed" his people. Sometime in the 1960s there came a gradual change. It had much to do with the growing up of a younger generation of people to whom the memories of comradeship in the war meant nothing, but also with the respect of the St. Radegunders for the widow who brought up her three orphaned daughters and managed their family farm in an exemplary way.

An important part in the recognition of Jägerstätter was taken upon himself by an American. I first read about Jägerstätter more than thirty years ago, in an article by Gordon Zahn, who was a conscientious objector during the Second World War, a committed pacifist and adherent of Dorothy Day's Catholic Worker movement. He had read something about Jägerstätter and chose to follow it up. The result was a fine book, In Solitary Witness, published in 1966 — for a long time the only book about Jägerstätter. Many more documents and details have come to light since then; yet Zahn's book has stood the test of time well — as Jägerstätter's biographer, Dr. Erna Putz, told me. I found her in Ostermiething, in the parish house (where she is the pastor's helper, busy with, among other things, bringing up two small Vietnamese children of the boat people), an hour or so after my solitary visit to St. Radegund.

The little white church of St. Radegund is lovely, perhaps remarkably so even in this part of Austria where onion-domed parish churches abound. I walked down to it on an alley of cobblestones. The church (founded in 1422) was open but empty. As in many other places of the world, in Austria there are now not enough priests to go around; the Mass is said and the other sacraments administered by the pastor who comes over from Ostermiething. Against the white wall of the church lies Franz Jägerstätter's grave. It has

*no marker except for the crucifix above it. But there is a
single bronze tablet set in the church wall to the left of it.
I translate its words from the German:*

✝

THANKS BE TO GOD FOR JÄGERSTÄTTER!
HE KNEW THAT ALL OF US ARE BROTHERS
AND THAT CHRIST'S COMMAND IS MEANT
FOR ALL OF US. HE DID NOT DIE IN VAIN!
MAY THE GREAT LOVE OF GOD
AND THAT OF HIS SON JESUS CHRIST
FILL THE HEARTS OF ALL PEOPLE!
MAY THIS GREAT LOVE MOVE THROUGH
THE WORLD, SO THAT THE PEACE OF GOD
ENTER INTO THE HEARTS OF ALL MEN. AMEN.

A BROTHER IN CHRIST
Missoula, Montana, U.S.A.
9 August 1968

I felt a sense of pride being an American.
*I went back into the church. There was a guestbook of
sorts, open near the entrance. It was filled with the
handwriting of people from far away: Irish, English, Poles,
Hungarians, Rumanians and many, many Germans. I copied
only one of the entries. "I was a German soldier. I know now
that Franz Jägerstätter was the one who did his duty to our
people." That afternoon in Ostermiething Erna Putz told me
that all kinds of people come to St. Radegund every ninth of
August, the anniversary of the martyrdom. On that day there
is a pilgrimage walk from St. Radegund to the church in
Ostermiething. This has become, she said, a local tradition
now — one hundred years after Adolf Hitler was born. I
thought of those few flowers on Hitler's parents' grave in*

Leonding and of the somber fact that, alone among the historical figures of this century, Hitler had no grave. On that cold March day in St. Radegund, Franz Jägerstätter's grave was covered with fresh flowers.

⚜

We still live at a time when the most powerful political force in the world is nationalism. We must keep in mind that Jägerstätter's calvary was not only due to his rejection of the authority of the state; what was even worse, he was, at least for a time, rejected by his *Volk*. Hitler was one of those who breathed a new spirit into nationalism, inflating it into a populist nationalism that was strong enough to inspire some people even today. But Jägerstätter's solitary witness was more than the martyrdom of an opponent of a tyrant and of his government. It was the living proof that religious faith and that kind of nationalism were incompatible — which is why his spiritual inspiration survived and will survive Hitler's.

⚐ IX ⚐

THE STATE AT
THE END OF THE MODERN AGE

AT THE END of the twentieth century — indeed, toward the end of the Modern Age — a new and strange conjunction has come about. Nationalism is still very strong, in places it is rising, while the authority of the state has begun to decline.

Many people cannot easily distinguish between country, state, nation. Understandably so: because during the last one hundred years at least, state and nation have become nearly identical. But, except in a few places, they were not identical before, and they may cease to be identical soon.

The state, as *we* know it, arose at the dawn of the Modern Age (as Burckhardt's chapter title in *The Civilization of the Renaissance in Italy* put it: "The State as a Work of Art"). It had nothing to do with nationality then.

That is not yet my point. It is that nothing in this world is totally independent; that every thing is defined by its relationship with other things that it is not; that every thing is definable and existing because of its limits. The emergence of the modern state was inseparable from the emergence of the first state system — that is, from the emergence of other, similar states and from its relationships with them. That happened first with the Italian city-states of the fifteenth century, when they established permanent relationships with one another, with permanent representatives in one another's courts, for the first time. The beginning of modern diplomacy (as we now use that word) was a part, but only a part, of that development.

Early in the sixteenth century this Italian web, this round-robin state system within Italy, was disrupted. (That century was a transitional century, leading into the Modern Age — just as the twentieth century has been a transitional one, leading away from it.) But at the end of the Thirty Years' War, in 1648, the modern European state system came into being. The erstwhile Italian practice became continental (soon including even England, though not yet Russia). This continental webbing emerged together with the authority of sovereign states, with the precise definition of state frontiers and with the so-called balance of power.

That lasted three hundred years, ending in 1945. Its paramount importance has been underestimated lately, by economic and sociological modes of thought. During three hundred years — and in many ways even now — the principal factor in the history of the world consisted of the relations of states, not of peoples, let alone of classes. The wars between states and their consequences have been more decisive than the internal conflicts within states. As early as the eighteenth century the rise of Russia and Prussia and of the United States, achieved through wars, may have been more consequential than even the French Revolution. The years 1770 to 1848 were an age of great democratic revolutions but also of great wars. What followed for a century, 1848 to 1945, was an age of greater and greater wars. Bismarck knew that when he said in 1848 that Germany would not be united by constitutional assemblies and by the speechifying of professors but by blood and iron. There *were* revolutions during the century before 1945; but they were the consequences of wars — as was the Russian one in 1917 largely the result of an unpopular war.

By 1900 the European state system and balance of power were transformed into a larger, global balance of power, with the appearance of the United States and Japan as World Powers. (Politically speaking, the world had not become round until 1900, four hundred years after the geographical discovery of that fact.) But even before that, something more important was happening. This was the internal, rather than the external, transformation of the structure of states and their systems. Gradually, and then gathering speed and mass, the framework of states began to be filled up with the content of entire nations. As late as the early nineteenth century, in most of Europe national sentiments (as we know them today) did not really exist, except here and there among the middle classes; surely not among the peasantry — that is, among the mass of the population and the bulk of the foot soldiery when needed by the rulers of states. But by 1914 entire nations were fighting each other. The First World War became not only a war between great states but between great nations. Its duration and bloodletting were the consequences of that.

The first half of the twentieth century was marked by the great world wars. After the Second World War the history of the world was marked by another, new phase. For forty-five years we have had no great wars. At the same time there came the dissolution of entire empires and also of states into smaller components — a phenomenon going on at the very present, foremost within the former Soviet Union, the inheritor of the previous Russian empire.

Often (but not always, and not everywhere) the nation came before the state. For a while it became near-identical with the state. To many people and in many places it is still so. But that identity won't last forever, probably not even through the twenty-first century. Nations — whether nationalist or not — will endure for a long time; but what will become of the state?

. . .

That nations had preceded, and that they may survive, the existence of the kind of states to which we are accustomed is important, and so is the recent, almost incredible proliferation of small national (or tribal) states. But the decisive importance of the relations between powerful states is still extant.

We (and perhaps especially Americans) are inclined to regard the states of Europe as ancient. Yet most of the present European nations were not capable of achieving their statehood by themselves. Despite their vocal nationalism, they were dependent on the intervention of other, greater states and powers. They needed foreign help, foreign armies (foreign volunteers were not enough). This is even true of Italy, whose great statesman Cavour had proclaimed that Italy would do it alone, *l'Italia farà da se;* but that was not what happened. The unification of Italy and the expulsion of the Austrians from its north were made possible because of the help of the French armies in northern Italy and, later, because of Prussia's defeat of Austria elsewhere. During the one hundred years before 1920 Greece, Rumania, Italy, Bulgaria and Albania became independent states — but they had been unable to accomplish their independence without foreign help. Add Finland, Estonia, Latvia, Lithuania, Czechoslovakia, Hungary, even Poland. They became independent states after 1918. That was possible only because of the then breakup of the Austrian and Russian (and, in Poland's case, also because of the defeat of the German) empires. Most of the states in the Balkans had come into existence because of the earlier retreat and dissolution of the Ottoman Turkish empire.

In the Americas, too, the independence of *all* of the Central and South American states was a result of the piecemeal dissolution of the Spanish (and Portuguese and, in the case of Haiti, the overseas French) empires — because of the inability, or the unwillingness, of the rulers of the mother country to enforce its sovereignty across the Atlantic. That condition was inseparable from the refusal of Britain (and, at least indirectly, of the United States) to support Spain but to favor the independence of the new Central and South American states instead.

As time went on, the achievement of the statehood of certain nations (and not only of former colonial ones) was the result of the weakening of imperial convictions in an age of democracy and liberalism. (Thus Sweden conceded the independence of Norway in 1905, and the British gave their reluctant agreement to an Irish Free State by 1922, at the cost of partitioning John Bull's Other Island.)

After 1945 came the dissolution of the remaining great colonial empires. At the end of the twentieth century the great majority of independent states are former colonies of the Great Powers. But how "independent" are they, and how "sovereign"? (They are all members of the United Nations. But the very name of that "international" organization is false. It is an organization of states, not of nations.)

Thus the vast majority of the present states of the globe declared their independence only during the last one hundred and seventy years. In many cases their independence led them not to prosperity or even freedom but to protracted misery and recurrent tyrannies of their own.

This has not been true, fortunately, of the United States — for many reasons. Not necessarily because of its Declaration of Independence, which contains some high-flown and inaccurate phrases, and which is no longer unique — since most states of the world, and just about all ex-colonial states, have produced their own declarations of independence. The freedom and the prosperity of the United States owes much to its Constitution. Yet even that excellent Constitution broke down in 1861 — not because of slavery but because of secession. While the Constitution was, and still is, clear about the procedures for the admission of states to the Union, it was not clear about their rights for a voluntary secession from it.

Abraham Lincoln was an American liberal nationalist. During his presidency his invocation of "nation" became increasingly frequent. James M. McPherson noted how after 1861 Lincoln employed the term "Union" less and less, "nation" more and more. In his first message to Congress (July 4, 1861) Lincoln used "Union" thirty-two times, "nation" three times. By the time of the Gettysburg Address (November 19, 1863) he used "Union" not at all, "nation" five times. In perhaps his greatest speech, his Second Inaugural (March 4, 1865), he said that the war had begun because one side had sought to dissolve the Union and the other side had fought to preserve the nation. This is very true and telling. And there may be even more to it. Lincoln knew that the Southerners belonged to the same, then still largely Anglo-Celtic-American, nation. What he would not allow was the prospect not of two nations but of two states. The Southerners knew that. The cause of popular sovereignty and of American nationalism remains strong among them to this day; but after the Civil War no Southerner would ever speak about secession.

The sovereignty of the state and the sovereignty of the people are two different matters. The first blossomed fast and furious into existence in the beginning of the Modern Age; it is in visible and palpable decline now. The second grew into universal acceptance during the last one hundred or one hundred fifty years; it is, and still remains, unquestionable now.

The sovereignty of the state had been bound to the sovereignty of the monarch. (That was different from ancient patriotism as well as from democratic nationalism.) Exactly four hundred years ago Henry IV united France into the first modern, centralized state. One of his main political instruments

was his then relatively rare promulgation of religious toleration. By tolerating the French Protestants he not only wished
to end a chain of religious and civil wars but to unite the state,
establishing the primacy of loyalty to the centralized kingdom.

By coincidence, in the same year a very different monarch,
under very different conditions, paid homage to the sovereignty of the rulers of states. In 1591 in his bull *Inter Alia* Pope
Gregory XIV, wanting to correct and limit the many irregular-
ities extant under the surviving medieval principle of sanctuary offered by churches, promulgated that all rights of
sanctuary be withdrawn from "highwaymen, ravagers of fields,
homicides who kill or mutilators who maim in holy places
[churches and cemeteries] *and traitors against their sovereign.*" * The italics are mine.

During the eighteenth century monarchs "came to see
themselves not *as* the state — in the manner of Louis XIV † —
but as *the first servant of the state* — in the manner of Frederick of Prussia." ‡ Near the end of the century Joseph II, the
heir to the Habsburg throne, answered his mother, Maria
Theresa, who had warned him that "toleration" meant "carelessness about religious truth, and that it would damage and
destroy religion." Joseph's answer is remarkable. It shows that
for this early liberal and prototype of an enlightened monarch,
the state was above everything. "The sole cause of our dis-
agreement is the definition of the word *toleration.* May God
preserve me from thinking that it does not matter whether our

---

* Owen Chadwick, *The Popes and European Revolution.* Oxford, 1981, p.
49. How different that was from the early Fathers of the Church, for example
Tertullian, who in the third century declared that the church was the antith-
esis of the state. But that was before Constantine.

† If he said that at all. The origins of that *mot* — whether *bon* or *mauvais*
— are unsure, as was its meaning. Attributed remark before the Parlement de
Paris, 1655.

‡ John Clarke, *British Diplomacy and Foreign Policy, 1782–1865.* London
and Boston, 1989, p. 30.

citizens remain Catholic, or change to be Protestant. . . . I would give all that I possess if thereby all Protestants of your states became Catholics! By the word *toleration* I mean that I, in all temporal matters, would employ anyone without taking notice of his religion, would allow him to own property and follow a profession, and be a full citizen, *so long as he was suitable and could help the state and its economy.*" *

Another one hundred years later Nietzsche wrote that the state was a "cold monster," the coldest monster of all. Yes, many crimes have been committed in the name of the state; many personal liberties have been suppressed by the powers of the state. Yet there were many examples then, and since, where the authority and the laws of the central government of the state (and often of a monarch) would protect those liberties, when the rule of the state was less oppressive than provincial misrule or neighborhood tyranny. The history of the United States provides innumerable examples of this — not to speak of modern Italy where, in the south, Mafia and 'Ndrangheta and Camorra rule, rage and prosper because of the inefficiency of the central government.†

Governments in the twentieth century, however, have not hesitated to collaborate with criminals for their own purposes. Even in the United States the CIA would, on occasion, employ, finance and arm various criminals and their organizations, ranging from the Mafia to Levantine, Oriental and Caribbean

---

* Chadwick, p. 434. My italics.

† In June 1992, as I write this, a remarkable phenomenon. In Palermo a vast crowd of Sicilians demonstrate for the enforcement of the law, against the Mafia and against the weakness of the Italian government in fighting it. In New York a smaller but more violent crowd of Italian-Americans demonstrate for the convicted Mafioso and assassin John Gotti, *against* the enforcement of the law and against the authority of the state that prosecuted and convicted him. There is another difference: the Italian-American demonstrators in New York wave American flags, convinced as they are that they represent true American nationalism.

drug dealers. In the administration of the concentration and extermination camps of the Third Reich the favored inmates were non-political criminals, many of them Kapos, whose co-operation was indispensable for maintaining order. In the prison camps of the Soviet Union criminals were not only indispensable; in many instances they virtually ran the camps themselves. During the last thirty years of the USSR the government party itself was hardly more than a class of mafiosi, running the state and its institutions for their personal power and profit.

The idea of totalitarianism (another imprecise and leaky word) obscured much of this. "Totalitarianism" is not quite synonymous with state rule. It is true that all modern, and especially twentieth-century, dictatorships ordered and practiced extreme police measures to ensure the subjection of the individual citizen to the state. But the authority of the Fascist, National Socialist and even Communist states was never total. One element in this was the uncontrollability of individual lives. *Total* control over every man and woman is impossible anywhere, even in prisons and concentration camps (which does not mean that the practices meant to enforce it are not horrible or cruelly effective). Another element was the confusion of party and state: the parallel, though of course often overlapping, authorities of the state apparatus with those of the single parties ruling the government. Hitler's Third Reich was a *Volksgenossenstaat,* as well as a *Beamtenstaat* and a *Parteistaat:* a people's state, a (still) bureaucratic state, and a party-state. The identification of the party with the state and the promulgation of the authority of the first over the latter were especially true of the Soviet Union (though only in the first two decades of its existence); they were also prevalent under Mussolini and Hitler.

But that was not all. Hitler may have cared more for the *Volk* than for the state; he was a powerful nationalist demagogue; Stalin was an astute Caucasian tyrant. Yet their astonishing successes and conquests were largely due to the condition that they also possessed considerable abilities of statesmanship.

Above all other political matters, even in World War II, stood the relations of states. It was still a war fought primarily by states, not by classes, and not even by ideologies. It was a war fought by Germany and Poland and France and Britain and Italy and Russia and the United States and Japan; not by Democracy and Communism and "Fascism." Hitler, Mussolini, Stalin, Churchill, de Gaulle, Roosevelt and Chiang were statesmen first of all. They subordinated their philosophical and political preferences to what they thought were the interests of their states. That primacy of state interests appears significantly in the history of the Soviet Union, of a state that millions still consider to have been a party-state, dedicated first and foremost to the utopian cause of world revolution. Stalin's real interest was security, not revolution; territory, not ideology. This tyrant cared not a fig for Communists abroad. Their activities, including espionage, in the interests of the Soviet Union were merely fringe benefits, secondary and unworthy of principal consideration. At times it was hardly more than a lunatic-fringe benefit; sometimes it was more than that; but Stalin knew that no one could pull the rug from under Hitler (or Churchill) by tugging at the fringe. In 1921 Lenin went through tortuous motions to isolate the handful of Americans who had gone to Russia in order to distribute large amounts of food during a famine. In 1941 Stalin asked for British and American divisions to come to Russia under their own commanders: if the price for the survival of his state was the presence of foreign imperialist armies on its land, with all of the prospects of capitalist contamination, so be it.

Such were the facts of life. By 1939 the official Soviet vocabulary reflected this. Terms such as "state matters," "state relations" and "state interests" became sacrosanct, in a stiff parvenu sense. When Stalin or Molotov would employ them, it was instantly recognized that these were the matters of highest importance, while references to the class struggle or to the cause of the revolution belonged to an older category of Communist pieties.*

Thus during the Second World War the authority of the state remained unquestionable and enormous. But during the last fifty years there came a gradual, though often hardly visible, change everywhere. This may be due to the condition that the unquestionable and unquestioned respect for the sovereignty of states is essentially a monarchical and aristocratic phenomenon, surviving into the democratic age; but in a democratic world people will identify, or confuse, the nation with the state, whereby that unquestionable and unquestioned respect for the primary principle of the state will diminish.

We have seen that in the Soviet Union the very opposite of Marx's dictum was happening: Communist rule was unquestioned but the state did not wither away — quite the contrary. Thirty years after Stalin another phenomenon became apparent: the party, because of its corruptions, began to wither. Andropov and Gorbachev saw this. In order to reform the country they wished to curtail and reduce the power of a corrupt and corroding party apparatus. Gorbachev's historical merits were, and remain, very great. Yet he not only failed to recognize the democratic and nationalist dangers to the authority of the state; he also failed to see the extent to which the authority of the state had been undermined during nearly

---

* Evelyn Waugh to Diana Duff Cooper, February 1948: "Churchill and Eden thought at Yalta — that Stalin was just old Tsar writ large. And it was that frightful mistake which landed us . . ." etc. But of course Stalin *was* a Tsar writ large. Only not that shuffling, bumbling, kindly Nicholas II type, with his spade beard, resembling that of George V of England; but a monstrous Tsar writ large, a new Ivan the Terrible.

seventy years because of its association with the party. Hence the final irony, a revelation of Lenin's dogmatic shortsightedness: the collapse of the Communist party preceding that of the state; the party withering away, and dragging the state with it.

Even now the monumental problem of the former Russian empire is not what kind of government will emerge there; it is, rather, what kind of state. That is not only the main problem of the peoples of the Russias but of our world at large, and not only because of the nuclear weapons scattered across their vast territories.

Another monumental problem is the present devolution in Europe, without precedent in its history. The end of the Modern Age has come to Europe politically. Fifty or more years after the end of the European state system the functioning, the authority, perhaps the very existence of the modern state that had emerged in Europe five hundred years ago, are weakening.

In Western Europe there is the movement toward an international or a supranational (these two things are not the same) bureaucratic organization. There is a common market, a European parliament, a European supreme court of sorts, a coordination of various economic, social and financial regulations, including an agreement toward the creation of a common Western European currency by the end of the chronological century. But the most important matter is missing. A common market will not a state make. There is no European state, and there are few signs that, in the foreseeable future, there will be one.

The states making up the present European "community" have agreed to relinquish some of the attributes of their sovereignty to this vague pudding of a Western European, and largely economic, community; but the pudding remains shapeless, having only a few, and not altogether essential, attributes of a form that must be as real as it is solid. For one thing — and it may be *the* essential one — there is no authority, no instrument to enforce these agreements, laws and regulations if one or another of the member states would reject or refuse to abide by them. As long as the principle and practice of popular sovereignty are unquestioned and unquestionable, this possibility exists and will always exist, since every democratic government now depends on the will of its people, expressed by its elected majorities.

Something new (and probably unexpected) will emerge in Western Europe during the next few decades. What this will be I do not know. What I know is that *if* something like a united European state comes about, the nature and character and limits of its sovereignty — as defined, for instance, by its frontiers and by its army; that is, by the evidence of its authority — will be very different from the past and very different from what people are imagining now. (If they imagine anything at all. In 1992 the enthusiasm of Frenchmen, Germans, not to speak of Englishmen and Englishwomen, for a new European union is fainter than before.*)

Meanwhile in East-Central Europe, in the Caucasus and elsewhere the sizzle and clangor of tribal wars have arisen. The response of the Western powers and states is as ridiculous as it is fretful. They "recognize" the "independence" — that is, the sovereign statehood — of Bosnia-Herzegovina and Macedonia and Azerbaijan instantly, as if that were a step in the

---

* *December 1991.* One example. The German government says that it will recognize Croatia and Slovenia within a few weeks, *whether the other members of the Council of Europe go along with that or not.* This is telling: a break between the Germans (who are supported by Austria, Italy, Hungary, and others) on one side and France, Britain and the United States on the other. A few days later a feeble compromise is struck: the Germans retreat a bit but the others retreat more: recognition is postponed for about three weeks, after which the Germans will have their way. This development has a slightly ominous portent: the Germans having their way in Eastern Europe, as in times of old. Yet the Germans still do not want to go it alone. This is new. The

right direction — which in most cases it isn't. It exacerbates problems, one of the reasons being that recognition, once given, is difficult to withdraw. Recognition means approval, which is why in the past it was tendered only after considerable deliberation and experience, whereby recognition was an important instrument of influence, which is hardly the case now. At the same time the European "community," or the Council of Europe, is incapable of exerting any authority over the civil war in Yugoslavia, (or the Russian government over the tribal wars in the Caucasus). The thought occurs to me that perhaps this may work itself out for the — relative — best; that perhaps a new generation of Serbs, Croats, etc., may someday recognize some of the merits of their interdependence as they find that the smoking rubble of their destroyed villages and towns came about because of tales told by nationalist idiots, full of sound and fury, fighting for an "independence" signifying nothing. But that is far from being certain.

Meanwhile an ominous thought: Sarajevo. In 1914 in that wretched Balkan town the spark was set that led to the First World War, to the end of that greatest and most prosperous of all centuries the nineteenth, to the end of the European Age. In 1992 it is in Sarajevo that the end of the "European" idea begins. In 1914 the terrorist murder of the Austrian archduke at Sarajevo led to a fatal miscalculation that was promoted, irresponsibly, by a foppish Austrian foreign minister and by the aggressive assertion of will by certain men in Vienna fear-

---

Germans still wish to remain respectable, a psychic, behavioral and political priority that West Germany had followed since the end of the war. This is all to the good, except that Kohl's pro-Croat and anti-Serb decision corresponds with strong German popular inclinations. That suggests that a time may come when, fifty or more years after 1945, the German desire for respectability among its Western neighbors and partners may no longer be a priority in its foreign policy. There may be some kind of a European political authority to which they would be bound, not very tightly but perhaps inescapably. Or they may do what they want, also because they would have all kinds of allies who would side with them.

ful of a further weakening of the multinational Austrian monarchy. In 1992 the murderous events in Sarajevo provide startling evidence of the absence of a "European" will, of the incapacity of the institutions of the European "community" to intervene, let alone impose their will, in the Balkans. (As late as 1913 the prestige of the European Great Powers — no matter that they were arranged in opposite alliances — was still such that they could impose a peace after two Balkan wars. Such was even then the influence of states.) What is now happening, or not happening, in Yugoslavia reflects the weakness of the European "community" (indeed, of the European "idea"), which flounders between the irresponsible recognition of multinational (and thereby hardly visible) new statelets and the incapacity to do anything save make anemic declarations. Sarajevo 1914, Sarajevo 1992 — suggesting the unpredictability of history but also that coincidences are spiritual puns, and in this case ominous symbols.

Farther to the east, Ukrainians (and others) say, and vote, that they will have their independence, including a national flag, a national parliament, a national government, and also their own army, their own currency (presumably their own national church) and their own ambassadors abroad and foreign embassies in Kiev. Some — like perhaps the Kazakhs and Uzbeks — may do without some (though never all) of these. Yet no one knows, they themselves do not know, where the limits of their "independence," of their "sovereignty," will be, where it will come to rest, if at all (consider but the geographic question of their often disputed frontiers). Of course it is not impossible that something new and unprecedented will evolve within the former Russian empire. But in the East history tends to repeat itself more than it does elsewhere. In Western Europe and in the United States relative prosperity and even national cohesion could exist in the nineteenth century to-

gether with the then greatly limited powers of a central administration. In the history of the Russias this has never happened,
and it is unlikely that it will.

In 1940 Molotov barked at the foreign minister of Lithuania:
"Be realistic and realize that the time of small nations has
passed." Molotov was a wooden dolt (according to John Foster
Dulles, Molotov was the smartest diplomat he, Dulles, had
ever met), but he was not alone. Standardization, Efficiency,
Consolidation, Streamlining, Regionalism, Internationalism,
World Economy, World Federalism, One World, and on and on
— these all are shibboleths of the twentieth century. Very different people, German geopoliticians, English historians,
American presidential candidates — Albrecht Haushofer, E. H.
Carr, Wendell Willkie, even George Orwell — foresaw what
to them was the inevitable coming of giant continental superstates, together with the disappearance of smaller states. None
of them paid enough attention to nationalism except for Orwell (and he, too, not in *1984*). None of them foresaw the
breakup of entire empires into statelets, the opposite of their
seemingly so rational predictions.

Still, they may have been right — but only in a very distant
future, when international anarchy will have to give way to
international tyranny of a new kind, of a kind not even imaginable now.

Meanwhile at the end of the twentieth century a degenera-
tion in the conduct of the relations of states goes on. When I
see or hear or read the language or the behavior of foreign
ministers and ambassadors, I am a witness of an enormous
decline, not only of intelligence but of diplomatic practice
(including decorum) and human common sense. I write "enormous," since the symptoms of a babbling barbarism are all
around us. That will last for a while but not forever. What may

succeed it is the rule of tougher barbarians who will not, because they need not, babble.

Fifty years ago there were few ambassadors and embassies. Most of the diplomatic representations of states in the capital cities of other states were legations, led by ministers. (The United States did not have ambassadors *anywhere* before 1893.) Now there are ambassadors and embassies everywhere — another result of the inflated nature of everything in the twentieth century. For Venezuela to have an embassy in Lithuania is a ridiculous practice, as it is for Bulgaria to have an embassy in Mexico. Consider only the cost of one hundred embassies in the budget of a small state. But the post of ambassador is coveted by ambitious people everywhere. It is more sought after and more prestigious than almost any other rank — oddly enough at a time when the functions of ambassadors have greatly declined, when they are hardly more than ceremonial.

That is only one consequence of the still prevalent practice of the state. The acquisition and possession of a high position in the state hierarchy includes advantages and privileges that only the state can confer, involving ceremonial luxury, frequent travel, state banquets, official automobiles and the important benefit of assured parking.*

In the new states and statelets such are the starry perquisites for the men and women of the new governing class, almost always members of the government party. But such vanities

---

* This is not a frivolous point. In the past, too, state officials considered themselves to be privileged and fortunate in having an official vehicle at their disposal. Now the streets of capital cities are choked with traffic, even in Eastern Europe. Save for special occasions, the official automobile cannot travel faster than any other car. Yet that official car has become much more valuable than it ever was before — because of parking. The advantage of the automobile has always been that its user is master of his time; he is not dependent on timetables, he can leave when and where he wants and arrive

exist elsewhere, and I am thinking of more than the desire of rich men to purchase ambassadorships. During the last fifty years we have seen the rapid development of an imperial presidency in the United States. Some of that imperial role and its functions were of course unavoidable, consequent to the United States' having become the greatest power in the world, during and after the Second World War. Yet the real nature of these imperial vanities appeared not under Roosevelt but thirty years later under Nixon. Some of their trappings had emerged earlier, but it was Nixon who in 1971 planned to dress the White House guards in special ceremonial uniforms, resembling those of a Ruritanian or Bolivian palace guard, after he had been first confronted and impressed by the sight of such palace troops on his state visits abroad. Fortunately he was persuaded to let that go; those uniforms, ready to be displayed, were eventually sold to a high school band somewhere in Wyoming, I believe. Yet this was a significant episode. It went hand in hand with the American discovery of the grand attraction of state ceremonies, involving foreign affairs. Perhaps for the first time in the history of the United States presidents such as Nixon and Reagan (and Bush) thought and spoke as if foreign affairs (or, as they said, "the Leadership of the Free World") were their principal achievements, more important than their leadership of government at home. The pomp and ceremony offered to the President abroad were more than merely pleasurable occasions during visits to foreign capital cities. There such occasions were unalloyed by domestic con-

---

when and where he wants. In a city crowded with automobiles this is possible only for someone who has a driver. While fewer and fewer businessmen can afford chauffeurs nowadays, high state officials are provided with them. Their driver will leave them at their destination and the car will be ready for its august passenger at the required time and place the latter calls for. To have your own car, to have your own garage, matters less and less. What matters is that only the high officials of the state can now use the automobile in the way the automobile was meant to be used.

cerns and politics; they were offered to the head of the American state, meaning something more and higher than the headship of the national government.

This confusion of state and government is an American phenomenon. It is evident especially among Republicans and "conservatives" who argue incessantly against Big Government, while at the same time they are the most fervent advocates of the extension of the powers of the state — including those of the White House, the armed services, intelligence organizations and their clandestine (and often illegal) activities.

One of the consequent dangers is the gradual replacement (or rather, the subordination) of qualified, independent men and women in the state bureaucracy by people whose main qualification is their loyalty to the government party and their contempt for its opposition. In Chapter VI I wrote about the dangers of a new kind of democratic tyranny in Eastern Europe, involving the rule of the majority party-state. Yet we had recent instances of this in the United States too. The Watergate episode was a petty affair, even though in the end (because of his own mistakes) it brought President Nixon down. The worrisome element in it was the effort of this President and his men to cover up the affair by advancing the argument of "national security" (and attempting to secure the assistance of the national security apparatus). During the Reagan presidency the total ideological loyalty of the director and staff of the Central Intelligence Agency and of the National Security Council to the President and his party were obvious requirements. They were serving a party-state. They were found out, and some of this danger passed (such dangers, of course, will occur again and again, whether under Republicans or Democrats); but it harmed the CIA and the NSC sufficiently so that with all the fool's gold and real gold, all the terrific machinery and money and intelligence gadgets at their disposal, they did not (perhaps because they did not want to) foresee the coming sudden crisis of Communism in Eastern Europe and in Russia at all, even though the evidences were all around.

Democracy and the interests of the state — what is often inaccurately called national interest — are not necessarily incompatible (though Tocqueville had foreseen that a democracy will have great and inherent disadvantages when it comes to its practice of foreign affairs). What are incompatible — not always, but surely in the long run — are the sovereignty of the state and the sovereignty of the people, meaning the absolute and unquestionable acceptance of majority rule. There are many reasons for this. A king or a dictator, an aristocracy or a ruling minority, may be wrong, but a majority may be wrong too. When the majority is right, the fact that it is the majority does not make it so; when the majority is wrong, the condition that it is the majority should not obscure that fact. Another troublesome condition arises from the circumstance that, contrary to accustomed beliefs, both "the people" and "the majority" are abstractions. Popularity is something that can be fabricated and thereby falsified, surely in the short run. "People say," "people want," "people do not want," etc., may accord with popular sentiment or they may not: for a statement by "the people" is almost always a statement made in the name of the people — one important step removed from reality. What is abstract cannot be sovereign. This is even more so when it comes to "the majority," dependent as that is on electoral practices and the inevitably restricted conditions of popularity polls.

I have written about this elsewhere.* Here I must confine myself to the problem of the authority of the state at the end of the twentieth century, when there is another danger on the

---

* See my *Historical Consciousness*, pp. 69–92.

horizon. That danger is inherent in the increasing inefficiency of and the subsequent impatience with parliamentary rule. We must keep in mind that parliamentary democracy has been primarily an outcome of nineteenth-century liberalism, the principles and practices of which are now in a state of devolution throughout much of the world. One consequence of this is the abovementioned novel form of a "tyranny of the majority," in the form of the democratic party-state. The other, allied danger is the inclination of the ruling party to do everything to maintain its majority — if necessary by adopting some of the rhetoric and the policies of extremist (usually nationalist) parties, so as not to run the risk of losing that majority to its opposition, whether in parliament or in a forthcoming election. If democracy means nothing else but majority rule, that is one thing; but parliamentary and liberal (and also conservative) democracy means, or ought to mean, the respect for the rights of minorities, including the government's opposition, with its potential right eventually to succeed the governing party in power. The founders of the American Constitution were by and large in accord with that — which is why their near-contemporary, the High Tory Coleridge, advocated the primacy of the authority of the state for the sake of preserving liberty. The identification of the interests of party government with the interests of the state only confuses that issue. In sum, the unquestioning and unquestionable acceptance of the primacy of popular sovereignty may be more dangerous than the acceptance of the sovereignty of the state.

Now we have as many as, if not more than, two hundred states and statelets in the world. The tribalism that developed into statehood in Africa, Asia and Oceania after the abdication of colonial empires is happening in Eastern Europe and in the Russian empire now. (It may even affect Western Europe and

Canada sooner or later * — who knows?) Let us not even consider the absurdity of minuscule statelets consisting of one or two small islands, replete with embassies and having a vote in the United Nations equal to that of the United States, for example.

Let us consider instead the present conditions of "sovereignty," which, in the case of every state, has already been compromised by the airplane. No state has control of the skies above its territory, surely not beyond certain heights. Hundreds of satellites whir above and around the globe. The once sacrosanct sovereignty of the state no longer reaches up to the heavens. Yet territorial sovereignty still remains. There can be no sovereignty without the control of one's land. There can be no independence without definite frontiers on land. The condition of sovereignty for a state *is* its control of its own real estate, as is the condition of the privacy and the freedom of a family or of a person.

At the end of the twentieth century two new problems arise. In Europe, both sides, even during the worst phase of the cold war, agreed on one thing: the inviolability and the unchanging nature of the frontiers established in 1945, after the Second World War — many of which had been established in 1918, after the First. But this century, and the landscape of a world formed after the two world wars, is now over. Time and people do not stand still. It is shortsighted and futile to believe that the frontiers of 1945, indeed of 1918, will remain forever. In Yugoslavia and the former Soviet Union they are already

---

* It may, I fear, even affect the United States in the twenty-first century, at a time when some of our southwestern states (and perhaps southern Florida, too) will be populated by overwhelming Hispanic majorities. Keep in mind that "the United States of America" is an imprecise term (as was "the Union of Soviet Socialist Republics"). I sometimes dare to speculate about the eventual merits of a North American Union (or Confederation), including the present United States and a Canada bereft of Quebec, with a capital moved to Minneapolis or some such place.

changing, and dramatically so. Elsewhere they are being challenged by force. No one knows how the political geography of Eastern Europe will look fifty years from now. At the same time something else is happening, in Western Europe but also elsewhere. Some borders are becoming "spiritualized" — that is, they are losing their importance. One can travel from France to Germany without stopping at the frontier, without passports or controls. Yet there must be a limit to all that. Frontiers cannot disappear altogether. Their total disappearance would mean the total disappearance of the authority of the state. A state that has no control over its borders is not only a weak state, it is no state at all — just as a man who has no control over the entrance door of his house is both lockless and luckless; he is the owner of his house in name alone, and even that not for long.

At the end of the Modern Age we face a new phenomenon, unknown for many centuries. This is the migration of large numbers of people across frontiers. During the second half of the twentieth century many democratic governments acted as if it behooved their liberal and democratic nature to accept all kinds of foreign immigrants, whether political refugees or workers, whether temporary or not. This period is now largely over, except for the United States. During the crucial second quarter of the twentieth century (more precisely, from 1921 to about 1950) the United States was the Great Power with some of the most stringent immigration regulations. During the last thirty-odd years it has had the least stringent ones — while its practical control of its southwestern and southern borders hardly exists at all. That, too, cannot and will not remain so for long. Not only the interests of the state but the demands of its native population will force the government to restrict an uncontrolled immigration.

Thus in the United States as well as in Europe (and also elsewhere in the world) the last, desperate attempts to strengthen the frontiers of states are about to occur at the same time when the meaning and the condition of those frontiers have changed drastically — because of many circumstances, including the increase of migrations. Surely at the end of the Modern Age the age of the sovereign state is coming to an end.

For five hundred years the army was the main instrument of the state: to maintain law and order if needed, to protect its boundaries constantly and to advance them when opportune. That, too, has changed, beginning about fifty years ago. During the Second World War all kinds of armed bands came into existence, roaming and fighting independent of the great national armies in the field. Again, Yugoslavia provides an early example. In 1941 the German army crushed the Yugoslav state army in less than a fortnight. Yet the Germans did not conquer the people, and I do not mean only spiritually. The Yugoslav state ceased to exist (while the pro-German state of Croatia came into existence), but soon armed bands sprang up, fighting the Germans here and there, and each other, too, incessantly. The Germans could not subdue most of them. In sum, guerrilla war returned to Europe for the first time in centuries. These forces had forerunners, foremost among them the Spanish bands attacking the French in 1808, after one of Napoleon's armies had conquered Spain and the Spanish royal army had been eradicated. (That, it will be remembered, was the first nationalist rising, rather than the limited draft decreed by the French Revolution.) The very word "guerrilla" ("little war") came out of Spain at that time, entering the vocabularies of many languages. Such guerrilla wars, tribal wars, are now frequent, and they may be even more frequent in the near future, in the Caucasus, in Asia and in South America.

Meanwhile the once clear and definite distinction between armies and civilians, combatants and noncombatants, has largely ceased to exist. That distinction and its observance was one of the greatest achievements of an advancing civility during the Modern Age. It was valid even at the beginning of the twentieth century, during the First World War. During the Second World War more civilians (including women, old people and innocent children) than soldiers were killed. The people of the United States, alone among the warring states of the Second World War, escaped that fate. This is no longer so. (The once brave and proud right of the American people to possess and bear arms, inscribed in the Constitution, has become a deadly danger to American law and order. As so many of the institutionalized achievements of the eighteenth century, that right has become largely meaningless, with its original purpose turned against itself.)

For nearly half a century after 1945 we have lived through a period unmarked either by great wars or by great revolutions. Many things indicate that the absence of great wars and great revolutions may continue, perhaps for a long time. Yet a new question arises, a question that is sadly appropriate in view of the growing evidence of a New Barbarism all around us. When life is endangered, when everyday life may be punctuated by instant and incalculable attacks of savagery, by tribal battles or by mob riots, no less dangerous than were wars that we still remember or can imagine — is that way of life preferable to an era when wars, with all of their dangers and horrors, were confined to definite periods of time, with a marked beginning and end, and when a definite distinction between armies and civilians corresponded to the definite distinction between war and peace? The answer to this question is not yet. History does not repeat itself. The new barbarians are not like the barbarians of sixteen hundred years ago (well, the latter had at least some virtues, whereas the present ones . . . at least, not yet); and the United States and/or the Western world at the end of the twentieth century is not really like the Roman Empire.

But while history does not repeat itself, certain historical conditions do. The summation of the thesis of Ramsay MacMullen's valuable book, *Soldier and Civilian in the Later Roman Empire*, is worth considering, perhaps especially for Americans: "Partly as a result, but more because of the violence of the later Empire, civilians had to arm themselves for their own protection. Civilian turned soldier, soldier turned civilian, in a *rapprochement* to a middle ground of waste and confusion. By the process, each influenced the other, but one direction of influence, the militarization of civilians, was particularly significant, and did much to change society."

However, there is more than a measure of consolation inherent in one of the profoundest chapters of Tocqueville's *Democracy in America*, with the title "Why Great Revolutions Will Become Rare." There that great seer, the Plato-cum-Aristotle of the coming age of democracy, perceived something that was the opposite of what in the 1830s the aristocratic and conservative critics of democracy feared. They feared that the rule of democracy would mean incessant radical agitation and endless revolutionary disorder, since it is in the nature of democracy to swing from one extreme to another. No, Tocqueville wrote: in an age of democracy and equality many people can acquire possessions; they bind themselves to material standards of life that may be petty and selfish but that precisely therefore makes them rather immune to radical and revolutionary ideas. Consequently the democratic age may lead to a slowing down of minds, to an intellectual and institutional stagnation that is only obscured by the incessant but essentially superficial agitation of petty minds and matters promoted by publicity. The cultural and intellectual history of the twentieth century illustrates this in manifold ways. It may not be a source of spiritual or mental comfort, but there it is.

What Tocqueville foresaw, too, was that democracy, though apparently universal, will not have the same content everywhere. "My aim has been to show, by the American example, that laws, and more especially mores, can allow a democratic people to remain free. But I am very far from thinking that we should follow the example of American democracy and imitate the means that it has used to attain this end, for I am well aware of the influence of the nature of a country and of antecedent events on political institutions, and I should regard it as a great misfortune for mankind if liberty were bound always and in all places to have the same features." When Tocqueville wrote *Democracy in America*, the word "nationalism" did not yet exist; but he was well aware of different national characteristics and national tendencies. He would not have been (and here and there in his other writings we can see that he was not) surprised by its increasing prevalence, by what would happen when nations fill up the ancient and creaking framework of states, and when that very framework is liable to crack and weaken.

We have seen that in the Russias it was not the state but the party that withered away to nothing, and that the collapse of the party soon dragged down the state with it. In the United States something else has been happening. During the last fifty years the power of the American state has been rising, beyond almost all American traditions and previous practices. Because of the Constitution and because of the older inclinations of American democracy, the clandestine and police powers of the national government, unlike in Europe, had been weak — indeed, for a long time they were almost nonexistent. The Secret Service came into being only in 1900, the FBI in 1925, the CIA in 1947. However, it took only a few years for the FBI to become very popular. (Something of the same occurred with the CIA.) By 1940 J. Edgar Hoover was the most powerful policeman in the United States, with great political influence at his disposal, which he used on occasion rather freely, and without compunction. Still, his influence on the course of the American ship of state was small. But by 1955 Allen Dulles was one of the chief officers, if not the chief pilot, on the bridge of that enormous American ship. Neither "national" nor "security" were particularly venerated patriotic American terms one hundred years ago. But during the second half of the twentieth century "national security," including its institutions, became an unassailable term. The national security establishment and the CIA became principal, and not merely secondary, instruments of the state. Those instruments of the American state — its defense establishments, its armaments and their contractors, its foreign intelligence and information services, together with its domestic governmental agencies — have grown enormous. At the same time they have become more inefficient and vulnerable, mostly because of their bureaucratic (and politicized) character.

At the end of the twentieth century we see, almost everywhere, overextended and heavily bureaucratic governments vacillating atop societies whose cohesion is lessening visibly, with the former cement of civility, morals, common sense and law and order dissolving in places, failing to hold them together. At the end of the Modern Age the size of the state increases along with the decrease of its authority, because of the decreasing respect and the decreasing efficiency of its powers.

☙

18 October 1990. *Dinner at the White House. S. and I are invited to a black-tie state dinner, given for the Hungarian prime minister Antall. We arrive as poor relatives, not in a limousine but in a taxi, the Haitian driver of which keeps missing the proper entrance gate to the White House, so that we arrive late, while the cocktails are going on.*

In sixty-seven years of my life I have been in a few high places, but I have the definite impression that nowhere on the globe is there more pomp and circumstance, an atmosphere more powerful and ceremonious, than such a state dinner in the White House now. This must include Buckingham Palace and the Elysée. The interior of the White House is most impressive and beautiful. Its successive inhabitants have had, of course, nearly two hundred years to collect the best of American furnishings (though this elevation of the contents of the interior took place mostly during the last thirty or forty years). The dinner and the wines are exquisite and faultless. (Much superior to the state banquet for Antall at the Four Seasons in New York that I had attended a few days before — that banquet consisted of 32 people, this one of 160. The waiters, however, are a bit harried, as are banquet waiters everywhere.) Music excellent. Dinner followed by a musicale, Van Cliburn playing — a bit too theatrically, but never mind. A little dancing to the Marine Band afterward.

Mrs. Bush at the receiving line; superb American manners. Her husband taller than I had imagined him to be. S. seated at Barbara Bush's head table, with an empty seat between them; they chat very agreeably. I sit next to Brent Scowcroft, who is thoughtful and intelligent — and, I am pleased to see, with a sense of humor. When waiting in the receiving line, he overheard me saying that I badly needed a drink, and he brought one instantly. I behave well, I think, and make only one malicious remark, as someone points out that toad Edward Teller at the next table: "The Zsa Zsa Gabor of physics," I say (and not softly, either).

But through all of this — and I enjoyed myself very much — a deep feeling of sadness,

media de fonte leporum
surgit amari aliquid quod in ipsis floribus angat

(Lucretius: In the midst of the flow of delices rises a surge of bitterness from within those very flowers).

I feel that all of this opulence only masks — or, more directly, it does not correspond to — the decline, and to the decline of the very cohesion, of the United States. Of course the guests, especially the Hungarians, do not know this. Edith J. is dazzled, her pretty eyes shine wide. "If only the children could see this," she says to me. It is a great day, a starry peak in her life. But the United States at the end of the twentieth century no longer leads the world, is no longer at the zenith of its history. This is how a state dinner may have been in the palace of the Roman emperor in the third or the fourth century A.D., not in the first or second. The fanfares, the strong military presence — so many pleasant young Marines, men and women in their striking uniforms, plenty of gold braid. Much of the now present protocol and this kind of staffing and the features of this kind of state dinner began in the Eisenhower and Kennedy period. It must have been very different in the Roosevelt and the Truman years, even though it was then that the American republic had risen to the top of the entire world, with Washington having become the capital city of the globe.

❧ X ❧

THE END OF
THE MODERN AGE

THE TWENTIETH CENTURY was the American Century. Shortly before its chronological beginning the American people and their politicians decided that the United States must become a World Power. They were no longer content with being the greatest power in the Americas. In 1898 the United States conquered Cuba and Puerto Rico and leaped across the Pacific. That was an isolated prelude to the First World War, but a prelude nonetheless. In 1917 the United States, allied with Britain and France, entered the First World War and helped to defeat Germany. Less than twenty-five years later the United States, allied with Britain and Russia, entered the Second World War and helped to conquer Germany, while conquering Japan almost alone. In 1945 the American flag, flying on American warships, ruled the seas from Tokyo Bay to the Bosporus. There followed the confrontation with Russia over the spoils of the Second World War. Here and there the leaders of America and Russia felt constrained to mitigate that confrontation, until in the 1980s the Russians decided to abandon it altogether, giving up their European conquests.

The twentieth century was the American Century not only because of the overwhelming power of the United States but also because of the overwhelming influence and prestige of things American. The American dollar became the universal standard of currency throughout the world. Many of the most valuable objects of European art and many of the greatest European artists came across the Atlantic to the United States. American universities became global centers of research and study. American customs, American practices, American music and American popular culture were emulated in the farthest corners of the globe. As early as 1925, millions of people in Europe knew the names and faces of American movie stars while they knew not the name of their own prime minister. Much of this is still going on. Yet many of these movements — movements of power, of prestige, of presence — continue no longer. It seems that the twenty-first century will not be an American Century. There is nothing particularly ominous in that prospect, and I mean for Americans. What is ominous is that the end of the twentieth century, the end of the American Century, is part and parcel of the ending of the entire Modern Age.

On the thirty-first of July in 1898 Bismarck died in Friedrichsruh, on the same day when the American war with Spain practically ended, as the armistice and peace proposals arrived in Washington. Bismarck had a premonition of the century to come. A few years before his death he was supposed to have said that an important fact in the coming century would be that the Americans spoke English. His meaning was obvious. An alignment, perhaps even an alliance, of the United States with Great Britain, of the English-speaking nations, could become the greatest power of the world. Other, very different men and women glimpsed some of the same around that time: Rudyard Kipling, Admiral Mahan, Theodore Roosevelt, W. T. Stead, Andrew Carnegie and Cardinal Gibbons among them, besides Russian journalists, French diplomats, Spanish intellectuals. The Kaiser, William II, Bismarck's jealous lord, failed to comprehend that sufficiently, as he had failed to pay sufficient attention to Bismarck's warnings on other matters, to his eventual loss. In 1900 the chronological century began with a sudden development of Anglo-German antagonism, without precedent in the history of those two great nations. That antagonism was not the principal factor in the outbreak of the war in 1914; but it was the principal factor in its escalation into a world war. The very term "world war" was an American usage, appearing first in 1915. A year or so later Americans and their government began to convince themselves that if Germany were to defeat Britain, that would pose an immediate and perhaps mortal threat to the United States. By and large they thought the same in 1940–41, even before Pearl Harbor, even though the Kaiser and Hitler were quite different men.

There was an element in this world historical development that underlay all calculations of global strategy and political power. By 1900 the American resentment and suspicion of Britain that had led to the War of Independence and to the War of 1812 had, by and large, disappeared, except among certain minorities. By 1900 the majority of the American people no longer consisted of men and women of English, Welsh, Scotch and Scotch-Irish ancestry; but the political, social, financial, intellectual and cultural leadership still consisted predominantly of such people. During the twentieth century, and especially during its second half, the presence, the proportion and the influence of this leading class was weakening. By the time the silly acronym "WASP" was coined, in the 1960s, the tone of American society and culture changed, perhaps irrevocably. Winston Churchill himself had not understood this sufficiently. He would have agreed with Bismarck, whose life ended in the very year when Churchill's public career began: throughout that long career Churchill's vision was that of an eventual confederation, if not a union, of the English-speaking peoples of the world, securing for most peoples of the globe a long sunny afternoon of peace, somewhat like Rome in the age of the Antonines (as Churchill himself once said). But that was not to be.

It must not be thought that the decline of American power came about only because of the decline of its once predominant ethnic component. The decline was probably preordained because of the decline of the age of superpowers, superstates.

During the Second World War the main instrument of Germany's defeat was the Russian army. The main instrument of Japan's defeat was the American navy. At the end of the twentieth century the Russians have retreated from Eastern Europe, and the American retreat from the western Pacific has begun.

Does this mean that Germany and Japan are rising again? Yes and no. The Era of Good Feeling in American-Japanese relations is over. This has worrisome consequences. Yet Japan, while an economic giant, is still a political and military pygmy; and it is uncertain whether the Japanese will be able (or even willing) to translate their economic power into political and military expansion. The problem of Germany in Europe is similar, though not identical. Unless the eventual collapse of the present government in China results in the kind of weakness and chaos that China experienced during the first half of the twentieth century, there will be no vacuum of power in the Far East from which Japan could profit, for the purpose of helping to establish pro-Japanese governments on the East Asian mainland. There is such a vacuum in Eastern Europe, where there already exist states and governments that are, or will be, beholden to Germany rather than to the United States or Britain or other Western European states. (We ought to remember that during the Third Reich Hitler was more interested in securing the vassalage of certain governments and states than in acquiring territories from them. By "vassalage" I mean nominally "independent" states but without much of an independent policy of their own.)

But the present German government and the German people are no mere continuations of the Third Reich. More than virtually any of the others who had lost the war, more than the Japanese, more than the Italians, the German government and the German people have repudiated their leadership and their behavior during the Second World War. Their governments solemnly and officially accepted the loss of large, and once largely German-inhabited, territories to other states in Central and Eastern Europe. They paid considerable reparations to people who had been injured and dispossessed by the Third Reich. Their constitution and their institutions are unexceptionally democratic. Their adherence to European organizations, indeed their willingness to be a definite partner and part of an eventually unified Europe, still prevails. As far as Germany's position in the world goes, there is a queer, though limited, similarity between the very beginning and the very end of the twentieth century. Around 1900 the German decision (or call it inclination) to assume the status of a World Power began. She was defeated in a world war and she rose again. That rise would have occurred even if there had been no Hitler, who accelerated that rise with a fantastic measure of success, until he had much of the world against him, and then his Germany was conquered in toto. But contrary to accepted ideas, Hitler did not want to conquer the world. He wanted to dominate most of the European continent, and European Russia. No one in Germany now thinks of anything resembling that. There will be, however, some kind of German preponderance in Europe, especially in Eastern Europe. The question will be that of its extent and quality: what kind?

The piecemeal withdrawal of the United States from the far western Pacific will be followed by its withdrawal from Western Europe, including Germany. (The erection of Disneylands in Western Europe will not counterbalance that.) The withdrawal of the Russians from Eastern Europe, including Germany, will be followed by their withdrawal from the Far East. This has already begun, with the state of Mongolia (a twentieth-century Russian and Soviet creation) having become virtually independent of Moscow. Meanwhile the Russian influence in China has dwindled to nearly nothing. Whether the Russians release to Japan the four small islands off northern Japan that the Russians occupied in 1945 will be significant, not because of the minuscule territory of those islands, but because it will mark the result of a test of wills between Russia and Japan.

Nearly ten years ago I wrote this concluding paragraph at the end of a book: "For more than one hundred years after the establishment of the United States most Americans saw themselves as representing something that was the opposite of the Old World and its sins. After about one hundred years this vision gradually transformed: the United States was the advanced model of the Old World . . . and perhaps of the entire world. Neither of these visions is meaningful any longer. Will the American people have the inner strength to consolidate, and to sustain, the belief that their civilization is different not from the so-called Old but from the so-called Third World, and not merely its advanced model? At the beginning of the third century of American independence this is — or, rather, this ought to be — the question." * At the end of another book, I wrote more than thirty years ago: "Toward the end of the last century Bismarck said that the most important factor in the next century would be that Americans, after all, spoke English. The most important factor in the second half of this century

---

* In *Outgrowing Democracy: A History of the United States in the Twentieth Century*, p. 404.

may be that, after all, the Russians are white."* Perhaps not in the second half of the twentieth century, though probably in the twenty-first.

It is a curious coincidence that the last ten or twelve years of each of the last five centuries were marked by decisive, indeed monumental, changes.

At the end of the fifteenth century Columbus discovered America, and Vasco da Gama sailed around Africa to discover India. The expansion of Europe began. The Mediterranean age of world history came to an end. For five thousand years the Mediterranean was the main theater of history. For two thousand years the Italian peninsula had been at its center. But in 1494 the French invaded Italy, and in 1492 the Spanish conquered the last Moorish kingdom on the Hispanic peninsula. The great Atlantic powers began to rise: Spain, France and then England. The nations bordering the Atlantic were becoming the main actors, and the Atlantic the main theater of the history of the world.

Twelve years before the end of the sixteenth century, in 1588, the English destroyed the Spanish Armada. One result of that was the rise of Holland, another seaborne power on the eastern shores of the Atlantic. In 1590 France became the first united modern state, under Henry IV. The long decline of that once astonishing and enormous Spanish Atlantic and Western European empire (whose rise had started during the last decade of the preceding century) began.

During the last twelve years of the seventeenth century there was another tremendous coincidence of great events. In 1688 the Glorious Revolution in England established a new form of government, emulated for the next two centuries, at least, in other places in the world: the constitutional mon-

---

* *A History of the Cold War*, p. 268.

archy, with its contractual definition of civil rights. At the same moment the struggle of England and France, which had become the two greatest powers of the world, began for the domination of the Atlantic — that is, for the inheritance of the weakened (and bankrupt) Spanish empire. In 1689 England and France embarked on a series of world wars that would end with Waterloo. In that very year Peter the Great became the Tsar of Russia. In the 1690s Russia began to rise and the Ottoman Empire retreated in Eastern Europe, another momentous development with the greatest of consequences.

The Glorious Revolution (it was not that glorious in Ireland and Scotland) coincided — and corresponded — with the glorified culmination of the so-called scientific revolution. What Copernicus, Kepler, Galileo and Descartes had begun, Newton completed in 1687, with the publication of his *Principia*. That the globe was round and that the universe was very large and that the earth moved around the sun were known by a few scholars, while it made no difference in the lives of people. What made the difference was that Newton's system had not only coincided with but in a way corresponded, too, with the new system of 1688: it transformed God into a constitutional monarch of the universe, with its laws dependent less on a divine rule resting on faith than on the rules of mathematical reasoning. That Newtonian system seemed complete and leakproof, with the technical achievements, functions and thought processes of the world depending on it even now — even though we in the twentieth century know (or ought to know) that it is neither leakproof nor complete, or even completable.

Eleven years before the end of the eighteenth century came the French Revolution in 1789. At the same moment (as a matter of fact, five days before the French National Assembly met in Versailles to begin the demolition of the ancient monarchy) George Washington in New York was inaugurated as the first President of the United States of America. During the last eleven years of the eighteenth century the rhythm of world events accelerated, with great changes occurring in wars and societies, in statecraft and art, in ideas and styles.

The 1790s were some fin-de-siècle, all right. Yet no one thought in terms of a fin-de-siècle then, not in Paris nor anywhere else. Precisely in 1890, at the end of the nineteenth century, the phrase appeared for the first time, in Paris. As the *Oxford English Dictionary* puts it: "1890. [Fr.] A phrase used as an adj.: Characteristic of the end of the [nineteenth] century: advanced, modern; also, decadent." That is just about right. In the 1890s the then overdue reaction against the Victorian era began, surely in Paris but also in London and elsewhere. "Avant-garde and decadent": the latter adjective may be arguable, but only in retrospect. *Our* fin-de-siècle in the 1990s is larger in scope, and different in meaning. It is anti-decadent, but its anti-decadence may only mask a decadence of another, deeper tendency. The fin-de-siècle of the 1890s was anti-bourgeois, neo-aristocratic and bohemian-elitist, at least in its pretensions. Our fin-de-siècle is superficially conservative and populist. However, in the more important sense, our fin-de-siècle is already over: for, save chronologically, the twentieth century ended with the events of 1989.

We must not attribute any functional importance to something that is nothing more than a chronological coincidence. Like the mechanical clock (invented at the beginning of the Modern Age), the exact hundred-year-long century was itself a modern idea, a human invention. As in the life of a single man or woman, in the historical life of a nation, a race, a continent or an entire civilization the chronological markers of the end of a year or a decade or a century are only milestones. The decisive events of their lives, their turning points, do not correspond to arithmetical markers. Why we, in the history of the Western world, have had these coincidences of great changes ten or twelve years before the chronological termination of each century we do not know. More than that we cannot say. The rest is astrology — if even that.

A millennium, too, is an arithmetical term, but one with a strong metaphorical suggestion. At the end of the first one thousand years A.D. many people in Europe were gripped by a wave of mystical fear. At the coming of A.D. 2000, among the peoples of the world such a reaction will probably not occur.

Yet the history of the world (and especially of Western civilization) around 2000 is already marked by a condition that in the year 1000 had not existed in the consciousness of people. People in A.D. 1000 — and indeed for centuries thereafter — did not know that they lived in the Middle Ages. Things are different now. We are more aware of historical time than was any previous generation in the history of mankind. This is the outcome of the development of historical consciousness, one of the most important and least recognized developments of the Modern Age.

The condition that we know that we are living not only at the end of a century but at a time of great turning points is relatively new and interesting enough. But we ought to know that we live at a time of something even greater and perhaps more ominous — at the time of the passing of a great historical epoch, the passing of the Modern Age.

That we live forward while we can think only backward is a perennial human condition. But the awareness of that condition has changed through the history of mankind. During the Middle Ages no one knew that he was living in the Middle Ages. We — for more than two hundred years — know that we live in the Modern Age; but the continued acceptance and use of that term will no longer do.

"The Modern Age" is a misnomer. The passing of the Middle Ages came gradually. So does ours. No single event or cluster of events marks the exact passing of an age, because a historical epoch never disappears entirely. Each age begins to wane earlier and lasts longer than a single marker may indicate. When its institutions, its social structures, its customs, its expressions and representations and ways of thought and belief are gradually abandoned, that occurs together with the development of new institutions, new structures, new ways of thought and belief. In Western Europe the two hundred years from about 1490 to 1690 were such a time of transition. Such transitions are suffused with violence, because most people find it more difficult to abandon or change their accustomed ways of thinking than to change or to abandon their material possessions. This is not new. What is relatively new is the subtle difference between the mental tendencies of people now and those of five hundred years ago. We, or at least some of us, know and sense that an entire age is passing. During the fifteenth century no one knew that "the Middle Ages" were passing. It was not recognized until most of that era was over, until the concept of the three ages: Ancient, Medieval and Modern began to spread together with the recognition that "the Middle Ages" (seen then, wrongly, as a long dark trough separating the shining ideal past of Antiquity and the beckoning uplands of Modern) were definitely gone. "Modern," both in the original Latin and in its literal sense, means "today's," "present." That use of the term began around 1580. But its adaptation to history, crystallizing about a century later, was inexact, because of its inherent suggestion that this new and present age will be always with us: a new and enlightened age, lasting unforeseeably long, perhaps forever.

There was more to this than shortsightedness, even though the historical optimism (which was not as dominant as people often think) of the Enlightenment, of an Age of Reason, played a part in it. An example is Edward Gibbon, the great eighteenth-century writer whose very work, style and vision represented the blossoming presence of a then relatively new historical consciousness. The idea of writing a book about the decline and fall of the Roman Empire came to him on an October day in Rome in 1764, when he sat on the grass above the sunken and partly buried monuments of the Roman Forum. (Archaeology, the other by-product of an increasing historical consciousness, had begun only around that time: it had not yet reached the Forum.) That day in Rome sparked Gibbon's inspiration to write not only about a great imperial city or state but about a great civilization. Several years later, in the middle of his work, Gibbon wrote his chapter "General Observations on the Fall of the Roman Empire in the West." *We* ought not to be apprehensive, he wrote. "We cannot determine to what height the human species may aspire in their advance toward perfection; but it may be safely presumed that no people, unless the face of nature is changed, will relapse into their original barbarism. . . . We may therefore safely acquiesce in the pleasing conclusion that every age of the world has increased, and still increases, the real wealth, the happiness, the knowledge, and perhaps the virtue, of the human race." (Reading this eloquent passage carefully, we ought to note the qualifiers of Gibbon's phrases: "their *original* barbarism," and "*perhaps* the virtue.") Still, that kind of optimism we no longer have. Gibbon's modern belief in the modern idea of progress sounds naive to us. Of course he was writing in the eighteenth century, near the zenith of the Modern Age. We have fewer illusions, if any. In any event, he was writing and thinking only of the threat of barbarians from the outside. That is now possible — indeed, more possible than even fifty years ago. But what Gibbon failed to imagine is what threatens the essence of what remains of our civilization, including our very lives. This is the growing presence and the rising threat of barbarism and barbarians within our cities and nations, internal challenges of savagery to our domesticity, inspired and spawned by some of the features and institutions and popular culture of our modern civilization itself.

So in the 1990s we also know what people five hundred years ago did not know: that we are approaching the end of an entire historical era. This book addresses the end of the twentieth century, not the end of the Modern Age, which is not yet. But many of the main features of the Modern Age, which began around 1500, have come to, or very near to, their end. The expansion of Europe. The conquests of the white race. The colonial empires. The Atlantic at the center of history. The predominance of sea power. Liberalism. Humanism. Bourgeois culture. The predominance of urban and urbane civilization. Permanence of residence. The respect for privacy. The Newtonian concept of the universe and of physical reality. The ideal of scientific objectivity. The Age of the Book.* Many of these conditions and ideals have now weakened. Some of them disappeared altogether. None of them proved to be perennial or leakproof. They were created by and incarnated in institutions that still exist and function, but in ever more different ways and for different purposes; and many of them have become antiquated and sclerotic.

It is significant that sometime after the middle of the twentieth century the very word "modern" was losing its shine. As late as sixty years ago "modern" was an unquestionably positive adjective, especially in America. By now it had lost most of its appeal, on all fields and all levels of life, including art. (The now current adjective "postmodern" is merely one inadequate example of this devolution.) In architecture, furniture, fashions, painting, literature, sculpture and music, the 1920s

---

* Etc., etc. I am compelled to add: the slowly increasing respect — since about 1500 — for women. This seems to me to have come to an end, too — or perhaps it has debouched into a cul-de-sac, since the extension of legal and sexual "rights" to women has little to do with the deeper and more important qualities of the respect and the protection due to them.

were actually the last (and in some ways perhaps the only) "modern" decade. The purveyors and promoters of "modern" art have been living off its ever more decaying and crumbling forms ever since that time.

During the last few decades this passing of an entire epoch has become increasingly visible. We are not yet at the end of an age. But we are already in mid-passage, in a time of transition to a new epoch to which our descendants will give a new name someday.

Besides the historical categories of Ancient, Medieval, Modern, there exists another view of history that we must recognize — because it is a great vision, and because it belongs within the scope of this book. This is the vision — more, the governing idea — of Alexis de Tocqueville, known mostly for his *Democracy in America*, and recognized as a political and social thinker. In reality, the range and the heights and depths of his mind were larger than that.

Tocqueville did not question the triune division of Ancient-Medieval-Modern. Yet to him the history of mankind was marked by a tremendous, providential and still largely unchartable passage from Aristocratic Ages to a Democratic Age. From ages when most of the world was governed and ruled by minorities, by small classes of privileged people, to a new age when the egalitarian ideals of democracy were becoming so prevalent that nothing would or could stand against their oceanic advance.

At the end of the twentieth century, nearly one hundred and fifty years after Tocqueville's death, the triumph of democracy has become worldwide. During the five centuries of the Modern Age what we see (or what we ought to see) is a progress toward democracy, a monumental change that no decent (and no religious) man or woman should deplore — until now, when democracy has become as ubiquitous as it is oppressive, because of the unquestioned acceptance of the rule of popularity, often dependent on the lowest of common denominators, when popularity itself is manipulated and may even be manufactured by the machinery of publicity. In the United States, for example, the elective practices of republicanism devolved into democratic popularity contests after the last founders of the Republic had died (at the very time when Tocqueville visited the United States). But in the twentieth century there was a more insidious devolution. The popularity contests became publicity contests. A decline of taste and judgment, of truthfulness and reason, was inseparable from this devolution * — together with the disappearance of the last vestiges of aristocratic values and standards.†

The achievements of the last five hundred years were those of a civilization in which aristocracy and democracy coexisted, though not always peacefully and not always beneficially. That mixture — it was increasingly a mixture rather than a compound — of aristocracy and democracy was the condition of advancing civilization. As the power and wealth and conviction of the aristocracies declined, their physical, social, political and intellectual intermarriage with the aspiring classes beneath them increased. This varied from country to country, as indeed the composition of the aristocracies varied. Many of the members of aristocratic societies proved unworthy of their

---

* Which devolution, of course, corresponds to many things beyond politics: for example, from the then relatively new and noble (another product of the early Modern Age) ideal of universal education to the nineteenth-century practice of compulsory schooling that eventually degenerated, again especially in the United States, to the condition in which schools for adolescents are primarily custodial institutions, and where most young men and women in their twenties, after having spent *twenty* years in successive schools, can no longer be expected to know how to read and write reasonably well.

† At the beginning of the twentieth century Edith Wharton could write about the patrician society of old New York that the bottle was now all empty but something of the aroma of the lees still remained. At the end of the century that is gone.

privileges. But in the largest (and necessarily imprecise) sense of the term, the prevalence of and respect for certain aristocratic standards were beneficial for the maintenance and development of civilization. These standards meant something beyond exquisite manners or a high quality of civilized living. They meant living evidences of high-mindedness and generosity. They meant the recognition of the primacy of a sense of honor over that of a passion for fame. That these did not necessarily require their incarnation by a ruling or even by a landed nobility is evident by the fact that already more than two hundred years ago the ideal of the English "gentleman" (the word as well as the behavior) was emulated throughout Europe. The gentleman was not necessarily a titled person. There was no aristocracy in America: George Washington could be called an aristocrat only by stretching that term unduly; the Adamses and the Roosevelts were bourgeois patricians, Lincoln and Truman not even that; but every one of these men had some of the essential characteristics of an American gentleman, because there *was* such a thing as an American gentleman.

During the twentieth century a few shining exemplars of statesmanship were the great defenders of Western civilization: democratic aristocrats such as Churchill in England, a Mannerheim in Finland, the German noblemen who tried to overthrow Hitler. "Democratic" here does not mean that they had compromised their inheritance and their convictions by resigning themselves to the inevitability of popular standards and popular rule. There was more to them. By defending their nations, these great patriots were defending something that moved them deeper: the traditions of Western civilization in the centuries of the Modern Age. In June 1940, in his "Finest Hour" speech, Churchill evoked the prospect not of a return to the Middle Ages but of a lurch into a new Dark Age. While Hitler was a visionary of a new, heroic, pagan and scientific world, Churchill was a defender of the traditional and increasingly antiquated but still surviving standards of the Modern Age. He was a defender of Western civilization rather than a champion of progress.

We ought to know that in the Middle Ages the very terms "civil," "civilized" and "civilization" did not exist. These words and their meanings arose only in the seventeenth and eighteenth centuries. "Civilize," in English, appears first in 1601: "to make civil; to bring out of a state of barbarism; to instruct in the arts of life; to enlighten and refine." A century later (1704) appears the word "civilization."

"To bring out of a state of barbarism": that was apposite to the beginning of the Modern Age. Near the end of the Modern Age our task — and our problems — are different: how not to accept the descent to a New Barbarism. We know something that people at the beginning of the twentieth century could not even imagine: that the advance of technology and barbarism are no longer irreconcilable. Goebbels realized that as early as 1939: "National Socialism had understood how to take the soulless framework of technology and fill it with the rhythm and hot impulses * of our time." Not National Socialism: rather, the New Barbarians of whom the Nazis were but one variant of forerunners.

Two hundred years ago the brilliant anti-revolutionary Rivarol wrote: "Les peuples les plus civilisés sont aussi voisins de la barbarie que le fer plus poli l'est de la rouille": The most civilized people are just as close to barbarism as is the most polished metal close to rust. But that is a maxim of universal truth, less relevant to our times, when there is ample reason

---

* I cannot avoid mentioning one disturbing symptom here. "The rhythm and hot impulses": the New Barbarians, including neo-Nazis and "skinheads," are fervent addicts of rock music, whereas during the Second World War, in Germany and elsewhere, the love of American music was an anti-Nazi manifestation current among those who despised the Nazis.

to fear that with the passing of the Modern Age the very word "civilized" may soon lose its meaning. There are already hordes of young people everywhere to whom the word is unknown and its meaning incomprehensible. But it is time to stop here, for many reasons, one of them being that this writer is a historian, not a prophet.

In any event, it is as a historian that I wrote three years ago: "Near the end of the twentieth century — indeed, near the end of the so-called Modern Age — two dangerous circumstances threaten the world. One is the institutionalized pressure for material and economic 'growth' — contrary to stability and threatening nature itself. The other is the existence of the populist inclinations of nationalism — contrary to a greater and better understanding among peoples, often debouching into barbarism. One is the thrust for increasing wealth; the other, for tribal power. One issues from the presumption that the principal human motive is greed; the other, that it is power. To think that the former is morally superior to the latter is at least questionable; but to think that the progress of history amounts to the triumph of money over force is stupid beyond belief."

In any event, here is one great difference. Five hundred years ago (and for centuries thereafter, since the rediscovery of some of the achievements of the Middle Ages did not begin until about two hundred years ago) thinking people looked back at the Middle Ages with disdain. Their eyes were fixed farther back. Their admiration concentrated on Rome and Greece, those models of the Renaissance, with standards that they thought they could never reach. (They did better than that.) They invested the classical age with the attributes of perfection, of a Golden Age. That was historical and unhistorical at the same time. Our nostalgia and our respect for the achievements of previous times are different. We do not reject the art, the thought and the achievements of the nineteenth or eighteenth centuries. To the contrary: our nostalgia is evoked by the creative spirit, by the security of the institutions, by the music and art and literature, by the language and culture of an age that is still visibly, sensibly, palpably within hailing distance of us. One of our reasons for this is our evolving historical consciousness, of a kind that our ancestors five hundred years ago did not possess. The other reason is that the last five hundred years did incarnate perhaps the greatest but surely the most widespread progress in the history of mankind. That is why the passing of the Modern Age may still last for a long time; and that, apace with its passing, the respect for its culture and civilization among thinking men and women will continue to grow.*

And now it is really time to stop, for the reason expressed in one of La Rochefoucauld's maxims: that things are never as bad — or as good — as they seem. Not to speak of the condition that despair is not only a sin; it is also useless — and untrue. Despair is an abandonment of trust in God, in His Providence. But it is also an abandonment of belief in ourselves — an underestimation of the meaning of one's existence. Democracy may have begun with an overestimation of human nature; but that was infinitely preferable to the present danger of the very opposite, by its underestimation (evident in

---

* And that is why the doubting Thomases — a Hobbes in the seventeenth and a Carlyle in the nineteenth century — were only half right; and that is why some of the great minds of the last fin-de-siècle, reacting against the philistinism and liberalism of the bourgeois nineteenth century — a Hamsun or a Nietzsche — are now not much more than period pieces: radical prophets, rebel voices that sounded strong and clear at a certain time but who have little to say to us now. To those of us who know that we live in a world at the edge of the sinking Modern Age, now when all the real bourgeois virtues, their interiority and probity, have remained enduring, real, lovable and admirable, like a piece of family furniture that is both finer and more solid than we once thought, a more and more precious heritage as we are carried farther and farther away from its time. As a matter of fact, our only *tangible* heritage.

so many things, including our educational practices). If history teaches us anything, it is that continuation is as powerful as is change, because human nature does not change. This means not only the difference between Evolution and History, but the recognition of reality, and of the responsibility that every human being has and that he will not — and, more important, that he cannot — abandon.

1989–1992

Kirkus Reviews described **John Lukacs** as "a master of narrative history on a par with Barbara Tuchman and Garrett Mattingly." Professor Lukacs, a recipient of the Ingersoll Prize, is the author of seventeen previous books, most recently *The Duel: 10 May–31 July 1940, The Eighty-Day Struggle Between Churchill and Hitler*. He lives in Phoenixville, Pennsylvania.